Discovering Sindh's Past

SELECTIONS FROM THE JOURNAL OF THE SIND
HISTORICAL SOCIETY, 1934–1948

Discovering Sindh's Past

SELECTIONS FROM THE JOURNAL OF THE SIND
HISTORICAL SOCIETY, 1934–1948

Edited by **Michel Boivin**
Matthew A. Cook
Julien Levesque

OXFORD

UNIVERSITY PRESS

Oxford University Press is a department of the University of Oxford.
It furthers the University's objective of excellence in research, scholarship,
and education by publishing worldwide. Oxford is a registered trade mark of
Oxford University Press in the UK and in certain other countries

Published in Pakistan by
Ameena Saiyid, Oxford University Press
No.38, Sector 15, Korangi Industrial Area,
PO Box 8214, Karachi-74900, Pakistan

First Edition published in 2017

ISBN 978-0-19-940780-4

Printed on 80gsm Offset Paper

Printed by Le Topical Pvt. Ltd, Lahore

Contents

A Note on Spellings

THE EDITORS GIVE ATTENTION TO RETAINING HISTORICALLY accurate grammar and spellings (e.g., Kurrachee instead of Karachi). Spelling inconsistencies, particularly within quotations, reflect original source materials. While the editors adopt the contemporary spelling of 'Sindh', original source materials often use other spellings (e.g., Scinde, Sinde and Sind).

Introduction

Michel Boivin, Matthew A. Cook, and Julien Levesque

Means and meanings are inextricably intertwined.[1]

IDENTITY ENTAILS THE CREATION OF SOCIO-CULTURAL
meanings and the symbolic means to express them. Some Sindhis
describe their socio-cultural identities as the product of a 'strange
amalgamation' process that symbolically mixes 'everything that is
good'.[2] In scholarly terms, this process could be labelled and/or
described as 'syncretism'.[3]

Despite a seemingly positive connotation, syncretism is not
without its critics. At various moments in history, syncretism has
negatively described a 'jumbled and confusing mixture of religions'
and/or distinguished '"hybrid"—and thus "lesser"—religions
from what is "pure" and "authentic".'[4] Accordingly, Carl Ernst
and Tony Stewart caution against using the term. They describe
how syncretism can result from violent domination: when one
group conquers a different group, syncretism can 'describe the
product of the large-scale imposition of one alien culture, religion,
or body of practices over another that is already present'.[5] In such
situations, the subjugated group often reconstructs its identities
by borrowing symbols and meanings from those who dominate
it. Syncretism can thus negatively imply that the borrowing group
is 'dependent, lacking in creativity, and fundamentally incapable

1

of defining itself'.[6] Among the metaphors used to describe syncretism, Ernst and Stewart are particularly concerned about its 'Alchemical Model':

> The more common alchemical model of syncretism, however, is that of the mixture, a colloidal suspension of two ultimately irreconcilable substances. The result is a temporary mixture that will invariably separate over time because the component parts are unalterable and must remain forever distinct and apart.[7]

Ernst and Stewart argue that 'explanations that hinge on syncretism really serve only to concretize the initial religious or cultural categories presumed to be self-evident'.[8] By linking self-evident 'orientations that are normally disparate, if not disjunctive', syncretism reaffirms differences of identity by implying an 'inappropriate' combination of 'intrinsically alien' socio-cultural symbols and meanings.[9]

Considering Ernst and Stewart's critique, it is worth re-evaluating the idea that Sindhi identities are syncretic. Sindh can be described as a 'shatter zone' or a region 'through which large numbers of people passed either in military or peaceful invasion ... socio-culturally the area tend[s] to be more of a mosaic than a relatively unitary kind of social structure'.[10] The historical creation of such a mosaic in Sindh entails people reworking and intertwining shards of symbolic meaning. As a process, it involves 'taking things apart' just as much as it does 'putting things together'.[11] By linking convergence with divergence, this process resists creating identities from 'irreconcilable substances'.[12] Instead, it utilizes multi-voiced symbols and meanings to generate new socio-cultural 'solutions'. Comprehending these solutions analytically involves numerous 'side-long glances' toward different socio-cultural assemblages.[13] Such glances reveal how Sindhis create their identities *not* from the simple historical mixing of oppositions but a socio-cultural code-switching process that transgresses boundaries by intertwining them.[14] Such 'intertwined' identities point towards meanings in multiple socio-cultural assemblages and rarely 'speak', symbolically or otherwise, in singular voices and/or tones. Rather than simply conclude that Sindhi identity is syncretic, the region's intertwined socio-cultural character points toward seeing it as a zone in which people's lives are *not* constituted by a mixture of parts bound to naturally separate.

THE PRE-PARTITION POLITICS OF SINDH AND IDENTITY

Prior to Partition in 1947, Sindhis did not generally view the intertwining of identities as incoherent and/or disorderly. Free from negative connotations, these identities resisted 'vertical fallacies' that separated Muslims and non-Muslims into socio-culturally discrete columns based on Islam and Hinduism.[15] By *not* framing in-group solidarities and networks into discrete realms of religious belonging, such identities socio-culturally subverted clear-cut communal distinctions by failing to foreground differences between Hindus and Muslims as politically relevant. In other words, religious distinctions were not particularly important political categories of identification for people in Sindh as they did not translate into radically segregated faith experiences. This lack of segregation reaffirms the historical divergence in Sindh between political power and socio-cultural purism. Although Sindh's rulers before its annexation by the British in 1843 were Muslims, access to positions of power in the region was rarely pre-conditioned on exclusive membership in the area's majority Muslim population. The codes (i.e., 'principles for selecting variants from a range of possible choices') of power and purism in Sindh did *not* historically encapsulate each other.[16]

The relationship between political power and socio-cultural purism began to shift in Sindh during the 1920s and the immunity that intertwined identities provided against communal politics weakened. Following the deaths of non-communal politicians like Ghulam Muhammad Bhurgri (1878–1924) and Seth Harchandrai Vishindas (1862–1928), as well as the communal riots of Larkana

(1927) and Sukkur (1930), the holding of political power in Sindh increasingly hinged on being part of its Muslim majority population.[17] This shift manifested itself in the political demand that the British give Sindh provincial autonomy from the Bombay Presidency. Stressing Sindh's distinctive character, Vishindas argued in 1913 that the region deserved autonomy because it possessed 'several geographical and ethnological characteristics of its own, which give her the hallmark of a self-contained, territorial unit'.[18] Vishindas, as well as Bhurgri, sought the backing of the secular Indian National Congress for Sindh's provincial autonomy. However, this unity of opinion between Muslim and non-Muslim politicians dissolved after communal riots in Larkana and Sukkur. Rather than becoming minorities in an autonomous province, Sindh's non-Muslims shifted their support for autonomy and advocated that the region remain part of the Bombay Presidency.

At the same time, Muslim politicians in Sindh campaigned to make autonomy an all-India issue and gained the support of the All-India Muslim League (AIML) in December 1925. United under the banner of the Sindh Azad Conference, they continued to put forward the argument that Sindh's socio-cultural uniqueness justified autonomy. Prominent politicians like Shahnawaz Bhutto and Ghulam Hussain Hidayatullah maintained that Sindh deserved autonomy because of the 'racial and linguistic differences between Sindh and those of the Bombay Presidency proper'.[19] But the most elaborate argument in favour of Sindh's unique character came from Muhammad Ayub Khuhro, a young landlord and politician who highlighted the region's continuity as a socio-cultural and political unit from the Indus Valley period onwards. Although not explicitly referenced, Khuhro's pluralistic perspective pointed towards the importance of Sufism as well as Shah Abdul Latif Bhittai (1689–1752) as a symbol of Sindh's intertwined religious inclusiveness.[20] Both Muslims and non-Muslims promoted and participated in Sufism but—by the 1930s—communal politics increasingly obstructed its inclusiveness. So much so that, when Sindh became autonomous in 1936, it did so under the leadership of politicians who 'were, on occasion, openly hostile to the Hindus'.[21]

Despite communal overtones, Sindh's provincial autonomy from Bombay did not initially tax the resilience of its intertwined identities. Following autonomy, Sindh's first Chief Minister, Ghulam Hussain Hidayatullah, called for unity:

> What is most urgently needed above everything else is complete trust and confidence between various communities. We must refuse to believe that there is much deep-rooted hostility on the part of the majority towards the minorities, that the interests of the one can never be trusted in the hands of the other. If this attitude of distrust and suspicion is maintained, we might as well throw overboard all our schemes of nationalism. We call ourselves a nation and demand for ourselves the right of self-determination. But how can we possibly be one nation if we are so helplessly divided?[22]

The first provincial governments in Sindh under Hidayatullah (1937–8), Allah Bux Soomro (1938–40/1941–2), and Mir Bandeh Ali Khan Talpur (1940–1) all included Muslim and non-Muslim politicians. By respecting the region's socio-cultural mosaic, these governments illustrated how power codes after provincial autonomy were encapsulated more by class and landownership than those of purism.[23] Nonetheless, efforts to establish an inclusive politics in Sindh were challenged after autonomy: the landowner-dominated Sind United Party only ran Muslim candidates and it emerged as the largest winner in the 1937 provincial elections. The separation of political power and communal ideas concerning purism also received a severe jolt from the Manzilgah incident of 1939. This incident, in combination with Partition in 1947, dealt a body-blow to Sindh's intertwined identities from which they never fully recovered.

The seeds of the Manzilgah incident can be found in the failure of the All-India Muslim League to establish a firm foothold in Sindh until the 1940s. While the AIML had individual members in Sindh

prior to the provincial elections of 1937, the party had no proper
branch office. While political parties led by Sindhi Muslims had
contacts with the AIML, they did not lead to the foundation of
a provincial branch office. Establishing a foothold in Sindh was
also stymied by disagreements among Sindhi politicians as well as
those the AIML had with its local advocates.[24] The AIML's lack
of structure resulted in the party failing to secure a single win in
Sindh's 1937 provincial elections.[25]

Despite its electoral failure in 1937, some Sindhi politicians
continued to view the AIML in a positive light. Abdullah Haroon
(1872–1942), a prominent Karachi businessman and a member
of the Central Legislative Assembly in Delhi, organized the Sindh
Provincial Muslim League Conference in 1938. The AIML leader
Muhammad Ali Jinnah attended this conference at which the
Muslim League Assembly Party (MLAP) was formed. The MLAP's
aim was to lay the foundation for the AIML's electoral success
in Sindh by building and organizing a united political front for
Muslim politicians.[26] Nonetheless, regional politicians who wanted
to safeguard their influence and interests within Sindh were an
important block within the MLAP. While some MLAP members
(e.g., Haroon) prioritized the AIML's all-India agenda, others (e.g.,
Shaikh Abdul Majid Sindhi) used the organization as a vehicle to
promote regional issues. Such divisions within the MLAP resulted
in it frequently not consulting and/or coordinating with the AIML.
One important example of this lack of consultation/coordination was
the Manzilgah incident. The Manzilgah was a group of buildings
in Sukkur, which some believed was a mosque complex. These
buildings stood on the shore of the Indus River and across from the
socio-culturally intertwined island shrine of Sadh Belo.[27] Fearing
that prayers at the Manzilgah would impede access to Sadh Belo,
locals protested against the possibility of the site becoming a mosque.
Attempting to bring down the government of Allah Bux Soomro,
the MLAP backed making the Manzilgah a mosque. It supported a
civil disobedience protest that occupied the Manzilgah on 3 October

1939. The use of force by the police to expel protesters resulted in communal riots that killed 15 Muslims and 19 Hindus.[28] These riots represented a particularly intense challenge to Sindh's intertwined identities. After the riots, this challenge was further intensified by the assassination, on 1 November 1939, of Bhagat Kanwar Ram, a 'Hindu' Sufi singer with followers from across the communal divide. Hassaram Sunderdas Pamnani (a non-Muslim member of the Sindh Assembly from Sukkur) openly accused the Sufi Pir of Bharchundi of ordering Bhagat Kanwar Ram's death. Later, in July 1940, Hassaram Sunderdas Pamnani was also assassinated (purportedly at the direction of the Pir of Bharchundi).

By heightening communal tensions to new levels, the Manzilgah incident and its aftermath dealt a blow to Sindh's intertwined identities.[29] Although orchestrated independently from the AIML, this communal blow, in conjunction with the MLAP's generally successful creation of a united political front for Muslims, helped it expand its base in Sindh. This expansion led to the AIML forming a provincial government in 1942 under the leadership of Ghulam Hussain Hidayatullah. The AIML's formation of a provincial government in 1942 illustrated how holding political power in Sindh after the Manzilgah incident increasingly depended on being part of the region's majority population. The elections of 1946 further reaffirmed this fact when the AIML won a landslide victory with 82.1 per cent of Sindh's rural Muslim vote and 98.8 per cent of its urban Muslim vote.[30] After these elections, power codes in Sindh were increasingly encapsulated by the socio-culturally purist codes of communalism. The region's historically intertwined identities hit an additional turning point with Partition in 1947. Migrations into and out of Sindh after Partition significantly modified its socio-cultural mosaic: many non-Muslims left while Urdu-speaking migrants arrived from India. Rather than result in the further intertwining of identities, these migrations increasingly communalized them. As a result, the processes by which people created their identities in Sindh became less intertwined and more 'colloidal' after Partition.[31]

IDENTITY, HISTORY, AND THE JOURNAL OF THE SIND HISTORICAL SOCIETY

The Sind Historical Society (SHS) published its journal from May 1934 to January 1948. The articles printed in the *Journal of the Sind Historical Society* (*JSHS*) were first presented and debated at meetings of the SHS. The society's participants primarily included the educated elite of Karachi, both European and South Asian.[32] Its founding President, Hotchand Mulchand Gurbaxani, reflected Sindh's intertwined identities: a non-Muslim professor of Persian who knew Arabic, he was well known for his annotated translation of the Sufi poetic compendium *Shah Jo Risalo*. In a newspaper article, 'Writing the History of Sindh', historian Mubarak Ali states that the SHS was the key that unlocked 'modern' methods for understanding Sindh's past:

> The modern historiography of Sindh was introduced during the British rule when the Historical Society of Sindh [*sic*] was founded with the purpose of reconstructing the history of Sindh. The Society held regular meetings where the members presented research papers on different aspects of history, as well as published a historical journal which contained well-researched papers, thus contributing immensely to recording the history of Sindh.[33]

During the period in which the SHS met and published its journal, the socio-cultural and political ecologies of Sindh were increasingly communal. As products of their time, some articles published by the SHS had a communal tinge. However, most articles swam against the emerging current of communalism by detailing Sindh's socio-cultural mosaic. Before and after the region's autonomy from the Bombay Presidency in 1936, the SHS published articles about this mosaic that supported Vishindas, Bhutto, Hidayatullah, Khuhro and others who argued that Sindh deserved greater political independence due to its distinct socio-cultural identity. Through the Manzilgah incident and Partition, the SHS published research that reaffirmed Sindh's distinct character. However, symbolic of the region's increasingly colloidal rather than intertwined identities, the SHS disbanded in the wake of Partition and ceased publishing in January 1948.[34] With a sense of loss, the SHS dedicated the last edition of its journal to the memory of Gurbaxani (who died in January 1947). This loss was also represented by the last article published in the *Journal of the Sind Historical Society*: it was about the Lohana, a group that fled Sindh after Partition and the formation of Pakistan.[35]

This collection of articles from the *Journal of the Sind Historical Society* concentrates on precolonial and colonial Sindh. It focuses on indigenous and British actors. It also showcases Sindh's broad socio-cultural spectrum. Scholarship on Pakistan frequently overlooks the subjects and people in this collection. In part, this oversight is due to so few libraries in Pakistan (and around the world) having copies of the *Journal of the Sind Historical Society*. It is also explained by the fact that articles from the journal are not often reprinted in books. Beyond this collection, Mubarak Ali's *Sindh Observed* is the only book to reprint full articles from the *Journal of the Sind Historical Society*.[36] None of the articles in this collection are in Ali's *Sindh Observed*, nor has anyone reprinted them in their entirety since the 1930s and 1940s.

This collection is chronologically organized. Chapter 1 describes Sindh's Kalhora rulers and their eighteenth-century overthrow by the Talpurs. Chapter 2 addresses justice and its decentralization under the Talpurs. Chapter 3 focuses on two men, Gidumal (an *amil* or government administrator) and Naomul (a *bhaiband* or merchant) as well as their relationships with the Kalhoras and the Talpurs. Chapter 4 is about Mirza Khusro Beg, a Georgian and influential advisor to the Talpur rulers of Hyderabad. Chapter 5 tackles the British 'militarization' of Baluch tribes on Sindh's frontier during the late 1830s. Chapter 6 describes three less-known military clashes between the British and Sher Muhammad Talpur: the Battle of Hyderabad, the Battle of Pir Ari and the Battle of Shadadpur. Chapter 7 depicts, from a first-hand indigenous perspective, diplomatic interactions between the British and the Talpurs. Chapters 8 and 9 address the private opinions and correspondences of John Jacob, a key figure in the British conquest and early rule of Sindh. Chapter 10 analyses Baloch poetry and history in Sindh. Chapter 11 socio-culturally and historically examines Hyderabad's *amil* community. Chapter 12 details four popular Sindhi folk legends. Chapter 13 compares the Sindh census reports of 1931 and 1941.

Individually, the articles reprinted as chapters in this collection reveal much about Sindh's past. Collectively, these articles not only deepen knowledge about Sindh but also the history of Pakistan and the diversity of its people. They represent, like most research published in the *Journal of the Sind Historical Society*, 'forgotten' chapters in both Sindhi and Pakistani history. These chapters celebrate Pakistan's socio-cultural diversity as well as point toward how the histories of region and nation should be 'intertwined' rather than exclusive.

Notes

1. Jane Hill and Kenneth Hill, *Speaking Mexicano: Dynamics of Syncretic Language in Central Mexico* (Tucson: University of Arizona Press, 1986), 3.

2. Steven Ramey, *Hindu, Sufi, or Sikh: Contested Practices and Identifications of Sindhi Hindus in India and Beyond* (New York:

   Palgrave-Macmillan, 2008), 16 and 190.

3. Ibid. 7.

4. Vashuda Narayanan, 'Religious Vows at the Shrine of Shahul Hamid', in Selva Raj and William Harman (eds.) *Dealing with Deities: The Ritual Vow in South Asia* (Albany, NY: SUNY Press,

2002), 81.

5. Carl Ernst and Tony Stewart, 'Syncretism', in Peter Claus, Sarah Diamond, and Margaret Mills (eds.) *South Asian Folklore: An Encyclopedia* (London: Routledge, 2013), 587.

6. Ibid.

7. Ibid.

8. Ibid. 588.

9. Ibid. 586.

10. Bernard Cohn, 'Regions Subjective and Objective: Their Relation to the Study of Modern Indian History and Society', in Robert Crane (ed.) *Regions and Regionalism in South Asian Studies: An Exploratory Study* (Durham, NC: Duke University Press, 1967), 12.

11. Hill and Hill, 417.

12. Ernst and Stewart, 587.

13. In literary theory, an 'assemblage' is a text that, unlike syncretism, blurs rather than reaffirms distinctions between what is borrowed and what is original (Stuart Selber and Johndan Johnson-Eilola, 'Plagiarism, Originality, Assemblage', *Computers and Composition* 24.4 [2007], 381). For details about how this concept applies to socio-cultural analysis, see: George Marcus and Erkan Saka, 'Assemblage', *Theory, Culture and Society* 23.2–3 (2006), 101–6.

14. Such code-switching involves the 're-contextualization' of socio-cultural interactions (Celso Alvarez-Caccamo, 'Codes', in Alessandro Duranti [ed.], *Key Terms in Language and Culture* [Malden, MA: Blackwell, 2001], 25). This process may yield new forms of socio-cultural difference and/or lead to the repositioning of already existing ones. For examples and greater detail about codeswitching, see: Kathryn Woolard, 'Codeswitching', in Alessandro Duranti (ed.) *A Companion to Linguistic Anthropology* (Malden, MA: Blackwell, 2006), 73–94.

15. Barbara Metcalf, 'Too Little and Too Much: Reflections on Muslims in the History of India', *Journal of Asian Studies* 54.4 (1995), 959. In Sindh, such resistance did not always extend to socio-cultural distinctions outside of the communal domain (e.g., along vectors of caste, class and the urban/rural divide).

16. Hill and Hill, 100.

17. Prior to this period, political power in Sindh depended largely on the ownership of land (David Cheesman, *Landlord Power and Rural Indebtedness in Colonial Sind, 1865–1901* [London: Curzon/Routledge 1997]).

18. Seth Harchandrai Vishindas quoted in Alhaj Mian Ahmad Shafi, *Haji Sir Abdoola Haroon: A Biography* (Karachi: Begum Daulat Anwar Hidayatulla, 1942), 70.

19. Allen Keith Jones, *Politics in Sind, 1907–1940: Muslim Identity and the Demand for Pakistan* (Karachi and London: Oxford University Press, 2002), 16.

20. Discourses that link identity in Sindh with Sufism were also fueled by Sindhi writers influenced by the Theosophical Society (Michel Boivin, 'The New Elite and the Issue of Sufism: A Journey from Vedanta to Theosophy in Colonial Sindh', in Muhammad Ali Shaikh [ed.], *Sindh Through the Centuries II: Proceedings of the 2nd International Seminar* [Karachi: SMI University Press, 2015], 215–31; Michel Boivin, *Historical Dictionary of the Sufi Culture of Sindh in Pakistan and India* [Karachi and London: Oxford University Press, 2015]).

21. Nandita Bhavnani, *The Making of Exile: Sindhi Hindus and the Partition of India* (Chennai: Tranquebar Press, 2014), xxxiii–xxxiv. Muslim politicians frequently blamed *banias* (i.e., Hindu moneylenders) for the woes of rural peasants in Sindh (David Cheesman, 'The Omnipresent Bania: Rural Moneylenders in Nineteenth-Century Sind', *Modern Asian Studies* 16.2 [1982], 445–62).

22. Ghulam Hussain Hidayatullah, 'The Task Before Us', *Alwahid: Special Sind Azad Edition* (1936): 6.

23. Having an exclusively Muslim identity was not a precondition for participating in any of these governments. Two government ministers under Mir Bandeh Ali Khan Talpur were non-Muslim Lohanas (i.e., Nichaldas Chotmal Vazirani and Rai Sahib Gokaldas Mewaldas) from different endogamous moieties. Hidayatullah's government also included non-Muslim ministers, like the *bhaiband* merchant Mukhi Gobindram Pritamdas (a leader of the Sindh Hindu Mahasabha) and the *amil* Hemandas Rupchand Wadhwani. Additionally, Hidayatullah crossed the communal divide to support Bhojsingh Gurdinomal Pahalajani as Sindh's first Assembly Speaker in 1937. Allah Bux Soomro, while from an 'indigenous' Sindhi family, was only able to form a government with support from Vazirani in 1938. Subsequently, Vazirani became Public Works Department, Public Health, and Medical Minister. Allah Bux Soomro's second government (1941–2) also had support from non-Muslims and included Mewaldas as Minister for Local Government and Agriculture. It is also relevant to note that Mir Bandeh Ali Khan Talpur's power base was largely ethnic rather than religious: he led an alliance of Baluch–Talpurs. The family and personal histories of some key politicians from this period were also not always so religiously lengthy: Ghulam Hussain Hidayatullah came from a family that converted to Islam and Shaikh Abdul Majid Sindhi, a minister in Mir Bandeh Ali Khan Talpur's government, converted to Islam in his youth (Bhavnani, xxxi).

24. Jones, 160; Hamida Khuhro, 'Masjid Manzilgah, 1930–40, Test Case for Hindu–Muslim Relations in Sind', *Modern Asian Studies* 32.1 (1998), 50. For example, Shaikh Abdul Majid Sindhi's Sind Azad Party sought the AIML's endorsement but refused to identify itself as its branch.

25. This situation particularly stung the AIML since 32 out of 60 seats were reserved for Muslims and Sindh's population was 72 per cent Muslim.

26. Many politicians in Sindh had multiple party memberships. A major goal of the MLAP was to prevent politicians from shifting their alliances when favorable political winds shifted from one party to another party.

27. Swami Bankhandi Maharaj Udasi established this shrine in 1823. Swami Bankhandi Maharaj Udasi followed a religious sect that centered on the teachings of Sri Chand, the son of Guru Nanak (i.e., Sikhism's founder). Reflecting Sindh's intertwined identities, members of this sect also worshipped the *panchayatana* (i.e., Shiva, Vishnu, Durga, Ganesh, and Surya). Prior to the rise of the Akali or Gurdwara Reform Movement in the twentieth century, *udasis* were the key custodians of Sikh shrines and philosophy.

28. These riots were apparently started by jeering aimed to imply that protesters 'had gotten what they deserved' (Jones, 138).

29. Ibid. 145.

30. While the 1946 elections were a clear victory for the AIML, the results should be taken with a grain of salt since important candidates were excluded and/or prevented from filing applications to run (e.g., G. M. Sayed).

31. Ernst and Stewart, 587.

32. The lists of SHS officers and members at the beginning of each edition of the *Journal of the Sind Historical Society* reveals the socio-cultural spectrum of urban Sindh. It also explains why so few Muslims, who dominated the population of rural Sindh, contributed articles to the journal.

33. Mubarak Ali, 'Writing the History of Sindh', *Dawn*, 23 November 2014 <http://www.dawn.com/news/1145793>

34. This date is particularly meaningful due to the killing of about 200 Sikhs in Karachi during January 1948. These killings contributed to the exodus of upper caste non-Muslims from all over Sindh after Partition. Despite this exodus, many from the low castes (e.g. Kohlis, Bhils, and Meghwars) remained in Sindh.

35. T. S. Thadani, 'The Lohanas', *Journal of the Sind Historical Society* 8.3 (1948), 166–70.

36. Mubarak Ali (ed.), *Sindh Observed: Selections from the Journal of the Sind Historical Society* (Lahore: Gautam Publishers, 1993).

1

The Kalhora Dynasty and its Overthrow by the Talpur Chiefs of Sind

A. B. Advani

THE ORIGIN OF THE ABBASI KALHORAS[1] IS LOST INTO HOARY antiquity. We first hear of them in the tenth century AD. A descendant of Abbas by name Mian Odhanah, resided in Makran. Being a virtuous and pious man, a large number of followers gathered round him. One of the descendants of Mian Odhanah, Thal by name, separated from the original stock, and journeying towards the east, established himself in Kahrah Belah, the capital of Mekran. Thal's grandson Chinah or Jhunia Khan, after a dispute with his brothers over the question of succession, left his native place and, collecting a large number of followers, penetrated further east, fixing his abode at last at the village of Khambhath. The local chief of the place received him well and made him his son-in-law. To Jhunia, a son was born, whom he named Muhammad, and this Muhammad is considered to be the latest ancestor of the Kalhoras.[2] This was in the beginning of the thirteenth century. From 1204 to 1557, the Jhunia family appears to have sunk into comparative obscurity. The glory of the family was revived by Adam Shah Kalhora, the ninth in descent from Muhammad, Mian Adam Shah became the leader of the Kalhoras and resided in a village in Chandukah district.[3] In the year 1586, the celebrated Nawab Khan Khanan, the commander-in-chief of the Imperial Army of Akbar came to Sind and gave to Adam Shah the *zamindari* of the Chandukah district. Thus, the Kalhoras who had been religious mendicants before, now became landholders and gained strength accordingly. The landlords of the surrounding lands, at whose expense the Kalhoras were rising into prominence, grew jealous, and at their instigation, the Kalhoras were dispersed and Mian Adam Shah, then at Multan, was put to death. His dead body, according to his dying wish, was brought to Sukkur and buried there.[4] To the present day, the hill on which he was buried is called Adam Shah-ji-Takri (Adam Shah's hill) and his tomb at Sukkur is a conspicuous object.

During the next hundred years, the power of Kalhora chiefs slowly increased. Their attendants and adherents having grown into a large body, the Kalhoras found it necessary to have some permanent source of income. Necessity, combined with a highly developed sense of acquisitiveness made them possessors of lands, forcibly usurped from different landholders who, unable to cope with these sturdy saints, reported the matter to the Moghul Governors of the province of Sind. Some troops were sent against them, but the Kalhoras defeated the Imperial force. The local Moghul Governors reported this state of things to Prince Muizud-Din, eldest son of Bahadur Shah, the Governor of Multan. The Imperial troops were despatched to Sind and, after some determined fights, succeeded in putting the Kalhoras to flight. Their chief, Mian Din Muhammad Kalhora, was taken away as a prisoner and by royal command was 'chopped to pieces'. Din Muhammad's brother, Mian Yar Muhammad, prudently repaired [*sic*] to the Moghul court. He was received with great compassion, and a Jagir was conferred on him. He was also given the title of 'Khuda Yar Khan' or the friend of God. This occurred at the close of the seventeenth century.[5] By these fights the Kalhora sect acquired a military character and 'the patriarchal authority began to assume the appearance of an organized government'.[6]

Though in their eagerness to acquire temporal power the Kalhoras often resorted to violence and rapine, yet the most remarkable thing about them was their persevering industry in the cultivation of land. We are informed that, 'Wherever they carried their lawless self-assertion, they turned wastes into productive fields and laboured hard to justify the claim that none so well as they, could make a good use of ill-gotten gains.'[7] The digging of Ghar Canal, near the town of Larkana by Mian Shahal Muhammad Kalhora, is a clear proof of the agrarian pursuits of the Kalhoras.[8] They preferred the sickle, but necessity and self-defence often made them change it for the sword. Mian Yar Muhammad, after getting the *jagir* and the title of Khuda Yar Khan, became one of the Imperial agents in Sind. His rule lasted for 18 years of which the first nine years, that is from 1700 to 1709, were full of fights, due to which he extended his territory and increased his power.[9] The next nine years, were years of peace and plenty, except for a battle at Jhok in which the Sufi mendicants of that village were attacked and defeated by Mian Yar Muhammad.[10] He also founded the town of Khudabad, 17 miles north-west of Sehwan, which became the capital of the Kalhora Chiefs.[11] Mian Yar Muhammad died in 1718 and was buried in a beautiful tomb at Khudabad—a most beautiful example of Moslem architecture in Sind.[12] Mian Yar Muhammad Khan's reign was 'distinguished no less for activity and prudence than by the signal success with which those were ultimately crowned.' Mian Nur Muhammad succeeded his father Mian Yar Muhammad, but not without a struggle. His brother contested the succession for nearly three years, and this unnatural contest ceased only when Daud Khan, Mian Nur Muhammad's brother, was amply and honourably provided for. He too was given by the Emperor of Delhi—Muhammad Shah—all the *sanads* and offices granted to his father. The title of Khuda Yar Khan was also bestowed on him.[13] At this time, it may be noted, the Kalhora chief was the governor of a not very extensive portion of Sind. His territory was confined, only to some portion of Northern Sind. In 1722 Mian Nur Muhammad warred on Daudpotas, who had trespassed on the parganahs of Shikarpur, Khanpur and other places.[14] Twice did Mian Nur Muhammad invade Shikarpur, with the intention of reducing it, but the fort of Shikarpur was well defended, and the besiegers retired to their capital—Khudabad. After nine months, Nur Muhammad sent another large force under the command of his brother but this force too was defeated and slaughtered by the Daudpotahs. These defeats did not dishearten Mian Nur Muhammad. The next year saw another Kalhora force marching towards Shikarpur. The chief of the Daudpotas now was one Sadik Khan who, finding himself unable to fight with the Kalhoras, fled. 'So the Kalhoras gained peaceably what they could not gain by force.'[15] After subduing the Daudpotas, in 1730, Mian Nur Muhammad commenced hostilities with the Khan of Kalat, who called himself 'The Royal Eagle of Kohistan'. The expedition against the Khan of Kalat, was crowned with success. A pitched battle was fought at the village of Jandehar in 1731 in which the Royal Eagle of Kohistan—Mir Abdullah Khan— was slain, and Brohis utterly routed. Peace was made with the Brohis and the future good connections between the Kalhoras and the Brohis were guaranteed by the two sons of Mian Nur Muhammad Khan marrying the two royal ladies of the Brohi clan.[16] In 1730, the fortress of Bukkur and its dependencies were made over to Mian Nur Muhammad, who had already acquired Sehwan; and in the next year, Nawab Sadik Ali Khan, the governor of Thatta, being unwilling to retain the charge of the place, the 'Subha of Thatta', was also given to Mian Nur Muhammad.[17] Thus by 1737, the whole of Sind practically, came under the rule of Mian Nur Muhammad. The Kalhora rule, therefore, may be said to have started from 1737.

We have mentioned before, that the Kalhoras were addicted more to agrarian than to war-like pursuits. They, therefore, invited mercenaries from the mountainous regions to the northwest of Sind to take service in their armies. The Baloch tribes, including Talpurs, left their mountains at this invitation, and came down to Sind where they enlisted in the Kalhora army.[18] The coming of the Talpurs and other Balochis in Sind is thus described by that famous orientalist Richard F. Burton:

> When the Balochis arrived within fifteen miles of Khudabad, the prince sent out several of his ministers and nobles, with presents of clothes and horses with gold saddles, to receive and escort his distinguished guests to the capital. As the procession advanced, it met a troop of beggarly shepherds, followed by their flocks, and women mounted on asses. The ministers enquired for Mir Aludo and were much astonished when told that the ragged wayfarer with the Dheri in his hand and the Kambo on his shoulders, was the personage whom they were sent to conduct with such ceremony. However, they saluted him with courtesy, took the Dheri and Kambo from him, mounted him upon the best horse and accompanied him on his way to the capital.[19]

The above story of the Talpurs being originally shepherds and goatherds supports the etymological theory advanced by Ansari. The word 'Talpur', he asseverates, is a corrupted form of the word 'Thal-Bur', which in Persian language means the 'cutter of branches'; a task generally done by shepherds and goatherds.[20]

The latter Talpur chiefs deprecated this theory about their humble origin, and were emphatic that they were of the Arab origin, and were descended from 'Amir Hamzah, the son of Hasham, the son of Abul-Munaf'.[21] Whether of humble origin or of Arab pedigree is not so much to the point as the rise of the Talpurs to eminence. The immediate common ancestor of the Talpurs, was one Kuka or Begam. One of his sons Hotak, begot a son, Shahdad by name.[22] This Shahdad Khan, left his paternal home on account of some difference of opinion with his paternal uncle, Mir Sobdar. He migrated to the plains of Sind, where he took service with the Kalhora chief Mian Yar Mahommad.[23] A large number of Balochis followed him. Extensive lands were given to them, on account of their military service, in the neighbourhood of Brahmanabad. Shahadpur, called after this Mir

Shahdad, became their headquarters.[24] This must have occurred
at the close of the seventeenth century or in the beginning of the
eighteenth century, when Mir Shahdad Khan is heard for the first
time fighting bravely in the Derah Ghazi Khan and Derah Ismail
Khan on behalf of Prince Muizzudin. On account of his bravery his
position was raised and favours bestowed on him.[25] Mir Shahdad,
gradually became the chief adviser of Mian Yar Mahommed Khan,
and 'acquired a great deal of influence in political affairs'.[26] Mir
Shahdad died in 1734, and one of his sons, Mir Bahram, served
Mian Nur Mahommed Kalhora faithfully and well.[27] Hardly had
Mian Nur Mahommed enjoyed his rule for one year, when he heard
of the mighty Persian host, under the leadership of Nadir Shah,
rushing like a mighty torrent from the north-west and sweeping
away everything before it. Nadir Shah, it is narrated, got angry at
the refusal of the Moghul Emperor—Mahommed Shah—to deliver
up some fugitives who had fled and found asylum in India. The
rapid march of Nadir, the defeat of the 'effeminate' Indian Army,
the general massacre in the streets of Delhi, and the plunder of
every conceivable article in Delhi for 35 days are matters too well-
known to need any elaboration.[28] On 22 April 1739, the Moghul
Emperor, Mahommed Shah concluded a treaty with Nadir Shah
by which he ceded to him all the territories westward of the 'River
Attock'. He made over to Nadir Shah, 'The Castle Buckar, Sunker,
and Khoudabad, the rest of the Territories, Passes, and Abodes of
the Chokias, Ballches, etc., with Province of Tatta, etc.'[29] Mian Nur
Mahommed did not approve of this cession of Sind to Nadir Shah,
by the Emperor of Delhi as the ceded lands formed his territory,
and he committed the blunder of refusing to recognise Nadir Shah
as his sovereign.[30] When Nadir Shah came to know of this, he left
Kabul on 27 November 1739, and marched towards Sind. On
1 February 1740, he reached Larkana, where he learnt that Mian
Nur Mahommed had fled to Umarkot with his treasure. Mian Nur
Mahommed imagined that the desert, the forests and lack of proper
roads in Sind would prove too much for Nadir Shah, who would

therefore fail to reach him in the desert fastness of Umarkot. The
army of Nadir Shah, however, marched towards the desert and
on 16 February 1740 at 3 o'clock arrived in the neighbourhood
of Umarkot. Mian Nur Mahommed was captured by the Persian
advance-guard and was made to disgorge all his wealth, which he
had buried in the underground cellars of the fort of Umarkot. This
hidden treasure amounted to one crore of rupees. The Persian host
left Umarkot with Mian Nur Mahommed in chains and reached
Larkana on 3 March 1740. Nadir Shah pardoned the Mian,
and restored to him only Lower and Central Sind. The country
bordering Baluchistan was given over to Muhbat Khan, the chief of
that province, and Shikarpur was given to the Daudpotas.[31] This was
not all. A further penalty of an annual tribute of twenty lakhs was
imposed on Mian Nur Mahommed, and his two sons—Mahommad
Murad Yab Khan and Ghulam Shah Khan—were taken away by
Nadir Shah as hostages. After giving Mian Nur Mahommed the
title of Shah Kuli Khan, Nadir Shah and his army left Sind.[32] Nadir
Shah's invasion of Sind had disorganized the peaceful government
of the country, and some local tribes had shaken off their yoke of
obedience. The year 1741 was therefore spent in punishing these
rebellious tribes. In 1743, Nadir Shah sent Thamas Kuli Khan to
Sind to punish the Daudpotas. Mian Nur Mahommed deemed it
wise, to remain quiet and not take part in any matter. This resulted
in anarchy, as there was practically no government in the country.
After some time, the Mian went to the camp of Thamas Kuli Khan
and was given back his authority. But Thamas Kuli Khan compelled
him to give his third son, Attur Khan, as hostage. During the next
three years, after the departure of Thamas Kuli Khan, the Hindu
chiefs of Kakralla and Dharaja were chastised and subdued, and
once more, the Kalhora authority was established in Sind.[33]

Nadir Shah was assassinated in 1747 and his Afghanistan
territory was seized and retained by Ahmed Shah Abdali.[34] This
new sovereign and successor of Nadir Shah confirmed Mian Nur
Mahommad afresh as the ruler of Sind, and gave him the title of

Shah Nawab Khan. Soon after this, Mian Nur Mahommed's three sons returned from Persia, where they had remained as hostages.[35] Ahmed Shah Abdali, the founder of the Government of Duranis, was for the first few years of his rule too occupied with greater affairs than Sind and Mian Nur Mahommed, taking advantage of this opportunity, stopped paying the annual tribute of twenty lakh rupees fixed by Nadir Shah.[36]

In 1754, King Ahmed Shah, advanced towards Sind to enforce the payment of the annual tribute, which, as mentioned above, the Mian had foolishly evaded. The Mian fled to Jesulmir, where he died 'of quinsy or the inflammation of the throat'.[37] After the death of Mian Nur Mahommed in 1755 his eldest son, Mahommed Murad Yab Khan, succeeded him on the throne, which he enjoyed for only a short time. Ahmed Shah Abdali not only confirmed him in the rank and power of his father, but conferred on him the title of Sirbuland Khan. Mian Mahommed Murad Yab Khan's rule or misrule did not last long. He ill-treated the noblemen and oppressed his subjects, with the result that he was deposed and his brother, Mian Ghulam Shah, was seated on the *gaddi*.[38] His other brother, Mian Atur Khan, resented this and personally presented his case before the Durani king—Ahmed Shah. He succeeded in getting *firman* from the king appointing him as the ruler of Sind instead of Ghulam Shah. Atur Khan was joined by his brother Ahmed Yar Khan and both of them proceeded to Sind. Atur Khan being armed with the Royal Seal and a body of Afghan soldiers, the people of Sind deserted the cause of Mian Ghulam Shah, and turned towards the new nominee. The result was that having no other alternative, Mian Ghulam Shah fled to desert.[39] Then followed a period of incessant warfare between Ghulam Shah on one side and his two brothers, Atur Khan and Ahmed Yar Khan on the other, in which Ghulam Shah ultimately became victorious.[40] It is from 1762 that Mian Ghulam Shah's rule may be said to have commenced as it was in this year that he was confirmed as the ruler of Sind by the royal *firman*. Along with the royal *firman*, Ahmed Shah bestowed on him the title of 'Shah Wardi Khan', an elephant, a robe of honour and many other presents.[41] The rule of Mian Ghulam Shah marks the zenith of the glory of the Kalhora rule. He was the most capable and vigorous of the Kalhora rulers. His brilliant career and vigorous rule arouses further admiration when it is learnt that he was absolutely illiterate and was of lowly birth. If the oral tradition, quite popular in Sind, is to be given credence, then Mian Ghulam Shah was a gift of Shah Abdul Latif Bhitai, a local saint and poet who flourished in the days of Mian Nur Mohammed. Mir Nur Mahommed, according to tradition, possessed a beautiful dancing girl—Gulan. This girl was wont to dance before the famous poet every Friday night with exquisite grace. On one such occasion, when Gulan had danced with great artistry and abandon, the poet was so pleased with her that he desired her to ask him for anything. The dancer modestly asked for a son, and the poet, being endowed with supernatural powers, blessed her and promised her a son. In due course of time, the story runs, Mian Ghulam Shah was born to Gulan, and the saintly poet blessed the child, prophesying his greatness by saying:

گلان مان گل پیدا ٹیو
ڪي نٹڙيو ڪي نٹڙندو

From the garden Gulan was born a rose that has bloomed and is still blooming

There being nobody to subdue in Sind and nothing to conquest, Mian Ghulam Shah turned his covetous eyes, after his ascension in 1762, to the Cutch territory.[42] In 1763 Mian Ghulam Shah marched towards Cutch, conquering the frontier fort of Sindri on the way.[43] On the heights of Jarah was fought a terrible battle between the Sind army and the Rajputs of Cutch.[44] The Rajputs, according to their time-honoured custom, cut the throats of all their ladies and then donning saffron robes came out to fight unto death. For six hours, in a thick fog which obscured the light of day, the battle went on, and so terrible was the slaughter that 'stones a pound in weight were moved from the side of the hill by the streams of blood'. The loss of both the armies was considerable, and in the evening, both the armies made a 'precipitate retreat'. Next year, Mian Ghulam Shah again invaded Cutch and arrived near the capital of Cutch. The Rao of Cutch, however, sued for peace and pacified the Mian by offering him his two seaports of Basta and Lakhpat on the borders of Sind. In 1765, on account of his bravery, and successfully managing the affairs of Sind, Mian Ghulam Shah received a fresh title of 'Shams-ud-Dawlat' or 'The Sword of the State' from the king.[45] Two more facts require to be noticed in the career of Mian Ghulam Shah, namely, his founding the modern town of Hyderabad (in Sind) and his matrimonial connections with the Rao of Cutch. Khudabad, the capital city of the Kalhoras, had soon after its founding, in the beginning of the eighteenth century, been abandoned. Each successive Kalhora chief had thereafter founded a new capital, which, either to some idle whim or danger from the summer floods of the Indus, had to be abandoned. Thus Khudabad, Muradabad, Allahabad, and Shahgarh became capital towns for a short time, only to be deserted for new ones.[46] In 1768, Mian Ghulam Shah decided to change his capital. He chose the site of old Nerun Kot on the left bank of the Indus which, since many centuries, used to be called Nerun Kafri or the Nerun of the Infidels. The range of Ganja hills, lying far above the Indus inundations with the newly formed Phuleli river washing its base, guaranteed security and permanence, and the northern spur of the low range of Ganja hill was selected for building the new capital. The graves of certain Pirs or holy men, and the shapeless rubbish that once upon a time was the old fort of Nerun, were cleared away and a large fort was built on the site. And to this newly built capital, Mian Ghulam Shah removed his court in 1770 and called it Hyderabad.[47] In the same year, good connections between the Rao of Cutch and Mian Ghulam Shah were established by matrimonial relationship. The Rao of Cutch gave Mian Ghulam Shah the daughter of one of his cousins in marriage.[48] It appears that the Mian wanted the Rao's sister in marriage, but later on was content to have the daughter of the chief of Khanker.[49] The seaports of Basta and Lakhpat were returned to the Rao by the highly pleased Mian in consideration of this marriage.

In 1772 several tombs, situated on a hillock to the southwest of the fort of Hyderabad, were razed to the ground by Mian Ghulam Shah's orders with a view to construct a small mud fort on the cleared ground; while this mud fort was being built, the Mian was suddenly smitten with paralysis, which proved fatal. In two days' time, he was dead. His death, which took place on 2 August 1772, was attributed by the superstitious people to the sacrilege he had committed in destroying the graves of the venerated saints on Shah Makai's hill to build his mud-fort there.[50] He was buried in a beautiful tomb to the northern extremity of the town of Hyderabad. This tomb, 'though sadly dilapidated, is by far the finest and was selected by Lord Curzon as the only one that deserved to be restored and kept in repair at the public expense.'[51] On the next day, after Mian Ghulam Shah's death, his son Mian Mahommed Surfraz Khan was seated on the throne. King Taimur Shah, who had succeeded to the throne of Kandhar after the death of his father, Ahmad Shah Durani, recognized the Mian as the new ruler of Sind by sending him a robe of honour and conferring on him the title of 'Khuda Yar Khan'.[52] After setting the affairs in the northern districts of his territory, Mian Mahommed Sarfraz Khan led his army to Cutch, the ruler of which country welcomed the Mian. This submissive attitude of the Rao of Cutch pleased the Mian, who left the Rao in peace and went towards Gujrat. The Jarejah chief of that province, too, submitted. Then the Mian returned to Sind.[53] The submissive attitude of the Rao of Cutch and the Jarejah Chief is a statement by the Mahommedan historian which admits of some doubt. Dr Burnes has clearly stated in his book, *A Narrative of a Visit to Court of Scinde*, that Mian Sarfraz Khan invaded Cutch twice leaving behind a desolate and plundered country.[54] Had the attitude of the Rao of Cutch been submissive and humble, the entry of the Sind army in Cutch, would have been peaceful and there would not have been any devastation or desolation in its wake.

The Talpurs it will be remembered had risen to power in the days of Mian Yar Mahommed, in the beginning of the eighteenth century. After the death of Mir Shahdad Khan Talpur in 1734, his son, Mir Bahram, had continued to serve Mian Nur Mahommed as faithfully as his father. Mir Bahram, through ability, had come to occupy a very prominent position in the political affairs of Sind. It was through him that Mian Mahommed Murad Yar Khan was dethroned in favour of Mian Ghulam Shah[55]. On account of this, he had won the respect of Mian Ghulam Shah. After Mian Ghulam Shah's death, Mir Bahram Khan continued to serve the Kalhora family, now represented by Mian Mahommed Sarfraz Khan. One of the courtiers of the Mian, by name Rajah Likhi, began to sow the seeds of distrust in the heart of the Mian against Mir Bahram Khan. Mian Sarfraz Khan was not a fool, but the strategy of Rajah Likhi slowly began to work. The Mian began to evince distrust of the Mir and gradually became cold towards him. The advice of Diwan Gidumal, Mian Sarfraz Khan's faithful minister, was not listened to and the efforts of this Hindu minister to bring about a reconciliation between the Mian and Mir Bahram Khan failed.[56]

Mir Bahram was a shrewd person and he felt that his life was in danger. He therefore called his two sons—Bijar Khan and Sobdar Khan—in his presence and told them that he felt he would soon be destroyed by Mian Sarfraz Khan. 'You know we have sworn on the Koran [sic] to be faithful to him (Mian Sarfraz Khan) and he has sworn to be kind to us. If now, without any reason he causes some harm to us, we must quietly bear it, leaving him to the punishment of God.' The two sons were told to escape and save their lives while the going was good, leaving their aged father to his fate. The eldest son took the hint and started on a pilgrimage to Mecca, but the younger son—Mir Sobdar Khan—preferred to stay with his father and die along with him if the matters came to a push.[57] One day after this, Mir Bahram Khan went to the royal court to pay his usual respects. Mian Sarfraz Khan gave him a letter to read telling him that it was from his son Mir Bijar. While Mir Bahram was reading the letter, a servant, at a previously arranged signal, drew out his sword and killed the aged Mir Bahram Khan. Mir Sobdar Khan, who was standing outside, was then besieged by some courtiers and cut to pieces but not before his strong hand had knocked off a few heads. This event occurred in the year 1774.[58] Mir Bijar Khan being away on pilgrimage, his cousin Mir Fateh Khan collected an army of Baloches with a view to punish the treacherous Kalhora chief—Mian Sarfraz Khan. He attacked the fort of Khudabad, but Mian Muhammed Sarfraz Khan fearing the wrath of the infuriated Baloches, secretly fled from the Khudabad fort, and sailing hastily in a fisherman's boat he reached the fort of Hyderabad. After his flight his adherents placed Mian Sarfraz Khan's brother—Mohammed Khan—on the throne. Mahommed Khan was a ruler only in name because the real power lay in the hands of Rajah Likhi. Mir Fateh Khan, after having taken his revenge, retired to Shahdadpur, the capital of the Baloches.

The incapacity of Mian Mahommed Khan made a change in rulers necessary and the choice of Rajah Likhi and his companions fell on Mian Ghulam Nabi, who was a brother of the deceased Mian Ghulam Shah. In 1777, Mian Mohammed Khan was compelled to vacate the throne for his uncle—Mian Ghulam Nabi.[59] At this time Bijir Khan returned from his pilgrimage and summoned the Baloches to aid him in avenging his father and brother.[60] The evil counsellors of Mian Ghulam Nabi prepared to march out and fight with Mir Bijar. This was against Mian Ghulam Nabi's wishes who, being a peace-loving man, suggested that peace be made with Mir Bijar. To this, his counsellors would not listen and he was compelled to go with them and fight. At Lanyari in the Shahdadpur taluka, a battle was fought between the Baloches and the Mian's army. When the Mian saw his soldiers losing ground, he sent a message to Mir Bijar requesting him to get him out of the difficulty as he felt himself quite helpless in the hands of Rajah Likhi and his other counsellors.[61] When these wicked men came to know of this, they became very angry and murdered the Mian. The Kalhora army was defeated

and Rajah Likhi and others of his band fled. In the Hyderabad fort
at this time, Mian Abdunnabi, a brother of the murdered Mian
Ghulam Nabi, had the charge of four royal prisoners. They were
Mian Sarfraz Khan, his two sons, and his brother Mahmud Khan
who had been deposed in favour of Mian Ghulam Nabi. Learning
of Mian Ghulam Nabi's death, Mian Abdunnabi killed all these
four prisoners and thus removed his possible rivals for the throne
of Sind. After the battle of Lanyari, Mir Bijar laid siege to the fort
of Hyderabad, which Mian Abdunnabi stoutly defended. Peace was
however made between the two, by which the throne was given to
Mian Abdunnabi, and Mir Bijar became his chief minister.[62] During
the reign of Mian Abdunnabi, Sind was invaded by the army of King
Taimur under the leadership of Izzat Yar Khan Abbasi, who had
obtained from king Taimur the rulership of Sind to the exclusion
of Mian Abdunnabi. A battle took place in 1781 near Shikarpur
between the Afghan army and the Sind force in which, after much
bloodshed, the Afghan army was defeated. At this, king Taimur was
so incensed that he personally marched against Sind. Mir Bijar
Khan was not only brave but tactful too. He went forward to pacify
the king and succeeded in doing so, with the result that the angry
monarch not only went back to his country pleased but he confirmed
Mian Abdunnabi as the ruler of Sind.[63] On account of his ability
and political sagacity, Mir Bijar came to be the real ruler in the land,
Mian Abdunnabi being merely a puppet. The result was that Mian
Abdunnabi began to chafe under the tutelage in which he was held.[64]

In 1781, one day, two Rajputs came to Mir Bijar telling him that
they had brought for him a confidential letter from the Maharaja of
Jodhpur. Mir Bijar went to a private room accompanied by these two
Rajputs from Jodhpur. As he was busy reading the letter, these two
Rajputs, taking their daggers, plunged them in the sides of Mir Bijar,
who jumped up at this assault and cut these treacherous Hindus into
pieces with his sword. But the dagger blows he had received proved
fatal and he too fell down dead.[65] What could have been the object
of this murder? One theory is that Mian Abdunnabi, fearing the

growing power of Mir Bijar, hired two assassins from the Maharaja of Jodhpur for the removal of this Baloch warrior, the consideration for this foul deed being the fort of Umarkot which was given to the Maharaja of Jodhpur.[66] According to another historian, this murder was committed not at the instigation of Mian Abdunnabi, but his mother, in whose heart, the murder of her son—Mian Ghulam Nabi, in the battle of Lanyari—had caused the birth of bitter feelings against Mir Bijar, whom somehow she held responsible for her son's death. She communicated her grievances to Maharaja Bijaising of Jodhpur, who undertook to help her. He sent two Rajputs to Sind to murder Bijar Khan, promising their families, in case they perished in their task, an annual jagir of Rs. 30,000.[67] Lt Col. James Tod advances another theory, which exonerates Mian Abdunnabi from having any hand in the murder of Mir Bijar. Mir Bijar, according to Tod, had been presumptuous in demanding a daughter of the royal family of Marwar to be his wife. Maharaja Bijaising, smarting under this insult, hired two assassins to destroy Mir Bijar which they successfully did at the cost of their own lives.[68] But if the motive for this murder is clouded with doubt, the deed anyway is clear.

After the death of Mir Bijar, his son—Mir Abdullah—became the head of the Baloch tribe. Accompanied by his relatives, he went to Mian Abdunnabi to pay the customary respects. But Mian Abdunnabi, being guilty, feared revenge at the hands of the Baloches. He, therefore, fled to Kalat with his treasure and confidential servants. The throne being vacant, Mir Abdullah selected one Sadik Ali, a kinsman of the Kalhora rulers, and placed the turban of rulership on his head.[69] Sadik Ali, being religiously inclined, took little or no interest in the mundane affairs like the government of Sind. The result was that Mir Abdullah became the real ruler of the land to the satisfaction of the people.[70] Mian Abdunnabi wanted to get back the rulership of Sind so he appealed to Nasir Khan of Kalat and Maharajah of Jodhpur for aid. The result was that two armies, one of Kalat and the other from Jodhpur, began to march on Sind from the north and the east. Mir Abdullah prepared his army and marched out to oppose the Jodhpur army, which he totally defeated, gaining much booty. Without taking any rest, Mir Abdullah marched against the Kalat army, which also he defeated causing Mian Abdunnabi to fly for his life to Kalat.[71] While at Kalat, Mian Abdunnabi heard of the coming of the famous Afghan Chief—Sardar Madad Khan—to Bhawalpur. He solicited the Afghan Chief's help for getting back Sind. King Taimur Shah also wrote to Madad Khan to take the Afghan army to Sind. Madad Khan rushed on Sind like a hurricane, devastating the country from the north to the south. Madad Khan's sole object was to obtain the treasure and the loot which Mian Abdunnabi had promised him. When these were not forthcoming, he commenced plundering towns and villages. Then commenced a reign of terror, the like of which had not been seen or heard of before in Sind. Rich or poor, high or low, irrespective of sex, all were mercilessly beaten and deprived, as the native historian puts it, of all their property, 'even to the clothes on their persons, to the shoes in their feet, and to the mats in their houses'.[72] 'Madad Khan,' writes Elphinstone, 'laid waste the country with fire and sword; and so severe were his ravages, that a dreadful famine followed his campaign, and the province of Sind is said not yet to have recovered from what it suffered on that occasion.'[73] Mir Abdullah and other Talpur chiefs negotiated for peace but found out that Madad Khan intended treachery, so they prepared to fight with him. But Madad Khan and his savage Afghans, satiated with blood and ruin, left Sind forever, leaving Mian Abdunnabi to shift for himself as best as he could.[74] Mian Abdunnabi now sought to be reconciled to Mir Abdullah Khan. This he successfully effected by sending the Koran to Mir Abdullah on the margin of which he wrote, 'I hereby commit to writing and swear by the word of God that henceforth, I shall remain true to the Mir and will not prove treacherous.'[75] On this sacred promise, the reconciliation was brought about between the Mian and the Mir, but the Kalhora family was ill-fated. Hardly had the reconciliation been effected, and peace and good will restored, when Mian Abdunnabi began to seek an opportunity to have Mir Abdullah Khan murdered. And he had not long to wait. One day when Mir Abdullah and Mir Fateh Khan, the two Talpur chiefs, went to the court of the Kalhora chief they were asked by the attendants at the gate to unbuckle their swords and enter the court unarmed. The Mirs thought that either it was a foul plan or the Mian was merely testing them. They bravely handed over their swords, but as soon as this was done they both were surrounded by the Mian's men who immediately made them prisoners. The captive Mirs now realized that their end was near; so they started reciting the Koran. An executioner came on the scene and cut off their heads. This butchery took place in 1783.[76] This was the last proverbial straw which broke the Talpur camel's back. Again and again had the Talpurs reinstated the treacherous Kalhoras to power forgetting their feelings of revenge and repeatedly they had experienced ingratitude for their good will, and treachery for their faithfulness. Under the leadership of Mir Fateh Ali Khan (grandson of Mir Bahram who had been murdered in 1774), the Baloches rose and engaged the force of Mian Abdunnabi in the battle of Halani, defeating it. This battle took place in 1783.[77] For the next few years Mian Abdunnabi strove hard and repeatedly to get back the Sind rulership. He returned to Sind with the help of the Kalat army which, after plundering Abdunnabi's own camp in lieu of pay and provisions, deserted him and went back to Kalat. The dejected Mian then went before Taimur Shah of Afghanistan pleading for aid against Mir Fateh Ali Khan and other Talpur chiefs. When this news was received in Sind, Mir Fateh Ali Khan sent his envoys to the royal court to represent his case. Taimur Shah, at last, divided Sind into two halves, bestowing one half on Mir Fateh Ali Khan, and the other on Mian Abdunnabi. An arbitrator and an Afghan army were despatched to Sind to reinstate Mian Abdunnabi. The Mir's envoys had not been idle all this time at the royal court. They at last persuaded Taimur Shah to issue a *firman* appointing Mir Fateh Ali Khan as the ruler of the whole Sind and ordering Mian Abdunnabi to desist from attacking or invading Sind.[78] It is learnt that the consideration for obtaining this *firman* in favour of Fateh Ali Khan was nine lacs of rupees in cash.[79] The chagrin and despair of Mian Abdunnabi should rather be left to the imagination of the reader than described. After wandering from place to place, he finally settled at Jodhpur where he was well received, and where, to the present day, his descendants reside as middle-class Jagirdars.[80]

In 1793, Taimur Shah died and his son, Zaman Shah, succeeded him. The Talpur chiefs who had ruled Sind now for about ten years received recognition from him as the rulers of Sind.[81] Thus ended finally the Kalhora rule so promisingly started by Mian Nur Muhammed, and so gloriously maintained by his worthy son, Mian Ghulam Shah.

A general review of the Kalhora dynasty makes one wonder at the folly and villainy which both in the case of the latter Kalhoras are found striving hard for pre-eminence. For a period of three centuries these religious mendicants struggled for greatness. And hardly had that object so ardently sought for been attained when, by their folly and overweening ambition, they were hurled back in 1783 to their original obscurity. The latter Kalhoras were neither imbeciles nor thorough sadists. How then explain their murders? We believe that they were driven to these treacherous murders by a latent fear, inspired by the growing power of the Talpurs, that they were going to lose their rulership. That explanation makes their actions credible though not creditable.

With the recognition of Mir Fateh Ali Khan by Zaman Shah in 1793 as the ruler of Sind, the pretensions of the Kalhoras were finally ended, and the Talpur rule commenced.

NOTES

1. They are called Abbasi Kalhoras as they claim descent from Abbas, the paternal uncle of the Prophet Muhammad (PBUH).

2. Mirza Kalich Beg, *History of Sind II*, 135.

3. James McMurdo, 'The History of the Kalhora Family of Sindh', *Journal of the Bombay Branch of the Royal Asiatic Society* 1, 406; Kalich Beg (*History of Sind II*, 136n3) writes that the parganah round about Larkana is even now called Chandko.

4. Beg, *History of Sind II*, 136–7.

5. Thomas Postans, *Personal Observations on Sindh*, 166–7.

6. McMurdo, *History of the Kalhora*, 409.

7. Malcolm Haig, *Indus Delta Country*, 112.

8. Beg, *History of Sind II*, 137.

9. Ibid. 142–4.

10. Jhok is a small town in the Karachi district and contains the shrine of Shah Inayutallah Sufi; Beg, *History of Sind II*, 132–3.

11. Haig, *Indus Delta Country*, 114.

12. Beg, *History of Sind II*, 144.

13. McMurdo, *History of the Kalhora*, 413.

14. Edward Aitken (*Gazetteer of Sind*, 107) explains that Daudpotas, or sons of Daud, trace their descent from the Abbaside Khalifas through one Amir Ahmad who came to Sind via Makran and set up a kingdom; Beg, 145.

15. Shahamet Ali, *History of Bhawalpur*, 19–21.

16. Beg, 146–7.

17. Ibid. 147.

18. Commissioner's Office, *History of Land Alienations in Sind I*, 1–2.

19. Richard Burton, *Sind and the Races that Inhabit the Valley of the Indus*, 235. Dheri is a bit of stone or other such material, round which the raw wool thread is twisted. Kambo is a long cloth thrown over the right shoulder, and so fastened round the waist as to leave a place for the lambs that are too young to walk.

20. S. Ansari, *Muslman Races Found in Sind*, 29.

21. Edward Eastwick, *Dry Leaves from Young Egypt*, 358.

22. Commissioner's Office, *History of Land Alienations in Sind II*, 79.

23. Edward Eastwick, *Dry Leaves from Young Egypt*, 359.

24. Commissioner's Office, *History of Land Alienations in Sind I*, 2. Shahdadpur, the chief town of Shahdadpur Taluka, is at a distance of forty miles north-east to Hyderabad in Sind.

25. Beg 143–4.

26. Ibid. 165.

27. Commissioner's Office, *History of Land Alienations*, 79–80.

28. Hugh Murray, *History of British India*, 27–4.

29. James Fraser, *History of Nadir Shah*, 223–6.

30. Haig, *Indus Delta Country*, 116.

31. William Jones, *Histoire de Nader Chah II*, 88–94.

32. McMurdo, *History of the Kalhora*, 417.

33. Rao Bahadur Diwan Bulchand Dayaram (*History of Sind*, 27) identifies these two places as parts of Mirpur Bathoro and Mirpur Sakro Talukas now; Beg, 149–50.
34. Haig, 117.
35. Beg, 151.
36. Haig, 117.
37. Beg, 152.
38. Ibid. 153–5.
39. Ibid. 155–6.
40. Haig, 117–8.
41. Beg, 161.
42. Haig, 118.
43. Beg, 161.
44. This place is twenty-miles north-east of Lakhpat Bundar in Cutch.
45. McMurdo, *History of the Kalhora*, 423–4.
46. Beg, 142, 154–5, 158.
47. Haig, 119–21.
48. Beg, 163.
49. James Burnes, *A Narrative of a Visit to the Court of Sinde*, 151.
50. Beg, 163–4.
51. Aitken, *Gazetteer of Sind*, 113.
52. Beg, 164.
53. Aitken, 113.
54. Burnes, *Visit to the Court of Sinde*, 161.
55. Beg, 165.
56. This Hindu gentleman, according to Bherumal Mahirchand Advani's *Amilan-ji-Ahwal* (40–1), was the actual founder of the town of Hyderabad Sind. Mian Ghulam Shah gave him the necessary money, and he built the fort of Hyderabad.
57. Mir Bijar's conduct is rather surprising. Knowing that his father's life was in danger, he still went away to Mecca to save his own life obviously. The only conclusion for his lack of filial regard, according to me, is the bad spirit existing between the father and the son.
58. Beg, 166–8.
59. Ibid. 168–70.
60. Haig, 122.
61. This Rajah Likhi was the son of Rajah Likhi. He had taken his father's place after the latter's death which, according to Beg's *History of Sind II* (170), was due to fear at the news of the coming back to Sind of Mir Bijar Khan.
62. Beg, 171–6.
63. Ibid. 175–8.
64. McMurdo, 427.
65. Beg, 178–9.
66. Ibid. 180n1.
67. Ali, *History of Bhawalpur*, 65–6.
68. James Tod, *Annals and Antiquities of Rajasthan III*, 1289.
69. Turban is the common headgear in Sind. One of the customs, on the ascension of a new ruler on the throne was the tying of 'Pugree' round the head of the ruler by his minister or the most important person at the court in recognition of his having become the king. This was a typical Muhammadan custom, to which great importance used to be attached.
70. Beg, 179–81.
71. Ibid. 181–4.
72. Ibid. 184–185, 187.
73. Montstuart Elphinstone, *An Account of the Caubul and Its Dependencies in Persia, Tatary and India*, 561.

74. Beg, 186, 189–91.
75. Ibid. 191.
76. Ibid. 192–3.
77. Ibid. 193–5.
78. Ibid. 198–202.
79. Ali, *History of Bhawalpur*, 70.
80. McMurdo, 430.
81. Beg, 206.

2

Crime and Punishment in the Days of the Talpur Rulers of Sind (1783–1843)

A. B. Advani

TO UNDERSTAND THE PECULIAR DISPOSITION OF ANY RACE OF men, one way is to observe the popular crimes and the way in which they are punished by that race. If this last test were applied to the people of Sind in the days of the Talpur Rulers of Sind (1783–1843), it will be found that the Sindhis at that time were by no means bad people as compared to people in other parts of India.

Crimes then, and crimes now, have not changed, but the mode of punishment has definitely undergone a change. To judge the people of the past by the punishments current then, and to consider them barbarians and savages, is to err most grievously. Other times, other manners. Moreover it should be borne in mind that if the punishments meted out by the Talpur Rulers are deemed savage by us, the Talpur Rulers themselves are mainly responsible for such thinking. The Talpurs were a military tribe who had migrated from the mountainous regions to the north-west of Sind, somewhere in the end of the seventeenth century and had slowly risen to power. Except for a little reading of [the] Koran [*sic*], they were most of them illiterate and knew no other law but that of matchlock and scimitar. In the main, they delegated the administration of law to the *mullas* and the *panchayats* and betook themselves to *shikar* and such other earthly pleasures.

The Talpur Rulers could, at best, be compared to feudal barons of [the] Middle Ages in England. The mode of administering justice was no doubt arbitrary, but it was prompt and vigorous. It [was] aimed more at the punishment of the guilty than the protection of the innocent.

One of the popular crimes was murder. An offence of such a serious nature was adjudged by the Talpur chiefs themselves, with the help of the *kazi*. After the judgment, the murderer's arms were pinioned and he was given up to the victim's relations, who either cut his throat with a knife or struck off his head with a sword. Sometimes the murderer was tortured to death by sticks, stones, poison, or thrown into a deep well.[1] At times the murderer, instead of being hanged or otherwise put to death, was publicly shamed by having his head and beard shaved off and then after mounting him upon an ass, he was paraded through the town and was then made to seek forgiveness from the murdered man's relatives.[2] In addition to all this, he had also to pay a certain sum of money called *diyat* which amounted to Rs. 2,000.

If the murderer escaped, one of his near relations was *not* put to death, nor did the practice of *badli* exist in Sind as it did in other parts of India, by which a paid substitute took upon himself the blame and consequences of the offence. The Ex-Political describes a scene he witnessed at Thatta in the late thirties of the last century, where the murderer being a Sayyid, instead of being hanged or decapitated, was put in a large iron cage and there he remained till he lost the light of reason.[3]

The crime of mutilation or grievous hurt was punished according to the methods approved by Koranic law. If a man blinded his neighbour, the executioner was ordered by the judge to destroy his vision which he did by means of a mirror held up to the sun. If a tooth was lost, the blacksmith was summoned who, with a huge pair of pincers, extracted a similar tooth.[4] Theft was the most common offence unless done with arms in their hands. To call a person 'thief' was regarded as a very great insult. Some of the petty chiefs did not object or hesitate to order robbery and divide the spoils with the thieves. The robber chiefs on the frontier were paid by the Talpur Mirs, yet they levied blackmail from the travellers and not infrequently robbed them. Most of the cases of theft were punished with fines. If a thief could pay a fine double the amount of the property stolen, he was released on the spot. If he could not pay, then he was put in chains and remained in that condition till some influential persons interceded for him. The owner was required to pay one-fourth the value of the property to the ruler. Thus, the Talpur Chiefs found fining a most lucrative system of punishment.[5] The bodies of thieves were not mutilated. But there were numerous other penalties. A thief was imprisoned or he was compelled to fast for few days. Or again in lesser cases, a thief would be disgraced by having his head, eyebrows and beard shaved off, his face blackened and then he would be mounted on an ass, facing the animal's tail. Or the thief would be compelled to go about the town, with old slippers tied round his neck garland-wise.[6]

Forgery, coining, and using counterfeit seals were put in the category of political offences. If the political offences were of a light nature, the culprits were punished with fines, imprisonment or flogging. In grave cases, the punishments were barbaric. For extorting money from those offenders who were unwilling to disgorge their dishonest gains or extracting confessions, tortures were applied. The culprit, for instance, was placed astride on a cot. His feet were tied below the cot with a rope, as tightly as possible. The intense pain thus caused would make the guilty party howl for mercy. If he remained stubborn, then water was thrown upon the ropes which consequently shrank, causing unbearable pain. Or a heated ramrod would be placed between a man's thighs while he dangled by his thumbs from a beam, his toes just touching the ground. Langley mentions another mode of torture also and writes that it was common practice in Upper Sind 'to place some beetles of a peculiar kind in a saucer upon the naval of the victim, binding it tightly with a cummerbund.[7] The beetles immediately begin to gnaw the part, seeming to the wretched sufferer to be eating his very entrails, and thereby causing him such intense agony and terror that he in a few minutes gives in.'[8] Some other modes of torture may also be mentioned here, which, according to Burton, were applied for minor offences. A *tobra* full of well-pounded red pepper was put over the head of the culprit.[9] Or he was hung up to a tree by his legs, with pots of sand fastened to his arms. Or again a few scorpions would be introduced into his trousers.[10] These extreme measures were of course resorted to in extreme cases, and were more in the nature of exception than rule.

Intoxication, fornication and prostitution were not severely punished as laid down in Koran. They were lightly punished with fines, flogging or disgracing in public.

Something should be mentioned about the administration of justice. At the top, there were the Talpur Chiefs themselves in whom was vested the right of trying all cases and giving any punishment they deemed fit. But this was only in theory. In practice, the Talpur rulers delegated this power to their subordinate officers, reserving for themselves the trying of important cases like manslaughter and administering justice in a truly patriarchal manner. Their Highnesses only possessed the power of awarding death sentences. An exception had been made by the Talpur Chief of Lower Sind in the case of Nawab Wali Mohamed Khan Laghari, their vice-regent in Chanduks district, who also could give the punishment of hanging. In big cities, justice was administered by Kotwals. The under-trial prisoners were kept in the Kotwal's office, called *Chabutaro*. The place was well provided with *niyyara* (heavy chains), *hathoriyun* (hand-cuffs), *katha* (stocks), *gatta* (heavy iron collars for the neck) and other similar instruments.[11] While in prison, the prisoners were fed at state expense. In villages, *kardars* took the place of *kotwals*. These Kardars occupied the same position as the present day Collectors and Deputy Collectors do under British Government. The *kardar* in each district not only collected revenues for his master, the Talpur Chief, but also administered justice on his behalf. In those matters in which Mahomedans were involved and the case had to be decided according to Koran, the *kotwal* or the *kardar* would send for the *kazi* to give his decision. Hindus were invariably allowed to settle their own matters through *panchayats* or the Committee of the Hindu Elders, except in case of murder, in which case they came under the jurisdiction of the kotwal who referred the matter to their Highnesses, the Mirs of Sind.

In addition to these recognized authorities for dispensing justice, many a Baloch sardar or a *pir*, though claiming no such right, would yet exercise it and not be taken to task.

Administration of justice, it will have become apparent, was prompt and vigorous though arbitrary. In such a state of things, many a time there was miscarriage of justice, in which people with typical oriental fatalism acquiesced and live on the whole a contented life.

NOTES

1. R. F. Burton, *Sindh and the Races that Inhabit the Valley of the Indus*, 194–5.
2. *Miran je Sahibi-ji Pachari* (Sindhi Mss.).
3. Ex-Political, *Dry leaves from Young Egypt (3rd Edition)*, 22.
4. Burton, 195.
5. E. A. Langley, *Narrative of a Residence at the Court of Mir Ali Murad*, Vol. 2, 49.
6. Burton, 195–6.
7. Cummerbund is a long strip of cloth some ten, twelve yards long, which a person rolls round his waist tightly.
8. Langley, 50–51.
9. *Tobra* is a leather bag, filled with grain, which is tied round the neck of a horse when feeding the animal.
10. Burton, 339.
11. Ibid. 196.

3

Diwan Gidumal and Seth Naoomal Hotchand
A. B. Advani

THIS PAPER DEALS WITH BRIEF BIOGRAPHICAL SKETCHES OF TWO illustrious Hindus who have played a not unimportant part in the Modern History of Sind. Diwan Gidumal was an important political figure in both the Kalhora and Talpur periods and Seth Naoomal Hotchand was one of the chief personalities in the Talpur regime.

DIWAN GIDUMAL

The exact date of the birth of Diwan Gidumal is nowhere mentioned. In *Chach-Namah,* we read that in the year AD 1755 Diwan Gidumal was sent by Mian Noor Mahomed Kalhora as an envoy to Ahmed Shah Durani and succeeded in placating that angry king.[1] Surely a young person in [their] early twenties could not have been deputed for this important political mission. This makes us infer that in AD 1755 Diwan Gidumal must have been at least thirty to thirty-five years of age, well-versed in politics and enjoying the confidence of his rulers. From this conjecture we may safely deduce that Diwan Gidumal must have been born somewhere between AD 1720 and 1725. Born in some obscure village in the Punjab, Diwan Gidumal soon attracted the attention of the rulers there by his wisdom and

40

tact. Both Diwan Gidumal and Diwan Adumal took service under Mian Noor Mahomed Kalhora and left Multan for Sind, where the former rose to be the chief adviser and minister, while the latter became the Mian's chief swordsman.[2]

In 1755 while Diwan Gidumal was negotiating with Ahmed Shah Durani, Mian Noor Mahomed fled to Jasalmir, out of fear, and died there of the inflammation of [the] throat.

Diwan Gidumal was a faithful servant and after his master's death at Jesalmir, strove hard to have Mian Noor Mahomed's son, Mian Mahomed Murad Yab Khan, seated on the throne of his father. In this task also, he succeeded. Mian Mahomed Murad Yab Khan was an unpopular ruler. Tyranny and confusion were rampant in the kingdom with the result that Mian Mahomed Murad Yab Khan was ultimately deposed in favour of that romantic figure of Sind History, Mian Ghulam Shah, the son of the dancing girl Gulan.

Diwan Gidumal's name is also connected with the founding of the modern town of Hyderabad. Before 1768, the year in which Hyderabad was built, the Kalhora chiefs had changed their capital from one town to another. Originally, Khudabad was their capital but each successive Kalhora chief had shifted the seat of government to a new town which, either to some idle whim or danger of inundation from the summer floods of the Indus, had in turn been abandoned. In 1768 Mian Ghulam Shah Kalhora decided to change his capital and selected Nerun Kot. The ruins of Nerun Kot on the low range of Ganja hills, lying far above the Indus inundation, with the newly formed Phuleli canal washing its base, guaranteed security and permanence, and the northern spur of the low range of Ganja hills was selected for building the new capital. Diwan Gidumal was furnished with two country boats full of money and he came down from Hala to the bank of the Indus, where a small village sprang up called to the present day Gidu-jo-Tando or Gidu Bandar. The graves of certain *pirs* or holy men and the heaps of rubbish which at one time made up the old ruined fort of Nerun, were cleared away and a strong fort was built on the site. The new capital was called

Hyderabad in memory of Imam Haidar, the fourth Imam and son-in-law of Prophet Mahomed [PBUH]. The land outside the fort was given free to all who asked for it and very soon a busy little town sprang up. All this time, Diwan Gidumal was busy in supervising the building of the fort, with the result that on completion of the fort, most of the land was taken up. Diwan Gidumal selected a spot near the fort and built his house there, so that he should always be in the near vicinity of his rulers. This explains why Gidwani Lane today is so near the fort in Hyderabad.

Mian Ghulam Shah died suddenly at Hyderabad in 1772 and with him departed the glory of the Kalhora rule. During the next eleven stormy years, Diwan Gidumal played well his part of a faithful counsellor. His name occurs frequently in *Chach Namah* and *Fateh Namah* during this period. He is mentioned as 'the old and faithful secretary of the ruling family' giving some such sage advice to his master as under:

> My master pay no attention to what these mischievous people tell you. Those who fan the fire closely, run back, when it kindles into a blaze. Do not be rash and hasty to make an enemy of such a party, or else it will end in a revolt, and you will come to grief.[3]

In 1783, the Kalhora dynasty finally came to an end and the Talpur chiefs rose to power. But the change of rulers did not affect Diwan Gidumal. He continued to occupy the same position under the Talpurs as he had enjoyed under the Kalhoras. His prestige had not suffered and the passage of years instead of diminishing his mental vigour, had, on the contrary, given him sound and ripe experience which was of great value to his new masters. He enjoyed the unique privilege of direct correspondence with the Shah of Persia and even the haughty Talpur Mirs visited him at his place, which must have been a rare honour in those days.[4]

The death of Diwan Gidumal forms the subject matter of a very confusing controversy. The date, and the year of his death, like his birth, are nowhere to be met with, but we are inclined to think that his death took place somewhere in 1803, in the days of Mir Ghulam Ali Khan. The historians and the legends are both agreed that he was murdered by the order of Mir Ghulam Ali Khan, but they differ as to the motive of the murder. Historians like Shahamet Ali and Mir Hassan Ali Khan Talpur are inclined to think that he was put to death as he was planning the overthrow of the Talpur dynasty. 'The present chief,' says Shahamet Ali, 'was not uninformed of the roguery of his minister (Diwan Gidumal), but waited for an opportunity to punish him ... His first act after his return was to seize the Diwan, and to deprive him of his whole property and treasure, which was immense: but as he did not consider this disgrace enough, the Diwan and his brother were soon after put to death by his order.'[5] Mir Hassan Ali the author of *Fateh Namah* also concurs with Shahamet Ali.[6] Moonshi Awatrai, Mir Sobdar Khan's prime minister up to 1843, thought that Diwan Gidumal's murder had nothing to do with religious bigotry of the Talpurs, but that they grew afraid of the rising power of the Diwan and that he was clubbed to death by the order of Mir Ghulam Ali Khan.[7]

The other version of Diwan Gidumal's death reads like a romance and lacks any historical corroboration. The story has been handed down from mouth to mouth and from generation to generation and smacks more of a legend than a historical fact. It is something to this effect: Diwan Gidumal had no male issue but had been blessed with a beautiful daughter. 'No shaft pierced deeper into man's heart than the lashes that guarded her lovely orbs; her brow shown dazzlingly as the light of the day, and her hair gloomed deeply as the midnight murks.' To put it plainly, she was a sensational beauty but withal a highly virtuous girl. One of the Talpur princes, filled with passion for this reputed beauty, disguised himself in petticoats and ventured in Gidwani Lane with the intention of catching a glimpse of her. The *sheedees* (Abyssinian slaves) who were guarding the Diwan's house, saw through this disguise of the gay Lothario and ran to report the matter to Diwan Gidumal. The Diwan resented this action on the part of the prince and loudly ordered the *sheedees* to give a jolly hiding to this strange and unwelcome woman. Nothing loth, the servants did as they were bid and the young gallant bolted smarting with pain but more on account of thwarted desires and shame. Few days later, he sent for Diwan Gidumal in the open durbar and demanded publicly to be honoured with the hand of this girl in marriage. Diwan Gidumal went home and confessed to his daughter about his predicament. If she had no objection to marry the Mir, it was all right, otherwise he was in a deuce of a fix, what to do. 'What say you, my daughter?' the Diwan asked his daughter and for the first time burst into tears. The brave girl replied that death would be preferable to being polluted by a Mahomedan. Some say that thereafter she took poison and died.[8] Others affirm that at her request, Diwan Gidumal cut his daughter with his sword and that same night he carried his dead daughter to the cremation ground for the last rites. Realizing that his life was no longer safe the Diwan tried to escape but was apprehended and brought to the court. The infuriated Mir gave the fatal order and as soon as Diwan Gidumal entered the *durbar*, he was clubbed to death.

Thus died Diwan Gidumal, the wisest and the most pious Hindu minister of eighteenth century.

When did this incident take place, what was the real cause of Diwan Gidumal's murder, who was the amorous young Mir, what was the name of Diwan Gidumal's daughter, what was her age at the time of the murder; all these questions remain unanswered. The whole matter lies shrouded in a vague mystery. The accounts of Shahamet Ali and Mir Hassan Ali Khan cannot be depended upon, because being Mahomedans they are likely to have suppressed the real facts in connection with this murder and given reasons justifying his death. Moonshi Awatrai, though a Hindu, also is unreliable because when this incident took place he was not born and therefore his statement is mere hearsay.

The other version, as stated above, lacks any historical veracity and is too full of improbabilities to appeal to the historically-minded persons as true. It said that the Diwan had no male issues and that this girl was his only daughter. As she was unmarried, we may safely presume that at the time of his murder she must have been about fifteen years old and certainly not more than twenty years of age because amongst Hindus, late marriages were almost undreamt of. In 1803, Diwan Gidumal must have been over eighty years old. If this girl was less than twenty years, did Diwan Gidumal get this child at the advanced age of sixty? It is strange that up to the age of sixty the Diwan had no issue and then this tragic girl was born to him. We do not say that it is impossible to get a child at the age of sixty but that it appears to us as improbable. We are inclined to think that this story of the girl is a myth and that there were other reasons for putting Diwan Gidumal to death. Perhaps it was jealousy at the popularity of the Diwan, perhaps it was his wealth which brought about his death. Due to lack of information from historical books and contemporary sources we are unable to ascertain the real motive or the true account of this incident. However, both the versions are given for what they are worth.

SETH NAOOMAL HOTCHAND[9]

Seth Naoomal, second son of Seth Hotchand of Karachi, was born in 1804 or 1805. He belonged to a well-known [sic] family of rich Hindu merchants. Among the early recollections of Seth Naoomal was one of the terrible famine of 1811–12. During this famine Naoomal's family came to the rescue of the starved people and supplied the hungry people with corn from their huge granaries. When he was eleven years old, Naoomal was employed in doing accounts and correspondence work of the family firm at Karachi and he worked as he tells us in his *Memoirs,* from six in the morning to sometimes ten at night. In 1829, Naoomal went to Dwarka to perform some religious rites. From Dwarka he went to Porebundar where the Rana of the place personally welcomed him and seated him near the throne. Naoomal's family was held in great esteem at

Porebundar and Rana Parthiraj offered Naoomal the lucrative post
of the principal manager at Porebundar which he politely declined
as it would necessitate his absence from his own family. The Rana
permitted him to go back to Karachi and at his departure presented
him with 'gold bracelets, gold necklaces and shawls of wool and silk'.

The next important event in Naoomal's life took place in 1832
and this event indirectly had far-reaching results in as much as it
alienated all friendly feelings which Naoomal and his family had
cherished for the Talpur rulers at Hyderabad. The trouble started
with a young Hindu boy who while standing before a mosque was
persuaded to enter it. The Hindus became very angry at this and
observed a *hartal* in the town as a protest against this outrage. The
Mahomedans in their turn retaliated by polluting the wells from
which the Hindus obtained their drinking water and added insult
to injury by abusing them. The Hindus of Karachi could not take
this lying down and abused the Mahomedans in return. Thus, the
feelings between the two communities got estranged. One Syed
Nooral Shah started on the propaganda tour of Sind and by his
mischievous propaganda of vilification, aroused in the Mahomedans
of Sind indignation against the Hindus and a great desire to convert
them to Islam by fair or foul means. The blaze of religious fire
was lit and spread from village to village. One of Seth Hotchand's
sons was in some way implicated in this affair and fled to Jesalmir
to avoid trouble. Seth Hotchand, on being ordered by Mir Murad
Ali Khan, proceeded to Hyderabad. The Mahomedans wanted to
wreak their vengeance on him but Mir Murad Ali Khan, owing to
his good connections with Seth Hotchand's family, would not listen
to it. The matter was referred to the Kazi of Nasarpur who realized
that the Mahomedans were bent on mischief would not permit
any discussion of the matter. But the things got out of hand and
one day Seth Hotchand was forcibly abducted by these religious
bigots. He was carried to a small town in Shah Bundar district
where he is supposed to have been forcibly circumcised, though
Seth Naoomal in his *Memoirs* asserts vehemently that his father was

not circumcised, nor was he compelled to eat beef or say the *Kalmo*, but that he lived on a handful of parched grain, supplied to him by one of his faithful servants and remained as cheerful as ever. Mir Murad Ali Khan sent orders to the Nawab of Thatta to have Seth Hotchand at once liberated. Seth Hotchand was brought back safely to Hyderabad, and when asked by the Mir as to what he proposed to do, he replied that he was going to renounce the world. That same night Seth Hotchand escaped in disguise to Lakhpat and was heartily welcomed by the chief men of the Rao of Cutch, and there he remained for the next ten years. Thus was the seed of bitterness against the Talpur Mirs sown in the heart of Seth Naoomal. This was, we think, one of the reasons why Seth Naoomal, later on helped the British unflinchingly, even when his own life was in danger. He was even threatened by the Mirs for helping the British against them, but Naoomal believed in the ultimate success of the British power in Sind and cultivated their friendship.

Naoomal's friendly connections with the British date from AD 1832 when Colonel Pottinger, the British Resident at Cutch, made his acquaintance during his visit to Hyderabad to negotiate a commercial treaty with the Mirs. Later on Naoomal also made Sir Alexander Burnes' acquaintance. He was also of great help to Lt Leckie and saved the lives of Commander Carless and his party who had incurred the wrath of the Nawab of Karachi by having gone unwittingly on a hunting expedition to the adjoining hills of Karachi without obtaining any previous permission.

In 1838, the tranquility of Sind was disturbed by Lord Auckland's Afghanistan campaign. Colonel Pottinger appointed Seth Naoomal as the British Agent to arrange for provisioning Sir John Keane's Army of the Indus. The *Sind Correspondence* of this period bears eloquent testimony to the great services rendered by Seth Naoomal in those troublous times. Naoomal's time was fully occupied in purchasing and storing of the grain, hiring of the camels for transport and looking after the welfare of the British officers. And all this work was done with the full knowledge that the Talpur Mirs highly disapproved of it. In addition to helping Sir John Keane is his advance on Kandhar and Cabul through the Bolan Pass, Naoomal was also of great assistance to Brigadier Valiant who landed in Karachi in February 1839 with his Reserve Force. Major Outram and Lt Eastwick also became Naoomal's friends at this time. This was all a labour of love or rather a labour of hate. Seth Naoomal himself explains the motive for his assisting the British. 'I was not actuated,' he writes in his *Memoirs,* 'by any love of pecuniary gain in rendering political service, and I acted at the risk of great danger to my person and property, when it was sufficiently well-known that the Talpur Government, under which I lived and to which I was subject, were averse to the passage of the British Troops through Sind, and looked upon all assistance rendered as a mark of disregard of their wishes and disrespect to their authority. But my family felt themselves aggrieved by the wrongs inflicted upon them by the later Mirs in their blind zeal for their faith.'

In April 1839, Naoomal was at Hyderabad with Colonel Pottinger. Mir Nur Mahomed Khan one day sent Diwan Hiranand to Seth Naoomal, desiring him to visit the Mirs. At first Naoomal declined to go but Diwan Hiranand told him that Sind was still under the Talpur rule and that many of his relatives, who were in the employ of the Mirs, might suffer on account of his refusing to comply with the Mir's request. Naoomal accordingly went to the *durbar* of Mir Nur Mahomed Khan. On his entering the *durbar,* Mir Nur Mahomed Khan stood up to receive him and taking him by the hand offered him a *munji* (a low stool). It should be noted that the offering of the *munji* was considered in those days as a special mark of honour reserved for select few, with the ordinary visitors generally squatting on the carpeted floor. After the usual interchange of greetings, Mir Nur Mahomed Khan said, 'Seth Naoomal, have you now fully avenged the wrongs inflicted on your father?' Naoomal tactfully replied, 'Sir, why should you say so, and why speak thus?' How Seth Naoomal's heart must have glowed with pride to see at last these Lords of the Land so humbled before him?

Four years later, the Mirs were defeated at the battles of Meeani and Hyderabad, and Sind was annexed by the British. And Seth Hotchand returned from his exile at Lakhpat. Thousands of people gathered at Native Jetty to welcome the self-exiled Seth who was taken home in a huge procession. Seth Naoomal's revenge was complete and his cup of happiness full. The proud Mirs had paid heavily for conniving at the forcible conversion of Seth Hotchand.

After the conquest of Sind in 1843, Sir Charles Napier became the first governor of Sind. This fiery old man popularly called by his Indian troops as '*Shaitan ka Bhai*' (devil's brother) was prejudiced against Naoomal from the beginning. This was perhaps due to the fact that Naoomal was the protege of Major Outram, and Napier hated Outram, the Bayard of India. Then there was Lt Marston, the first Chief of Karachi Police Force, who had, at the instigation of one Sheikh Ghulam Hassan Fojdar, lodged a complaint against Seth Naoomal of interfering with the Police. On account of this vexatious charge, Seth Naoomal and his friends suffered. One day Napier burst out in anger saying that wherever he went, he heard people saying 'Naoomal, Naoomal', that he had conquered the country by sword and not Naoomal and he wondered what weapon Naoomal wielded that people attributed the success of the British army to Naoomal, instead of him.

In 1847, a false case was filed against Naoomal. Captain Young was the Judge Advocate-General. The trial lasted for seven days and Seth Naoomal was declared innocent. At this unjust trial, Seth Naoomal's enthusiasm for the British Government abated, and he left the court a sadder and a wiser man. But the humiliation of being dragged into the court of law prostrated him and he fell ill and weak. In spite of all this, Naoomal had no ill-feeling against Napier whom he calls in his *Memoirs* 'a simple-minded, pure-minded and religious gentleman'.

Sir Charles Napier soon left Sind and was succeeded by Sir Bartle Frere, who was more than kind towards Seth Naoomal. Frere at once recognized the sterling qualities of head and heart with which

Naoomal was gifted and always treated him with great consideration. We learn from Martineau's *'Life of Sir Bartle Frere'* that Naoomal 'was so valued by him that he gave orders that Naoomal was never to be refused admittance day or night, when he came to see him.'

Sir Bartle Frere was responsible for starting of Karachi Municipality. He took Seth Naoomal's advice on this matter. Naoomal called a meeting of the townsmen and persuaded them to agree to Sir Bartle Frere's suggestion of paying *ghee* tax at the rate of one and a half annas per hundred-weight, for the purpose of municipality. The first Managing Committee of the Karachi Municipal Corporation consisted of Captain Preedy, the Revenue Collector, Mr John McLeod, the Collector of Custom, and Seth Naoomal. Daily in the morning these three gentlemen used to go and inspect the town and to arrange for its proper sanitation.

In 1860, the Government of India passed a resolution sanctioning a pension of Rs. 100 per month on Seth Naoomal and his descendants up to the third generation. He was also to be rewarded with a *jagir* in perpetuity.

On 1 January 1867, Seth Naoomal was publicly honoured by being presented at Frere Hall with the Insignia and Grant of the Dignity of Companion of the Most Exalted Order of the Star of India. Sir Bartle Frere the then Governor of Bombay, in his speech on that day, said, 'You had great influence amongst your countrymen, you possessed information drawn from every part of Northern and Western India and you placed all unreservedly at the disposal of the Government. When many of your countrymen were appalled by the greatness of the danger, and believed that some catastrophe threatened the existence of the British Empire in India, you never faltered in your sagacious trust in the power of the British Government.'

Thus in the evening of life, honours were heaped on Seth Naoomal. Surrounded by his large family he passed the remaining years of his life in peace and plenty. His love for horses remained up to his death and his daily physical exercise consisted of a walk of two or three miles and a ride every evening. A man devoted to his faith, it was a pleasure to watch him at sunset, when the lamps were lit and the temple bells called, closing his eyes and joining his hands in prayer.

On 16 September 1878, at the age of 73 years, Naoomal died peacefully. We cannot do better than conclude this brief biography of this great man with Sir Frederick Goldsmith's eulogy:

... connected with what may be called the Intelligence Department of the Province from the first hour of British occupation, he remained until the period of his demise the most trustworthy informant and adviser of the several officers who administered the affairs of Sind ... his memory is specially noted here, for Karachi in its zenith, was not Karachi without Seth Naoomal.[10]

NOTES

1. Mirza Kalich Beg, *Chach Namah*, Vol. II, 152.
2. M. A. Bherumal, *Amilan-jo-Awal* (in Sindhi) first edition, 51, 79.
3. Beg, 66.
4. Moonshi Awatrai, *Miran-Je-Sahibi-Ji-Pachari* (Sindhi Ms.).
5. Sahamet Ali, *The History of Bahawalpur* (1844).
6. Mir Hasan Ali, *Fateh Namah* (Persian Mss.).
7. Awatrai, *Op. cit.*
8. Manghirmalani, 'Diwan Gidumal', *Modern Review* (March 1932), 270.
9. Following books have been freely consulted in preparing this biography: *Memories of Seth Naoomal Hotchand; Sind Correspondence, 1838–1843*; Martineau's *Life of Sir Bartle Frere.*
10. F. Goldsmith, *Asiatic Quarterly Review* (April 1888).

4

Mirza Khusro Beg
A. B. Advani

THE LIFE STORY OF MIRZA KHUSRO BEG IS ONE OF THE ROMANCES of Sind History.[1] It reads more like fiction than the cold facts of History. But verily truth is sometimes stranger than fiction. The word *Mirza* in Persian language means a secretary or a person whose occupation is to write and whose habits of life are civil. It also signifies a prince of royal blood because the word *Mirza* is a compound of *Mir* or *Amir* meaning *Lord* and *Za,* an abbreviation of *Zada* which means *Son.* In the case of Mirza Khusro Beg, both the meanings could appropriately be applied to him for he was a prince of royal blood *(vide,* the genealogical table at the end) and in Sind he was a civilian of higher grade.

Before starting with the biography of this remarkable gentleman from Georgia, I shall mention one moot point which I have not been able to decide. It is this: Was Mirza Khusro Beg an adopted son of Mir Karam Ali Khan or was he a Georgian slave who was treated by the Mir as his son? Dr Burnes has clearly mentioned that Mirza Khusro Beg was a Georgian slave but has added that he was treated as an adopted child.[2] It is also true that the other Mirs treated Mirza Khusro Beg as their equal, but never as one of them. For instance he didn't marry from the family of Mirs, and as far as it is known, he never sat on the raised *gaddi* or throne as the other Mirs used to sit.

52

He was, as it appears, a high dignitary who was much respected and trusted. On the other hand, in the *Memoirs of Mirza Khusro Beg*, it is clearly stated that Mir Karam Ali Khan at the time of the Mirza's coming from Persia to Sind embraced the Mirza and publicly announced that he had adopted him as a son. (*Frere Namah* does not mention anything about this adoption.) Mir Karam Ali Khan in his will also wrote that Mirza Khusro Beg was his son.[3] What was he really speaking [*sic*]? A Georgian slave or an adopted son of Mir Karam Ali Khan? I leave this matter to all those who are interested to work it out for themselves.

In 1783, the Talpur Mirs of Sind defeated the Abbasi Kalhoras and ascended the *gaddi* of Sind. The province of Sind, by common consent, was divided into three parts. The important part of which, with Hyderabad as its capital, was enjoyed by Mir Fateh Ali Khan and his three brothers—Mir Ghulam Ali Khan, Kaman Ali Khan and Murad Ali Khan. These four brothers on account of the great attachment for one another came to be known as Char Yar or the Four Friends.[4] Mir Karam Ali Khan had two wives.[5] His three brothers were also married and in due course of time became happy fathers, but this pleasure of being a father was denied to Mir Karam Ali Khan, in whose heart there remained a void on account of his childless state.

The Talpur Mirs of Sind had very friendly connections with the Shah of Persia, to whom they frequently used to send presents through their envoys. There were trade connections also between Sind and Persia. Through one merchant Mir Karam Ali Khan sent a message to Haji Ibrahim Khan, the Vizier of the Shah of Persia in the last decade of the eighteenth century, requesting him to be on the lookout for a boy of good family whom he would like to adopt as a son. This message was duly delivered to the Vizier, who promised to do as the Mir desired. Some years passed away [*sic*] and Fateh Ali Khan became the King of Persia. On his sitting to the throne, Mir Karam Ali Khan sent to him some presents through a trusted courtier, by [the] name Akhund Ismail.[6] Akhund Ismail was

also instructed to remind Haji Ibrahim the Vizier about his promise
of sending some boy of noble birth to Sind for being adopted by
Mir Karam Ali Khan as his son. While conversing with the Vizier,
Akhund Ismail's eye fell on a handsome young boy studying hard
under a Persian tutor. The Akhund became curious and inquired
from Haji Ibrahim about the parentage of the boy. He was told a
strange tale which was something to this effect.[7] For hundreds of
years, the rulers of Georgia, a small territory with Mount Caucasus
to its north and Armenia to its south-west, were at war with the
rulers of Persia. Gurgin Khan III was the ruler when Georgia's
capital Tiflis was attacked by the Persians.[8] Gurgin Khan had to
fly for his life and he left his two young sons, Humayun Khan
and Khusro Khan in a garden in the vicinity of Tiflis under the
protection of a small band of faithful soldiers. Tiflis was ruthlessly
ravaged and these two boys, nine and seven years old, were captured
by the general of the Persian army. Much booty had been obtained
in this attack on Tiflis and, as is common, there arose a quarrel
between the Persian soldiers over the distribution of the booty. The
matters were reported to Haji Ibrahim Khan, the Persian Vizier, who
ordered all the booty and the prisoners to be brought before him.
Among these prisoners was a handsome boy crying piteously. This
boy told the Vizier that his name was Khusro Khan and that he was
Gurgin Khan's son. He said that his elder brother Humayun Khan,
who had been ailing for some time past, had breathed his last on the
previous night. Haji Ibrahim was filled with pity and took Khusro
Khan under his protection. From that day, he began to treat him as
his son and the boy came to be known as Mirza Khusro Beg. Love
and kindness were showered upon the boy and special tutors were
sent for to train him up in the three R's. It was this very same Mirza
Khusro Beg who had caught the eye and fancy of Akhund Ismail,
the envoy from Sind. The Akhund ventured to suggest that if this
boy were sent to Sind, Mir Karam Ali Khan would be delighted to
adopt him as his son. Haji Ibrahim Khan was at first reluctant to
part with the boy saying that he had practically adopted him as his

own son, and that his wife would never agree to part with him. The Akhund mentioned the matter to his Majesty the Shah of Persia who persuaded his minister to give permission to the boy to go to Sind. Soon the preparations for departure were made and the time came for Mirza Khusro Beg to bid farewell to his protector the Vizier. The parting scene we read was very touching: 'Cries were heard outside (from the Vizier's *Harem)* and the old Vizier himself was shedding hot tears and the state of the young Mirza was not less pitiable.'[9]

By easy marches, Mirza Khusro Beg and Akhund Ismail reached Sind and were welcomed in a right royal manner in the *durbar* of Mir Karam Ali Khan, who called the young Mirza to himself, embraced him and publicly announced the fact of having adopted the Mirza as his son. At this time Mirza Khusro Beg was only nine years old, but he had such charming manners and such a sharp intellect that he won the hearts of all who came in contact with him. Mir Karam Ali Khan gave the young Mirza a separate house to live in and a number of attendants to look after his physical comforts. Akhund Ismail was appointed as his tutor in Persian and Arabic languages.

Though the young Mirza, as the adopted child of Mir Karam Ali Khan, had everything which wealth would buy and heart desire, yet he began to languish for want of suitable companions. To remedy this, Mir Karam Ali Khan sent his envoys and merchants to Persia, who in due course of time returned with some Georgian and other boys. Among these were Mirza Fredun Beg (father of the late Mirza Kalich Beg, the grand old man of Sindhi letters) and Mirza Kurban Ali Beg. In the company of such companions, and the atmosphere of love and affection which surrounded him, Mirza Khusro Beg began to wax strong, both physically and morally.

In 1811, Mir Ghulam Ali Khan, while hunting, received a light wound from a wounded buck. The wound swelled and in spite of the efforts of the local physicians proved fatal.[10] Mir Karam Ali Khan, being the elder brother, now became the Rais or the Chief of Sind. Under his rule Mirza Khusro Beg, having by now grown out of his teens, enjoyed great favours.[11] We learn from the *Memoirs* that he became 'a powerful and influential minister in every department of the State. No one ventured to do anything in connection with the internal or foreign policy of the country without first consulting the Mirza.'

The next event, worthy of note in Mirza Khusro Beg's life was his visit to Bombay in 1823 as the Sind envoy. This visit has been merely referred to by Dr Burnes in his book.[12] The details of this visit, though assuredly exaggerated, are to be found in the *Memoirs of Mirza Khusro Beg*. A dispute had risen between the British Government and the Mirs of Sind over some refugees who had taken shelter at Hyderabad in Sind. These refugees were from Jesulmir. The Mirs were required to pay Rs. 70,000 as compensation for the loss suffered by the Cutch State on account of these men. Later on, when these refugees went back to their native country of their own accord, the Mirs demanded the refund of this amount of Rs. 70,000. For this purpose, Mirza Khusro Beg was deputed to go to Bombay and settle this matter with Mountstuart Elphinstone who was the Governor of Bombay then. The Mirza had been ailing for some time also and he seized this opportunity with eagerness. The Mirza started from Hyderabad with a retinue of one hundred followers and sailed down the Indus to one of the mouths of the river. Thence he had to set sail for Bombay in large boats especially got ready [*sic*] for the purpose. After nine days' voyaging, Mirza Khusro Beg's boat anchored at Bombay. On his alighting from the ship, a salute of twenty-four guns was fired and some 2,000 troops presented arms. The Governor himself, accompanied by some officers, had come to receive the Mirza. After the usual exchange of civilities the Mirza rode in a four-horse carriage, seated on the right-hand side of the Governor. A big bungalow had been rented and Mirza Khusro Beg was lodged there. There were frequent exchanges of visits and presents and occasionally both the Governor and the Mirza went out for 'a drive'. The account of the Mirza's visit to Bombay would be incomplete without narrating an incident which is very amusing, as it shows Mirza Khusro Beg's complete ignorance of the

manners end customs of the *Feringhees* (Europeans). To quote from
the *Memoirs*:

> One night the Mirza was invited to a dance of Europeans and it was
> with great hesitation that he accepted the invitation. At the appointed
> hour the Governor came and took up the Mirza in his carriage and
> Muhammad Abid and Akhund Baka sat in front of them.[13] The
> latter had been ordered by the Mirza to carry two thousand rupees
> with them. As soon as the party arrived in the ball-room, the dance
> commenced and ladies and gentlemen began to dance by turns.
> When the lady of the Governor began to dance, the Mirza gave a hint
> to Muhammad Abid, who took up a purse of one thousand rupees
> and after waving it over the head of the lady placed it in the middle.
> The Governor told the Mirza that that was not the custom among the
> Englishmen. But the Mirza told him that that was the custom among
> the Mirs of Sind and among the princes of India. A few minutes later
> Muhammad Abid did the same thing over again, and the Governor
> remained quiet. When the dance was over the Governor took the
> Mirza and his two attendants back to their place.

The embarrassment of the Governor and his wife may well be
imagined, but they were all polite enough to put up with what the
Mirza termed 'the custom among the Mirs of Sind'.

Mirza Khusro Beg remained in Bombay for three months, during
which he spent no less than one lac and forty thousand rupees. The
matter regarding the refund of Rs. 70,000 was amicably settled, the
Mirza's health made wonderful progress, and the Mirza prepared
to go back to Sind. On the day of departure once again the salute
of guns was given, the troops presented arms, and the Governor
wished him 'Bon Voyage'. In due course of time, the Mirza arrived
at Hyderabad.

Mirza Khusro Beg's influence began to grow stronger and
stronger day by day. In all political matters he was the first to be
consulted and his sage advice was implicitly followed. People who

had earned the displeasure of the Mirs would solicit the Mirza's help to restore them once again to their former position and Mirza Khusro Beg was ever obliging. This popularity and the influence of Mirza Khusro Beg is evidenced by a statement made by Dr James Burnes, who visited the Court of Hyderabad Mirs in November 1827.[14] Dr Burnes writes as follows:

> The first of this class (that is to say courtiers who exert a personal influence from being constantly in private attendance on the Mirs) worthy of notice is Mirza Khoosroo ... whom his master (Mir Karam Ali Khan) now treats as an adopted child.[15]

Soon after the departure of Dr Burnes from Sind in January 1828, Mir Karam Ali Khan fell ill. Realizing that his end was near, he called Mirza Khusro Beg by his bed-side saying, 'O my son, I am dying. As soon as death occurs, you must break into pieces my sword, that I always carry on my waist and kill the horse and the camel that I always use for my riding ... after doing this, you must proclaim my death.' After the death of Mir Karam Ali Khan, the Mirza carried out the wishes of the Mir. He killed the horse, whose name was Azad, and the camel and then broke the sword on the stone fixed at the gate of the Mir's Harem-Sarai.[16] Mirza Khusro Beg felt the death of his master very keenly and was, for days, inconsolable. Mir Murad Ali Khan, the last of the Char Yar, who now ascended the throne of Sind assured Mirza Khusro Beg of his favour and wanted to entrust the affairs of the State to him as his brother the late Mir Karam Ali Khan had done. But the Mirza declined the honour on the plea that after his master's death he was not in his proper mood and therefore could not attend to State affairs.[17] Mankind has to be grateful to benign Nature which causes mental pain and sorrow to disappear after some time. Life otherwise would not be endurable. Time is a great healer and Mirza Khusro Beg once again began to take an active interest in affairs political. We next hear of Mirza Khusro Beg during that period of Sind history when the misunderstanding between the British Government and the Mirs of Sind had extended so far as to cause a war between the two parties unavoidable. It is evident from the volume of *Correspondence Relative to Sinde, 1838–43*, that Mirza Khusro Beg suspected the British Government of entertaining designs of Sind conquest. In a public *durbar*, in May 1839, Mirza Khusro Beg inquired from the British Deputation how long Colonel Pottinger (the then British Resident in Sind) was to be the Mirs' ruin.[18]

It is needless to go into the causes which finally brought about the Sind Conquest. We shall merely state that in January 1843 when Sir Charles Napier—after seating Mir Ali Murad Khan on the *gaddi* of Khairpur and blowing up the fort of Imamghar (considered by the Talpur Mirs of Upper Sind as their Gibraltar)— started marching on Hyderabad where Mir Rustam Khan and other refugees had gone, the Mirs of Hyderabad sent Mirza Khusro Beg and another gentleman, investing them both with full powers to treat with Sir Charles Napier and avert the war. These two deputies met Sir Charles Napier at Bhiria.[19] There was a long talk between these two envoys and Napier. During the course of interview, Mirza Khusro Beg got very excited and told Napier to beware of the fighting of the Baloches, which was not an easy affair: 'You should be sure that Sind is not a cold pudding that you would eat so easily,' said the Mirza.[20] These words exasperated Sir Charles Napier and [he] dismissed the envoys, saying, 'I am also for war; let us see how the swords of the Baloches resist the volleys of muskets and guns.'[21] The envoys were convinced that nothing but war would satisfy Sir Charles Napier, and Mirza Khusro Beg at once wrote to the Mirs at Hyderabad, 'The General is bent on war; so get ready.'[22]

The matters were put to the test in the Battle of Meeani fought on 17 February 1843 and the Mirs of Hyderabad lost heavily and surrendered themselves as prisoners of war. Four days later, a general order was issued by Sir Charles Napier regarding taking possession of the fort of Hyderabad and of all the treasure hoarded therein.[23] In accordance with this general order, some soldiers and prize-agents entered the fort and started to take possession of the vast treasures of the Mirs. Before the arrival of the soldiers, the ladies of the various Mirs residing in the fort collected their jewelry, ornaments and other valuable articles and buried them underground. Then they hid themselves in some other houses. Much of this hidden treasure was unearthed through the help of some faithless servants, who informed the British Prize-Agents that the ladies of the Mirs had hidden their treasure in the fort. They also informed them that Mirza Khusro Beg would be able to tell them where the treasure of Mir Karam Ali Khan was buried. Mirza Khusro Beg, who had been kept as a prisoner along with the other Mirs in the gardens on the bank of the river Indus, was accordingly sent for. On his arrival, he was questioned by Major McPherson, the Prize-Agent, about the buried treasure. Major McPherson however made a mistake and asked the Mirza to point out to them the treasure of Mir Zangi Khan instead of Mir Karam Ali Khan. The Mirza having never heard of Mir Zangi Khan, replied that he did not know. The British officers got excited at this reply and spoke harshly with the Mirza. They called him a liar and threatened to beat him. The Mirza's face flamed in anger at this insult and, leaping forward, he caught Major McPherson by the throat. With his left hand he took out the Major's sword and would have killed him but the other officers rushed to the Major's rescue and tied the Mirza with a piece of rope. He was tied for two hours in the fort and was afterwards released and brought back to the gardens on the bank of Indus.[24] Some days later, while the Mirs and the Mirza were still prisoners, Sir Charles Napier entered the fort of Hyderabad and inquired from an attendant about the Mirza's residence. He went over to the Mirza's residence and asked one Akhund Baka how many sons the Mirza had and what their names and ages were. Suddenly Napier told Akhund Baka that he was feeling hungry and, as there were children in the house, there must be some sweets in the larder. Could he get him some *halwa* or some eatables? The Akhund told him that there were no sweets available in the house: it is inferred that Sir Charles Napier asked the Akhund to give him some *halwa* because he remembered the words of the Mirza Khusro Beg at Bhiria; 'You should be sure that Sind is not a cold pudding *(halwa)* that you would eat so easily.' Now that Sind was conquered, the General wanted to eat some *halwa* to remind the Mirza of his boast. Next day, Sir Charles Napier purchased some *halwa* from the *bazaar* and sent it in a covered plate to the Mirza with the message that not only had he had eaten the cold *halwa* of Sind, but he was sending him something out of it to eat. The Mirza sent back a dignified reply saying that the *halwa* he had referred to at Bhiria was a moral and spiritual *halwa* which the General was not destined to taste. The dirty *halwa* sent to him by the General was fit for being given to dogs. And he threw it before a dog in the presence of the messenger.[25] In April 1843, the Mirs were removed from Sind as state prisoners. As their harems were not allowed to accompany them, the Mirs decided between themselves to request Sir Charles Napier to allow Mirza Khusro Beg to remain behind in Sind and look after their *derahs* or harems. Sir Charles Napier hesitated in the beginning as he considered the Mirza a likely person to cause rebellion in Sind, but at last consented to let the Mirza remain in Sind. After the departure of the Mirs, the Mirza took the *derahs* to Tando Saindad in the vicinity of Hyderabad. All the time that the Mirs were prisoners at Bombay or Calcutta, he was in frequent correspondence with them, sending them comforting messages or delicacies like snuff or Pishori rice. These letters between the Mirza and the Mirs clearly indicate the esteem in which the Mirza was held by this younger generation of the Mirs. He is invariably addressed as 'Dear Brother' or 'Of High position and kind, in the position of our uncle' or 'My kind and respectable friend'.[26]

Eleven years later in 1854, the Mirs were allowed to return from Calcutta to Hyderabad. Some of the Mirs had died in their captivity but the remaining Mirs were given pieces of land, along the bank of the Indus near Gidu Bunder, to fix their residence there. The *derahs* of the late Mir Karam Ali Khan, however, chose to live with the Mirza and they all came to live at Tando Thoro, a village on the bank of Phuleli canal in Hyderabad Sind.[27]

The Mirza had by now, become a respectable old man of 64 years, the patriarch of his family. After the conquest of Sind, the Mirza had led a life of retirement. Several times he was advised to approach Sir Charles Napier for some pension or *jagir*, but this was considered by the Mirza as undignified. While settling the political affairs of the country and confirming *jagirs* and allowances on nobles and other deserving persons in Sind, Sir Charles Napier sent for Mirza Khusro Beg and evinced a desire to grant him some *jagir*. But the Mirza refused to have anything for himself. After some years when Sir Bartle Frere came to Sind, he came to Hyderabad and called on the Mirza as the latter was suffering from boils and gangrene. Sir Bartle Frere was full of concern at the Mirza's ailment and at once sent him a European doctor. He assured the Mirza that he would get his sons some government jobs. He also recommended to the Government of Bombay that the gardens and other landed property enjoyed by the Mirza, before the Sind Conquest, should be returned to him. Of this landed property, only one garden on the bank of Phuleli was returned to the Mirza. Regarding the other property, which included that area of land on which the present Hyderabad Central Jail is situated, the Mirza was given monetary compensation.

The Mirza had reached the end of his life. The Mirs back from Calcutta, his sons settled in life, and having sufficient money to live in comfort and with dignity, he passed his days at Tando Thoro in contented retirement. For the last seven years of his life, the Mirza was confined to bed and he passed most of his time in reading Persian and Arabic literature. He died on 2 Jamadissani 1277 AH, equivalent to AD 1860, at Tando Thoro and was buried in a small tomb outside the tombs of the Mirs at Hyderabad in Sind.

THE GENEALOGICAL TREE OF THE ANCESTORS OF
MIRZA KHUSRO BEG

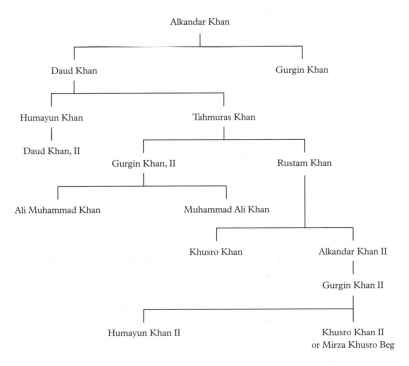

NOTES

1. The biography of Mirza Khusro Beg is mainly based on a manuscript in English entitled *Memoirs of Mirza Khusro Beg*. It was written in 1920 by late Mirza Kalich Beg and professes to be a translation of a Persian mss. which was written by one Wadalshah, son of Mian Yakubshah Alawi Kadri, in AD 1897. The *Memoirs of Mirza Khusro Beg* reads like a story, but I have referred to books like Malcom's *History of Persia,* Burnes' *Narrative of a Visit to the Courts of Sinde,* Parliamentary Blue Books containing correspondence relative to Sinde, and I find that the information given in the *Memoirs* is partly true. As a rule, a Mahomeddan chronicler is very particular to give dates when writing history,

but in this instance, this exactitude is wanting. Hardly any dates are given and the account of the Mirza's life at several places is contradictory to historical information which we know to be reliable. The author of the *Memoirs* in Persian has confessed that the incidents mentioned by him are based on hearsay. There being no documentary evidence we have to be satisfied with second hand information. There are several statements in this *Memoirs,* which for want of time, I have not been able to verify.

2. James Burnes, *A Narrative of a Visit to the Court of Sinde*, 110.
3. Mir Karam Ali Khan's will is to be found in the mss. *Memoirs of Mirza Khusro Beg.*
4. Burnes, 27.
5. This information was given to me by Mir Ali Bux Khan Talpur in June 1932.
6. John Malcolm, *History of Persia II*, 213–14.
7. *Memoirs of Mirza Khusro Beg* (Mss.).
8. Ibid.
9. Ibid.
10. Mirza Kalich Beg, *A History of Sind II*, 212.
11. Mirza Khusro Beg was born in Tiflis in 1790 AD and was brought to Sind at the close of the 18th century. At the time of Mir Karam Ali Khan's becoming the Rais, he had reached the dignified age of twenty-one years.
12. Burnes, 110.
13. These two gentlemen belonged to Thatta and had been asked by the Mirs to accompany Mirza Khusro Beg to Bombay (*Memoirs of Mirza Khusro Beg* [mss.]).
14. *Burnes,* 42.
15. Ibid. 110.
16. *Memoirs of Mirza Khusro Beg* (Mss.).
17. Ibid.
18. *Parliamentary Blue Book: Correspondence relative to Sinde (1838–1949).*
19. *Parliamentary Blue Book: Supplemental Correspondence Relative to Sinde*, 23 (No. 40).
20. The word used by the Mirza was *halwa,* a kind of confectionery. This word has been translated in English as *pudding.* This incident was remembered by Napier and he took an opportunity of humiliating the Mirza by sending him some *halwa* after the Sind Conquest to remind the Mirza of his boast.
21. Beg, *A History of Sind II*, 229.
22. James Outram, *The Conquest of Scinde: A Commentary*, 835.
23. Edward Green, *General Orders of Sir Charles Napier*, 73.
24. *Memoirs of Mirza Khusro Beg* (mss.); *Parliamentary Blue Book: Supplemental Correspondence Relative to Sinde*, 58 (No. 102).
25. *Memoirs of Mirza Khusro Beg* (mss.). The above incident reads like a story. I have been unable to verify it in the *Diaries and Life of Sir Charles Napier.* It may, therefore, be taken for what it is worth.
26. Ibid.
27. Ibid.

5

Lieutenant Amiel and the Baluch Levy
(with a map)
H. T. Lambrick

IN THE MAP ATTACHED TO POTTINGER'S *TRAVELS IN BALOOCHISTAN and Scinde* published in 1816, the province of Karachi, marked Kutch Gundava, bears a prosperous appearance. The names of numerous towns appear, connected by roads; the plain is traversed by mighty streams from the mountains of Khorasan. Pottinger's description of the tract, admittedly based on second-hand information, is also favourable. 'The villages of this fine plain are almost innumerable, and are increasing in number every year ... of Kutch Gundava, the soil is rich and loamy; and so exceedingly productive that it is said, were it all properly cultivated, the crops would be more than sufficient for the consumption of the whole of Baloochistan; even as it is, they export great quantities of grain, besides cotton, indigo, and oil rice will not grow in Kutch Gundava, although the soil affords the most luxuriant crops of every other description, nor is there any deficiency of water.'

On this map and this description the Government of India seems to have relied when planning the invasion of Afghanistan in 1838–39. It is notorious that the expedition was grossly deficient in the departments of Intelligence and Liaison between Politicals

65

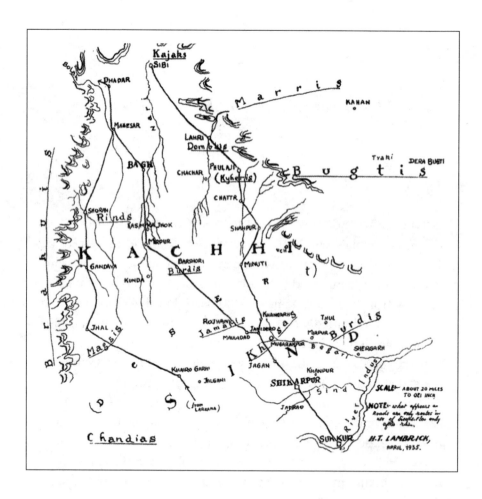

and Military: every narrative of the campaign, from whatever view-point written, affords evidence of blind movement forward in more or less complete ignorance of the country, its supplies, and the attitude of the tribes to be met on route. To sum up all in the words of W. J. Eastwick, 'there never was an enterprise of such magnitude undertaken with so little foresight and prudence'. It was, of course, well known that the Bolan pass was a trade route between India and Central Asia; moreover, Arthur Conolly had come that way on his overland journey to India in 1830 and had duly published an account of his travels, together with a map of 'the countries between the Arras and the Indus, the Aral and the Indian Ocean'. But Conolly had travelled by himself and in disguise. A man who had been robbed of all he possessed in Turkestan might well be indifferent to tales of robber-tribes in Kachhi: *Vacuus cantabit coram latrone viator*. And he had come through the pass and the plains in the cold weather. Burnes had visited Shikarpur at the same time of year in 1836–37 but he too does not seem to have realized the conditions under which the Bolan trade was carried on. The Government of India, oppressed with empty fears of a Russian advance in Central Asia, were too much engrossed in consideration of conditions at Khiva to give due attention to those of Kachhi; and seem to have fallen into the easy assumption that where a merchant's *kafila* could pass, there could be no obstruction to an army. For all practical purposes, knowledge of the theatre of the future campaign began above the passes; as for the route thither, the very improvidence of the commissariat staff-work on the expedition implies that reliance was placed on the glowing description of Kachhi in Pottinger's work.

The book was twenty years old. It was forty years out of date. Kachhi had indeed been comparatively tranquil and prosperous under the rule of Nasir Khan I of Kelat, who died in 1794. The great chieftain is said to have been powerful enough to prevent the Marri and Bugti Baluchis from plundering the plains; it is even stated that their internecine wars and feuds were checked by their Brahui over-lord, that they remained within and cultivated their

respective countries, and were held responsible for the protection
of caravans passing between Gundava and Multan. But Mir Nasir
Khan himself was baffled when, for some defiance of his authority,
he attempted to coerce these tribes within their hills; he destroyed
the alum mines in the Bugti country, and did as much damage as he
could but, at last, returned unsuccessful. We may assume at least that
Kachhi prospered under his reign; and that its prosperous condition
was, in the best tradition of Oriental [*sic*] camouflage, represented to
Pottinger as obtaining under the effete rule of his successor.

The actual state of affairs in Kachhi and Upper Sind in 1838–
39 has been described by so many writers, and in such vigorous
language, that a mere summary of the elements constituting
Pottinger's land of milk and honey may be given. Three-quarters
of Kachhi was a waterless desert all the year round except when rain
actually fell; and the *kafila* route to the Bolan passed through the
very worst of it. The whole area was subject, during the hot weather,
to the blasts of the *simoom*, a wind fatal alike to vegetable and animal
life. The villages, collections of miserable huts; the roads, vague and
illusory tracks, the only permanent indications of which were the
bones of men and animals whom they had beguiled; the cultivation,
patches of wheat or *jowari* precariously raised under the shadow
of the hills; all were the hunting-grounds of the predatory Baluch
tribes under whose reign of terror, not to mention the tyranny of
the Khan's officials, three quarters of the population had migrated
to Sind.

The most active among the marauders were the Dombkis and
Jakhranis. Their numbers were small, but the speed of their forays
gave them the reputation of ubiquity, and in consequence, great
numerical strength. The chief of the former, Baluch Khan, lived at
Lahri, and with a portion of his tribe remained quiet and respectable.
The more unruly spirits among the Dombkis acknowledged no head
but Bijar Khan; the lord of Wazirah and Darya Khan and Turk Ali,
the leaders of the Jakhranis, whose headquarters were at Sheranee,
also admitted his authority. Together they had taken possession of

the lands and strong-holds of the Khyberis, south of Lahri: Phulaji and Chattr; and the Syeds of Shahpur, still further to the south and within striking distance of the Talpurs' frontier, were under Bijar Khan's influence.

The condition of Upper Sind was little better than that of Kachhi. Since the city and districts of Shikarpur fell into the hands of the Mirs in 1824, the prosperity of both had declined. The extent and causes of this deterioration are ably discussed by Goldsmid in his *Historical Memoir* of the place. We consider that Shikarpuri merchants must have found their trade injured not a little by the transfer of authority. While their headquarters and their principal entrepôt, Kandahar, were subject to the same rulers, Hindu speculators enjoyed facilities now abruptly cut off and a lack of confidence in the Mirs may well have drawn oft some of the mercantile community to the Punjab.

Their mistrust was well-founded, for under the Talpurs' rule the standard of law and order in Upper Sind rapidly declined and in a few years, the contrast with the Kandahar administration was most marked. The former rulers had maintained effective measures for the security, not only of the town and neighbourhood of Shikarpur but the whole line of their border, by posts and patrols, affording a reasonable degree of protection to kafilas starting for the Bolan. The activities of the Baluch free-booters were consequently circumscribed; as for the route through Kachhi, a certain immunity could be secured by the payment of blackmail on a regular basis. Thus, the Shikarpur Sethia sending a consignment of goods to Central Asia calculated as a matter of course for blackmail charges to be debited; and the Jamalis of Rojhan, the Burdis at Barshori, the Marris and Kakars at Sibi, levied their 'sung' without evincing a disposition to kill the goose that laid such golden eggs. A present to the Khan of Kelat's Naib at Bhag must certainly have figured in this primitive system of insurance.

When the Afghan grip upon Upper Sind was relaxed, and disorder reigned unchecked from Shikarpur to Sibi, Bijar Khan Dombki was able to tap the dwindling stream of *kafilas* nearer to its source; and actually established himself temporarily at Khangarh. The Mirs' method of dealing with this menace to their revenues was characteristic; he was invested by both the branches of the Talpur House with dresses of honour, and some years previous to the appearance of the British in Upper Sind he held a jagir near Larkana, granted by the Hyderabad durbar, perhaps ostensibly for services rendered to the Mirs against Shah Shujah in 1833–34.

The predatory Jakhranis and Dombkis were essentially tribes of horsemen who secured the country for plunder from the Bolan to Shikarpur and from Lahri to Gandava. The villages and cultivated lands of Western Kachhi were well within their range; and the attacks on the columns of the Bombay Division, which marched by the route Khairo Garhi—Gandava—Shoran, may be ascribed to these two tribes rather than to the local Magsis and Rinds. As for the 'High Road', by which the Bengal Division marched and which remained the line of communications for the advance, the two predatory tribes found *kafilas*, richer than ever a Shikarpuri merchant sent to Khiva, passing week after week. They were strongly guarded, it is true; but the good Company's rupees, the innumerable camels, were an irresistible attraction and naturally the Sarcar's commissariat was harassed in preference to the country people. It was estimated that besides occasioning a woeful loss of life and seriously interrupting the communications of the army, the plunderers were responsible for a loss of actual property 'calculated in round numbers at about two and a half lacs of rupees'.

This doubtless explains in part Bijar Khan's scornful refusal to enter the service of the British Government upon the princely salary of three thousand rupees per mensem. The offer was made by W. J. Eastwick when he was officiating as Political Agent in Upper Sind, [with] Kadir Bakhsh Khan, the Khosa Chief, being the channel of communication; it is sufficient testimony to the impression of the robber baron's power. But for the most part the British authorities, military and political, remained for some months under the delusion that the country had risen against them and that every Baluch of whatever tribe was their active enemy. It seemed incredible and it seems so even now, that the robbers could come so far and so fast across that appalling desert. But the Baluch horseman and his mount were not governed by accepted rules and standards. Two descriptions of them will suffice to explain their methods. The Dombkis and Jakhranis were 'mounted on small but high-blooded fiery mares, swift and enduring to a marvel ... they were taught to drink only at long intervals, and were at times fed with raw meat, which is safe to increase their vigour for the time, and create less thirst.'

'When an expedition across the desert was to be undertaken, the mare's food was tied under her belly; the man's, consisting of a coarse cake and sometimes a little arrack, was slung across his shoulders, and was generally sufficient for ten or twelve days' scanty fare: but it was used only in necessity, for, the spoil the robber looked for subsistence.' So [states] Sir William Napier. E. B. Eastwick, who speaks with the greater authority of intimate personal knowledge of them at this period, writes: 'The Baluchis, of all men, can longest endure the want of water. On their most distant forays they drink but once, and never during the heat of the day. They undergo, in fact, a discipline of the most rigorous kind, and those who would cope with them must undergo it too. But no European can ever hope so to change his nature as to match them in hardihood. With the crown of the head bare, and a long roll of cotton cloth twisted loosely round his temples, on a wooden saddle of excruciating hardness, and mounted on a small, lean, ill-formed but indomitable mare, whose pace except when put out is a villainous short rough trot—the Biluchi rides on and on, fifty, sixty, nay seventy miles without a halt.'

The results of the 'horrid state of disorganization' in Kachhi and Upper Sind were experienced not only in attacks on the line of march and the lifting of camels wholesale, but in an almost complete lack of supplies. The army were very soon disabused of the vague idea that Kacchi would be found a granary. The irrigation works referred to by Pottinger had mostly been abandoned and an enormous proportion of the cultivators had fled the country. Another circumstance which seems to have been forgotten by those who planned the expedition was that the season for the spring harvest above the passes was two months later than in the plains. The advance under Sir Willoughby Cotton, after passing through the Bolan, soon exhausted the resources of the valley of Shal: the commander was naturally unwilling to fall back, while to advance and to remain stationary seemed equally impossible. Sir John Keane joined him with the main body and the position became critical. The army had to be fed from Upper Sind. The Bengal Army's Commissariat department was well organized. Not so that of the Bombay Army: middling and recrimination began as soon as the urgency for supplies on an unusual scale put a strain on the department; aggravated, of course, by the enormous length of the line of communications, the impossibility of feeding adequately the transport animals, the heat and shortage of water, and the constant harassment of the raiders.

The state of the army in the advance in April may be described in the words of a relative of the present writer, then an Ensign in the 23rd Bombay Native Infantry, stationed in Sukkur. 'Sir John Keane's army was starving; the fighting men allowed only half a seer of flour daily, and the poor camp followers one quarter. Beer was selling at 150 Rupees a dozen, and everything else in the same proportion.' The main duty for the Politicals in Upper Sind was to collect supplies by hook or crook, and to arrange some means for their safe arrival with the advance. They were asked to 'strain every nerve to push on all the camels that may come in your way. There is no certainty of our getting anything beyond the pass, or at least, in comparison with what we require. Send no camels unladen, if you have wherewithal to load them. We shall want grain, grain, grain to the end of the chapter. Let the escorts be very strong … I have little hope of this ever reaching you, but I must make the trial. Send camels and grain—grain and camels.'

There was a limit, however, to the strength of the escorts that could be given when the country round the base of operations at Sukkur itself was in a turmoil. W. J. Eastwick, brother of the 'ex-political' who wrote that fascinating book *Dry Leaves from Young Egypt* gives this account of the situation—the chaos from which he was expected to evolve order: 'The country round Shikarpur is in the last stage of disorganisation. Every man is anxious to cut our throats, and we have a few hundred infantry to protect the vast quantities of stores and treasure, to provide escorts, and secure the base of our military operations. It is really quite lamentable to see the want of wisdom and common judgment. We have murders and robberies every day. I am levying troops of the country on my own responsibility: thieves to fight thieves—an irregular corps of Biluchis.'

This was the beginning of the Baluch levy but before embarking on its history, it is necessary to glance for a moment at the final efforts of regular troops to pilot through to the Bolan, and to punish those that harassed them.

A convoy of two thousand six hundred camels crossed the desert in the middle of April, under the escort of the 31st Bengal N.I. and the officer commanding wrote to the authorities describing the sufferings of himself and his men from heat and want of water, and declared that it would be madness to attempt to send another, as the season was so far advanced. The Baluchis had harassed him incessantly, and he 'lost 52 horses from over fatigue, following those rascals'. It was now decided to make an example of the marauders and the unfortunate choice of the objective shows how much in the dark the politicals and military still were as to the identity of the raiders. Ensign Newnham, mentioned above, writes on 12 May from Sukkur: 'a detachment of the 5th regiment have gone out with a six-pounder to take a small fort in which the Baloochees have deposited their spoil. I hope they will give them a good rubbing.' Next day he hears the result—'that detachment of the 5th that left the other day have taken the fort ... on our side Subahdar Bukadoor and 3 privates killed, 1 ensign and 7 privates wounded; on the side of the enemy, 2 chiefs and 48 men killed, and 46 wounded and taken prisoners.' He adds later: 'The Brigadier put it in Orders that it would have met with his highest approbation if he (the officer commanding) had not spared one.' The spirit of indiscriminate vindictiveness, due to ignorance, had not taken long to grow.

Thus did Khangarh, afterwards to be known as Jacobabad, make its first appearance on the page of history. Eastwick's account is that 'the fort contained two hundred men, chiefly of the Khosa tribe. Some of them were said to have plundered our baggage, though the other Sindhis declare these Khosas were innocent and that the ill-deed was done by the Jakranis ... a great number of the Biluchis were bayoneted—and the rest were sent prisoners to Shikarpur, where they were afterwards released. If the Khosas were really guilty of the marauding imputed to them, they were terribly punished.' T. Postans, writing some months after this tragic event, roundly declared that these Khosas were our friends, and that from the error 'a want of faith was engendered which we could not re-establish'.

Perhaps some such doubt was in the mind of the newly appointed political agent, Ross Bell, when he planned another expedition, against Phulaji. This shot would really have been in the bullseye, as the fort was a stronghold of Bijar Khan Dombki, the most active of all the Baluch raiders, and, as we have seen, leader of his own tribesmen and of the Jakranis.

John Jacob's account of the disaster that overtook this expedition, long before reaching its objective, occurs in his Memoir on Billamore's Hill campaign and elsewhere among his writings. But he only witnessed one side of the whole tragedy; another detachment, designed ultimately to join that under his command, underwent an even fiercer ordeal, in the passage of the desert by the last of the great *kafilas* sent up to supply the starving army in Afghanistan. The tale of that crossing was told nearly thirty years afterwards, by Sir Thomas Seaton, then a captain in the 35th Bengal N.I., who being on his way to join his regiment, accompanied the convoy by a mere chance. The 'Athenaeum' critic refers to the book on 27 January 1866 in a somewhat patronising manner: the notice might almost have been written by Mr Arthur Pendennis—but at least he admits that: 'the fearful hardships of this march in the hottest part of the year exceeded anything that can well be imagined, even by the most experienced traveller.' Seaton omits to mention that any of the troops forming the escort were detailed for another duty as soon as they reached Dhadar, and went on up the Bolan to join the advance. The wing of the 23rd N.I. duly remained at Bhag and Dhadar under Major Newport, who had commanded the convoy but were denied the excitement of a punitive expedition. They were, in fact, no more fit for duty than the remnant of Jacob's detachment which reached Shikarpur.

Ensign Newnham, who had to be left behind at Bhag to recuperate, writes of the experience as follows:

A most severe and fatal march we have had, one that, I hope, will never be my fortune to witness again. The heat was dreadful, far exceeding that of Guzerat; even the natives of the country do not venture out at this season, when exposure to the sun is certain death. They all said it was madness our attempting to proceed. Nothing but the most dire necessity could have justified an immense *kafila* such as ours was, consisting of 4,500 camels, 400 cavalry, 600 infantry, and numerous camp followers, being sent when it was doubtful even if water was to be obtained at some of the stages … we started from Shikarpur on 23 May, and got on very fairly till we arrived at Rojhan, where we first felt the want of water. From Rojhan to Barshoorie, a march of 32 miles, across a desert where not a tree or a blade of grass was to be seen, the men suffered extremely from thirst. Our men having kettles got over it much better than the Bengalees. Nevertheless we arrived at Barshoorie at 6 o'clock in the morning without the loss of a man. Here the heat was so great, the thermometer ranging from 115° to 124° in the tents, and the water so bad, that the men began to fall rapidly, and died like rotten sheep.

From this place to Baugh only three marches, we lost out of the Europeans, 3 officers, one conductor, one sergeant, and Mr Tait's agent (and myself nearly dead, at one time: I thought it was all over with me and my campaigning at an end). They all say it is the greatest mercy to have escaped. The day I was taken ill we had buried two of the officers in one grave. Of the Natives, 60 men of the Bengal 42nd, about 50 or 60 of the Irregular Horse, and camelmen, and only 4 or 5 of our own men died an awful mortality in so short a time … the Brigadier has issued a flaming order begging to congratulate the surviving officers on their escape and said it was a case, however, to be regretted, that the sacrifice of life was warrantable, without which it was not expected the convoy would reach its destination.

Mr Ross Bell the Political Agent at Shikarpore, planned an expedition against Pullajee (the stronghold of the most powerful tribes) the other day, in which our detachment was to have taken part, the whole to be commanded by Clibborn of the 1st Grenadiers; but the following fatal march from Sukkur knocked it on the head. The Artillery and the details of the European regiments in the advance marched for Shikarpore to join the expedition. Somehow or other the officer commanding the Europeans got separated from the Artillery and lost his way. The consequence was that his men were exposed to the sun nearly the whole day, himself, 1 sergeant 2, corporals and 9 privates died that day, and a number afterwards in hospital; which I think ought to prove to the *wise* men in power that neither Europeans or Natives can stand this sun, and it is to be hoped that no more valuable lives will be sacrificed to the whim of such people as Mr Bell, and old Gordon.

This was, in fact, the last of the attempts to use regular troops against the Baluchis that season and the Baluch Levy was to hold the field against the predatory tribes until the cold weather. It is a convenient moment to make their acquaintance, for a number of the Levy accompanied Major Newport's detachment and their commandant, Lieutenant Amiel, saw them off from Rojhan. Amiel was an officer of the 1st Grenadier N.I. and before he was deputed to this duty, had done twelve years' service. He had already had some experience chasing Baluchis in the Janidero-Rojhan area, before the *kafila* marched on 29 May. A letter from Captain Smee, who had led the expedition against Khangarh and was now commanding at Rojhan, addressed to the Brigade Major, Sukkur, gives a picture of the miserable conditions of existence at this place:

Sir it becomes my duty to inform you for the information of the Brigadier that the detachment under my command has become so weak, both from cholera having broken out and the intense heat, that I have scarcely any men fit for duty. About 20 natives have died here within the last few days. I have lost one sepoy and two *naiques* from cholera. It has been out of my power to get the men undercover, the work-people all deserted except a few, who have been employed nearly all day burying the dead. Under these circumstances I shall await your reply to this letter. The heat has now become so great that it is almost impossible to move out during the day, and at night it blows quite a hot wind. There is not at present more than one Government Camel here, and it will take (a string) of twenty to move the tents, ammunition etc. should it be required. There is a very large amount of Government Grain in the Fort. It is with great difficulty that I am able to write this letter, being so unwell.

P. N.—Camels for the sick and to carry the provisions for the men will also be required should we move.

The regular troops were shortly afterwards withdrawn and Rojhan was occupied, from time to time, by detachments of Amiel's levy. He, meanwhile, had moved on the night of 3 June to Janidero, whence he writes to inform the Assistant Political Agent, Shikarpur, of the outbreak of cholera, which had caused the deaths of several of his Baluch Horses. He had only fourteen horses fit for duty and looking to these conditions, he asks for leave to build sheds to shelter the men!

We should, however, before embarking on the history of the Levy's activities say something of its origin and composition.

Lieutenant W. J. Eastwick, as we have seen, had started recruiting for his corps of Baluchis in anticipation of the Government of India's sanction. This he received on 18 April, Government observing that 'there appeared no improvement in the attitude of the people' and ordering him to raise 500 Baluchis as cavalry and the same number as infantry, through their chiefs. Enlistment on these lines was supplemented when on 16 June agreements were entered into by the Politicals with Kadir Bakhsh Khan, Chief of the Khosas, residing at Jamra, and Sher Mahomed Khan, Chief of the Burdis, at Shergarh. Each chief was to receive Rs. 300 per month, the former for protecting the road between Sukkur and Shikarpur and the latter as his territory adjoined that of the Dombkis and Jakhranis, to check plunder throughout his country. The Khosa Chief was to provide thirty horsemen at twenty-five rupees each, and Sher Mahomed ten men on a pay of ten rupees. It was also hoped that some Bugtis might be recruited.

Postans mentions a similar arrangement with Imam Bakhsh Jatoi, and observes 'in both cases the expense was incurred as a sort of *douceur* to keep these people quiet'—in fact, one of the most noted of all the border freebooters, Rahman Burdi, was in command of the quota from that tribe.

E. B. Eastwick's estimate of his brother's scheme is somewhat too flattering: 'In this manner,' he says, 'and acting on this foundation a body of police was gradually formed by the officer who first had the political management of Upper Sindh, which, as it employed the most active spirits and protected the communication between different parts and detachments, soon promised to terminate the old regime of anarchy and bloodshed, and to confer on the whole province the blessings of peace and tranquillity.' Meanwhile the Levy proper, six hundred foot and horse, had been enlisted at Sukkur and Shikarpur. They were described by Ross Bell (Eastwick's successor) in a report to the Government of India as mounted on *tattoos* (country ponies) and looking more like grass-cutters than a body of horse. He was prepared to raise their pay from Rs. 15 per month to Rs. 20 provided they produced better horses.

At Shikarpur, four hundred Khyris had been raised together with a number of Yusufzais: these men had been put under Amiel, and given the duty of protecting the *dak* across the desert to Dhadar. It is with these that we shall be mainly concerned.

The Khyris were a tribe which had originally occupied lands round Phulaji and Chatter. They were not Baluchis but Sheikhs, though they had adopted certain Baluch customs. For years they were subject to constant attacks by the Dombkhis aided at times by the Marris, and though they resisted bravely, they had finally been driven out of their lands by Bijar Khan about ten years before the appearance in Upper Sind of the British who found them settled in the neighbourhood of Shikarpur. From the first they proved friendly and faithful, hoping that the Faringhi would be able to instate them in their ancestral country, for which they had applied to the Khairpur and Hyderabad *durbars* in vain.

The business of knocking this material into shape was not easy. One 12 June, Amiel wrote to Ross Bell that: 'if ever they are to get into any state of discipline it must be done very gradually. Our first essay must be to conciliate and gain their affections, after which we may do anything with them ... placing three men in a row the other day and drilling them has frightened them all.'

The officers and men stationed at Shikarpur were still under canvas but by 14 July, Amiel could write to E. J. Brown, the Assistant Political Agent at Sukkur, 'I've commenced building a shed and on its being habitable I shall be able to get my papers and books into good order. I have only 9 bottles of beer left, and the road from Sukkur is impassable—pleasant, is it not?'

Bottled beer was, of course, the drink par excellence of British officers serving in India at this period. It was something more than a drink: the general belief was as stated by Ensign Newnham, writing home from Sukkur in May 1839 and justifying a modest budget under this head—'In this warm weather if you did not drink beer you would die of exhaustion.' A few years later Sir Charles Napier himself the most abstemious of men, wrote that his subalterns did not seem to be able to undergo privations, and were discontented without their usual wine and beer! They regarded it not as a luxury but as a necessity. The redoubtable Major Gahagan tells us (and so it must be true) that during his first year in Bengal with the Ahmednuggur Irregular Horse he drank two hundred dozen bottles of Hodson's Pale Ale. To turn from fiction to fact, Eastwick writes of E. J. Brown, to whom Amiel addressed the letter quoted above: 'It is true that he was an able officer, and possessed excellent natural abilities, but … no man who swallows from one to two dozen bottles of beer per diem can always scrutinize with sufficient exactness the infinitesimal limits of the expedient and inexpedient.' Richard Burton, who knew him later when serving as Secretary to Sir Charles Napier as Governor of Sind, speaks of him as 'Captain "Beer Brown" of the Bengal Engineers: poor fellow! He lived upon and died of a dozen of Bass per diem.' He died, indeed, of abscess on the liver, to the great grief of Napier, who was then Commander-in-Chief.

However, beer was indispensable: whether at the board of the Political Agent, where 'fourteen thousand bottles annually poured forth their foaming contents' in miserable forts on the borders of the desert, or under canvas in Shikarpur.

To return to the Baluch Levy. Our information concerning the Corps is derived in the main from demi-official letters written by Amiel to Ross Bell and others, but particularly the former, with very occasionally an official despatch.

It will be convenient to bring its history with an exposition of the Baluch plunderers' methods as related by Amiel in a letter to Ross Bell dated 4 July 1839 from Shikarpur.

Yesterday 30 camels belonging to Lieutenant Shaw were driven off by the Balochis. We sent after them and recovered the camels

two *coss* the other side of Jeneederah, 14 or 15 miles from this. The
horses could not overtake the plunderers and four died from fatigue
and heat. These Balooches travel quietly at night and arrive near the
grazing ground about gun fire. Their horses then have a good feed
and a rest. When they drive off the camels they manage to proceed
at a rapid pace, yet not sufficient to knock up their horses. Our
men arrive in sight with every animal tired and done up; they then
forsake the plunder and make their escape. I wish information could
be gained of an intended expedition, although we can never as the
camel men (at least many of them) are accomplices of the robbers,
giving them information and taking the camels in the direction they
know the thieves are. The horses and *tattoo* that have died are not
expensive ones, it would therefore be a desirable thing if Government
sanctioned a certain sum to be given in compensation, otherwise it
cannot be expected that a man whose only fortune is his horse will
exert himself and perhaps lose the animal by the possession of which
he obtains his livelihood.' Amiel proceeds to inform Ross Bell of the
progress made in building the Residency in Shikarpur which in the
following November Eastwick describes as a 'barn-like structure'.

Three days later, Amiel writes to say that another party of Baluchis
had driven off some camels belonging to a native and recommends
that a party of horse and foot should be stationed at Janidero with the
object of cutting off the plunderers on their return towards the hills
from the vicinity of Shikarpur; Minuti being another stopping place
of the raiders. Two more horses had died from fatigue at Khangarh,
and the rigours of the climate took a new form, as he concludes:
'Last night it blew such a gale of wind that my head aches from the
dust having penetrated my eyes and head.'
　　The tale of outrages and loss of horses continued almost daily.
On 10 July, Amiel reports two of his Pathan horsemen killed near
Rojhan. A party of Dombkis and Jakhranis attacked the *tapalis*
(postmen) near Mauladad, murdered them and carried off the
camels. Some of Amiel's men tracked the camels, and came upon

the raiders, only to be cut up by them. The survivors in their examination said 'we went after the camel about four *kos*. It was not a camel, but the Angel of Death who enticed us into the mouth of destruction.' Amiel took up again the question of compensation to families of men killed, and for horses dying on duty: by the 12th a report came in that four belonging to the party which had proceeded with Major Newport's *kafila* to Dhadar had died from want of forage and fatigue while detained at Bagh by Lieutenant Travers. 'Bagh,' says Amiel indignantly though incorrectly, 'where even water is not procurable without being paid for.'

Soon afterwards, water was in excess instead of defect. Amiel writes to Bell on 18 July: 'Here am I in Shikarpoor without a chance of seeing Janeederah without swimming there. The rain commenced on the afternoon of the 15th and has continued at intervals ever since. The country is a complete sheet of water and your house a mass of mud. We covered the walls with matting: this has been a slight protection, but I fear a few more showers will erase every appearance of its being brick. The natives are most miserably off ... I hope ere long to start and look about the country and hope to inspire a little wholesome terror into their minds.' The relief of the rain was only temporary. By the 23rd he is writing to Bell, 'The weather here is hotter than ever, and the natives say for two months more we shall have it day and night: for my part I doubt whether there is any cool weather in this country.' The forage problem, at least, was in a way to be solved. While at Rojhan under Captain Smee, they had been compelled to send for grass from Jagan; and similarly while at Janidero from Bungla, three *kos* distance. With the rain and inundation together, the grass soon shot up, and preparations for the tour were begun.

Khan Muhomed Umerani of Minuti met Amiel and offered his assistance in showing him the country. Amiel writes to Bell: 'if I take possession of this fort we might cut the Doomkies and Jekranies off ... the Balooches have destroyed the two sheds and my house at Janeedera: have I authority to erect a few sheds, as there is no shelter. I shall in all probability take up my residence at Kangur, as it is the largest fort and has shelter in the bastions for a few men.'

Meanwhile Ross Bell had been in correspondence with the Government of India on the subject of the Baluch plunderers, the disastrous result of the employment of regular troops at that season, and his hopes that for the time being the Levy would be able to restrain the raiders. He had also recommended that a body of Afgan Horse should be raised and employed against the Baluchis. Government replied that it would be necessary to use coercive measures against the tribes in the ensuing cold weather. Meanwhile two *rissalas* of Skinner's Horse and the Gwalior *rissala* of Anderson's Cavalry were being drafted to Upper Sind and 'the number and efficiency of the Balooch Horse renders the raising of Afgan Horse unnecessary.' In actual fact, the numbers and efficiency of the Levy left much to be desired. Amiel writes to E. J. Brown on 28 July that he only had 128 men out of 356 available for duty in Shikarpur. The remainder were distributed between posts at Dhadar, Roghan, Jagun and Sukkur, besides providing an escort for the Political Agent (to which Eastwick refers ironically). The main body at Shikurpur were not cantoned, but scattered witty their horses throughout the town, and the sawars gave considerable trouble. Amiel continues: 'I've a bad headache from drinking too much beer, and shall draw my letter to a conclusion. Sinclair who exceeded me, says, fresh salmon never agrees with me; curious, it never is the wine. P.S., I've just heard that the forty sawars sent to Dadur have been detained by Travers at Bagh on account of the fighting between the Balooches between that place and Dadur. I am afraid that for some time these men will not return (not within twenty days. One jamadar of foot who got some horsemen together and who I made a duffadar refused to go as far as Dadur. I've had *dreadful* work getting some men who never intended leaving Shikarpore to start: In time we shall find out the good and bad.'

On the 30th, Amiel reports that Bijar Khan, the head of the predatory confederacy, was said to be alarmed by his preparations to move out into the country, and that he might throw himself upon the Ameers. It should be remembered that the territories of the Hyderabad and Khairpur Mirs were inextricably mixed in the region of Shikarpur. Roughly speaking the country to the east and the north was under Khairpur. The rumour must have been deliberately circulated, for on the first August the *Dombkis* and Jakhranis took the fort of Rajan with the object of levying from it blackmail on the *dak* line.

Amiel gave orders to his men at Mubarakpur to retake the fort, and followed himself, to find that three tribesmen had been captured.

He now started on his tour. Only those who have moved about this tract in August (camping in well-constructed bungalows, and supplied with ice and stores of all kinds, in these degenerate days), can appreciate the hardships of Amiel on his pioneer trip. The country was altogether unknown, and, where it was not desert, covered with dense jungle; its inhabitants, if not openly hostile, unwilling or afraid to give assistance or true information; the Levy unproved, intriguing, and as soon became evident, addicted to tyrannising over and plundering the people; the only shelter ruined forts or 'kacha' sheds.

Amiel's first camp was at Janidero, where he arrived via Jagan. He found that it was impossible to remain there, as the Khyeri Horse who had vainly pursued the Dombkis and Jakhranis had consumed all the grass, though the juari crops which at the same season next year Eastwick found covering the country round for miles, and growing nearly twenty feet high, were coming on. Amiel decided to see Khangarh to consider its eligibility as a post, and in a letter to Ross Bell dated the 8th observes: 'If I had 500 horse and the 6 pounder I would try my luck against Chuttur and Poolajee'.

By the 10th, he was writing from Mubarakpur, which he describes as a bazar town, the fort of which was capacious and strong. He had seen Khangarh on his way eastwards, and had ordered his Khyeris to get banias to settle there. Among the advantages of this place were a house formerly occupied by the Killedar, and the fact that it was only a march from Minuti, an oasis in the desert, already mentioned by him as one of the principal routes taken by the raiders on their incursions.

Ross Bell seems now to have decided to employ Amiel in the capacity of a political or rather intelligence officer, for the latter replies on the 13th: 'thanks for obtaining for me an appointment not only congenial but well-paid. I am only afraid my talents are more in riding horses than writing letters.' He had found Mubarakpur a good place for grass and began to get his horses fit. His next move would be a visit to Thul. He proceeds, 'Rumour took me towards Khangarh, but I found no enemy, though I offered 100 Rupees for *pukka* information … only drawback is the heat and miserable sheds. I'm obliged to live in that in truth after a ride of 12 *coss* as this morning I'm more inclined to sleep than any other thing.'

He visited the villages and forts in the neighbourhood, and the appearance of the Sarcar's representative was noised abroad, for he received a letter from Bibi Sultan Begum of Shahpur (of whom he writes facetiously 'unfortunately she's old') containing a story of the miseries she endured at the hands of the robber bands. By the 17th the cattle of the Levy had eaten all the grass round Mubarakpur, and Amiel decided to move on Mirpur, three *kos* distant, where he hoped to intercept the raiders' camels which were sent there to obtain grain. It was rumoured in the country that Bijar Khan was trying to persuade the Syeds of Shahpur to intercede for him. Amiel sent a spy to Chattr. His Kyhris were now in expectation of having their old lands restored to them. He says, 'they are the only friends Government has in this country. I feel an interest in the men and should like to see Kamal-Khan once more in possession of his country.'

Amiel now moved on to Thul accompanied by Sher Mahomed Burdi, of whom he writes 'his advisor in the shape of a fat Syud is one of those men taught from infancy to conceal the truth. They are our servants, yet keep the camels they have taken either by force themselves or as lords of the land from others.' It will be remembered that Sher Mahomed Burdi was one of the two Chiefs whom we had taken into service in June to protect the country from the predatory tribes. As hitherto their efforts in this capacity had not been subjected to any real supervision, it was scarcely surprising to find them making capital out of their new position; but Sher Mahomed was now ordered to dance attendance upon the political authorities, and after the capture and execution of the notorious Saula, the Burdis ceased to be the scourge they formerly had been to the eastern half of Upper Sind. Amiel had now entered the territory of the Khairpur branch of the Talpur House, and he seems to have met its future ruler.

The Hakim of Meerpur, Allee Moorad, a very independent sort of character, built a bridge over a *nullah* which broke down and spoiled all my kit. After I had threatened, if another did so, to shave him, the bridges became strong and passable. These men have no gentlemanly feelings, to deal with them as equals is throwing away time. Those who really do our work we must take by the hand; the remainder must be kept down to the grindstone. The sheds become worse as I advance. Although this (Thul) is a town, yet inside the fort there is not a place equal to an English pig-sty.

Since having the Belooch Corps I have taken every means of ascertaining the dispositions of the different jemadars. From what I've observed the Khyrees and Purdesces would be the only people on whom any dependence could be placed. Abdul Kureem and his brother Abdul Ghunee Khan I would rely on. And from what I've seen Jemadar Abdul Haleem Khan is the only one who is not mixed up with the petty intrigues going on in this part of the country Jemadar Uliff Khan is Zamindar of the village of Zukriel and altho' not a partaker in the spoils yet he does not wish stolen property to be recovered, having threatened the scout in our employ to be revenged on him when the English left the coast clear. Jamadar Ghoolam Khan is a plausible soft-spoken Douranee, always vaunting of what his tribe could do. He is connected with all the Shikarporeans; many being under him, most of them perfectly useless as soldiers. He is always in arrears to myself and his sowars; in fact I've more trouble with him than all the remainder. It appears from what lean glean from listening to their conversation that he considers the service of the Feringees as a Pis-aller. At present reform is impossible: it must be done gradually. I shall not take (except Khyherees) and the characters whom I find useless can be gradually got rid of. These men may be individually brave yet as a body they are useless. To pursue Jekranees or Doomkees, or take the post to Dadur, Shikarporeans may do; for the purpose of forming a Russallah Hindus and Punjabee men are the fellows. We shall ere long know more of their work, as yet we've been in the dark. By employing Beloochees we add, in case of their becoming enemies to their efficiency in arms and horses, until the opportunity occurs of their turning against us.

The last half of this letter has only to be considered, in the light of subsequent events for us to realize the justice of Amiel's observations. He was indeed unduly optimistic of the Levy's ability to deal with the Dombkis and Jakhranis. The raiders had so far avoided him, and like everyone else at this time he did not understand the Baluch method of fighting; to evade coming to close quarters until in a strong superiority, and then to fight with dauntless valour. A taste of the real capabilities of the tribesmen was in store for him. But Amiel's estimate of the materials for a *rissala*, and his opinion of the undesirability of recruiting Baluchis for this service, anticipate in an interesting way the conclusions of John Jacob on this subject. Writing fourteen years later, on the Brahuis, Afghans and Pathans considered as recruits for our armies, Jacob makes it clear that his bad opinion of these races as soldiers extends also to the Baluch. He concludes his remarks: 'Were I proceeding on service against the Tribes bordering on our frontier I should consider the real strength of my force to be increased by the absence of such soldiers. They could not be trusted without imminent risk of failure and disgrace.' From the first, Jacob declined to enlist Baluchis and Afghans in the Sind Irregular Horse, for which he recruited almost exclusively Hindustani Mussulmans.

But to return to our pioneer. In a letter written from Mubarakpur on his return from Thul four days later, Amiel shows his estimate of Jemadar Alief Khan was correct. Some stolen government camels were recovered from Chana, and this worthy claimed them as his own. 'These men,' (the local population and the Jemadars) says Amiel with resignation, 'are all related to each other or friends.' Raman Burdi was a similar case. In the same letter he reports that the water in the Begari—then the size of a large *'karia'* and half choked with jungle—had risen again. By 31 August he was back in Shikarpur, arranging for the security of the *dak* to Bagh, and at length successfully persuading 'three miserable Hindoos' to reside at Janidero. His auxiliaries continued their double game. He reports: 'Sher Mahomed Boordee has patched up a treaty with the Boogtees; only a week hence he offered to march against them with his whole tribe. We shall never get these men to understand us until a few have their brains knocked out; they imagine we fear them, from paying them so well.' A report came in that Bijar Khan Dombki had sent his men to Rohjan to levy blackmail on the *dak* once more, and he sent one of the jemadars, Itbar Khan Khyri, from Mubarakpur to seize them. Amiel concludes his letter, 'I understand the General is taking the held next month. He'll find it very hot work: the plunderers will keep. I wish he would give me a few auxiliary horse and a six pounder. Without the latter it would be folly as the villages contain enclosures with embrasures for matchlocks. The time will yet come for our revenge, until which time we must keep quiet.'

One piece of information picked up by Amiel on his tour was that some Hindus of Mirpur farmed the trans-desert trade in tobacco, bhang, sweetmeats and cloth from the Hyderabad Government. To stop this would naturally cause loss to the Mirs; but though the *banias* pretended that they could take security for the sale of these goods on arrival at Chattr exclusively to Hindus, their customers were actually the Jakhranis and Dombkis. The tribesmen were also largely dependent on Sind for grain, the bare hills and the patches of cultivation on their border producing insufficient supplies except in the most favourable seasons; and the Bugtis at least, did not steal all that they needed.

A peaceable visit of some men of this latter tribe to Thul to purchase grain gave Amiel the opportunity of sending Jemadar Abdul Karim from Mubarak and he captured nine tribesmen and several camel-loads of corn. In the same letter as this questionable achievement is reported, he records a real success in the capture of a number of prisoners by the expedition to Rojhan referred to above, and requests favourable notice of its leader, Jemadar Itbar Khan Kyheri. Amiel recommended that the fort of Rojhan should again be permanently occupied by foot, not horse, as there was no forage there; the advantage being (obviously) the facility of gaining information of raids, and preventing the freebooters from obtaining water and food after crossing the desert. The Khyri foot were at this time at Khanpur, to protect their own families, as their old enemies had threatened to pay them a visit: doubtless annoyed by the growing strength and influence of the tribe whom they had driven from their ancestral lands, and so into British service. The problem of fodder was even more acute at Barshori, the next stage of the *kafila* route. We have already mentioned this horrible spot, surrounded by thirty miles of desert featureless as a calm sea, where the first disasters overtook Major Newport's convoy at the end of May. A post of twenty men was maintained here for guarding the *dak*. Eastwick, who visited Barshori in the following year, writes of it characteristically: 'This hole boasts of a chief, whose motto should be "better to reign in Hell than serve in Heaven", and this agreeable place, in which the delay of an hour seems protracted to infinite ages.' Amiel recommended that his men there should be given an allowance of Rs. 5 per man, since grain was only obtainable at prohibitive prices.

For some time after his return to Shikarpur, Amiel had to give attention to the western side of his extensive beat. The Jamalis round Rojhan were found to be hand in glove with the raiders from across the desert, and this was the explanation of an incident he recalls from the strenuous days in May, which he had spent in vain pursuit of robbers who had stolen camels. 'When the Russeldar and myself were come up with them he (Suleman Jamali) called out to the robbers: "you'd better be off, as Itibar Khan and the Khyerees arc close behind"—the robbers themselves related this at Minootie.' Another prominent man of this tribe Lashkar Khan, explained a suspicious absence from Rojhan by saying that he had been cultivating fields near Minuti; by a strange coincidence, no doubt, the Jammalis and other Baluchis had looted a *kafila* of Hindus' goods at just that time, in August and the unfortunate owners had gone to Rojhan to pay the blackmail.

Amiel got information that the Jamalis had concealed their loot at Rojhan in the fort while he was paying a surprise visit to Khangarh on the night of 10–11, when, in addition, he captured eleven Suhriani Khosas. He seems to have laid some of the Rojhan Jamalis by the heels, for on 12 September he writes: 'my menagerie is increasing every day: what is to be done with all these fellows? My trip has proved a good one, not so much from the number of prisoners as the information they have given us. I always doubted the Jamalees, altho' Eastwick called them as well as the Khosas quiet people. What fools the Baloochees must imagine us to be! I should like to hang a few; an example would be very thing; they would then know we were not playing with them. The information against Lushkur Khan is, plundering the *kafila* mentioned in my letter to Postans, the son of Luskur Khan having (stolen) sixteen camels when Major Newport's detachment marched; these he sold.' Amiel concludes: 'yesterday I was so completely knocked up for want of good for four days that at one time I doubted my ability of riding back again.'

A rumour now reached him that the arch free-booter, Bijar Khan, was intending to give himself up, together with Yar Shah, one of the Syeds of Shahpur, whose position at this period seems to have been (under compulsion) *Chursh* to Bijar's unique form of State. Amiel, in anxiety not to lose the fun, says he would like to know the Brigadier's plan of operations. By this time, he was alone in his command. Lieutenant Sinclair, his former coadjutor, had been derailed on the much less arduous and more profitable duty of proceeding in charge of a beautiful boat—a present to the new Sikh Maharajah Kharak Singh—for the successful performance of which he received (and was allowed by Government to retain) a sword with a jewelled scabbard and a charger! Amiel remained to plough a lonely furrow.

His next trip was to a village called Jalbani, about forty miles west of Shikarpur, where he had heard stolen Government property was concealed. He found the fort and village deserted; a horseman from Shikarpur had communicated news of his visit, giving time to remove everything. One of his Jemadars, Abdul Karim, assaulted a man when drunk with bhang. Amiel says: 'as a soldier I think he would fight like the devil, but these men have not been accustomed to control ... I hope by being constantly with them to find out many who have merely entered our service for the purpose of plundering whenever the opportunity occurs, and turning out such will be the most effective way of eradicating the evil.'

His words were prophetic, for his next letter to Bell, dated 23 September reports a fight between his men under Itbar Khan and some Burdis in Abdur Rahman Burdi's village, which seems to have been a squabble about plunder, though many government camels were recovered. Postans mentions that he went to Mubarakpur to inquire into the circumstances of this outrage, in which the Levy cut up a number of perfectly innocent Burdis; he secured the ringleaders but they managed to escape. Amiel arrived too late for the fracas but writes from Mubarakpur two days later that the Levy were quite adepts at plundering and that he had dismissed some of them.

More congenial was the task of getting information about the country beyond the northern desert. He says, 'Bijarkhan Doomki's "*dil*" has gone. He wished for an asylum in the Boogtie country but Beebruk said no. He then sought out the Murees, but they likewise politely declined the honour. In fact, it merely requires 500 sowars to go across the desert to do for him the men in this part of the country are in a fine state of subordination, and I'll wager my existence that a sowar of mine shall go from Shikarpore to Dadur without anyone endeavouring to hurt him, always excepting our friends the Doomkies and Jakranees; but their time is nearly out, and thereafter I anticipate splendid shikar.'

Again the over-confidence: what says the Persian proverb? 'When you set out to hunt the deer you should be prepared for the lion.' It did not occur to Amiel that possibly he might be the quarry! The letter continues: 'Last night a Khyree named Abdulla, a relative of Kamal Khan and Itibah Khan's came from Chuttur and gave himself up to the latter. It appears he was concerned in some robbery and fled to Beeja Khan. He is under restraint but his being a relation prevented me from sending him to Shikarpur as a prisoner; one man would not swell my list of prisoners and it would be the cause of much "Badnamee" being attached to Kamal Khan. He has not spoken about the man, and even Itigah Khan is willing to cut his throat should I give the *hookum*. I think some good information may be derived from keeping him and this is more valuable than his services working in irons.'

Such was the first appearance on our stage of the most useful and the most faithful auxiliary we had yet gained in this country. As guide to Billamore's expedition, of which more anon, and in 1840 to Brown, Clarke, and Clibborn, his loyalty never wavered even in the face of utter disaster to those he served. Eastwick describes him as 'a very handsome young man, with long dark brown ringlets, curling to his shoulders, and hazel eyes.'

But we anticipate Amiel's next letter, dated 24 September was addressed to Postans, then Assistant Political Agent, Shikarpur. It is in a truculent vein though the Levy had let its commander down badly. The jemadar (Ghulam Khan) and sawars sent to Rojhan to collect the Jamali prisoners improved the shining hour by looting the inhabitants of the surrounding Sind villages, collecting a large booty of goats, sheep, and other property and nearly causing a serious rupture between the British and the Mirs' government. Amiel had now to tell his jemadars that 'the first fellow found plundering will be strung up. This I shall carry into execution. It is useful, people who do not know these fellows making (suggestions?) and giving advice as to your conduct; they know nothing what it is absolutely necessary to do … these chaps are ruled by kindness and tyranny, the first for good men, the latter for rascals. If a man does not obey my *hookam* I've fifty fellows who'll cut him down, and it is the knowledge of this that makes them fear me. I intend administering an oath to the jemadars and men to fish up some concealed property … Mr Bell writes that he wishes for information of the country. To go in it is impossible without being allowed to cross the desert.'

To Bell, on this same subject of the looters, Amiel writes: 'these jemadars were employed from being the first to offer their services to Eastwick.' He also mentions that they had a practice of changing their men without consulting him. As to the state of the country for the rejected expedition against the robbers, he observes, 'I'm afraid water and grain will totally fail. Even at this time the 'Begarrie' the largest *nullah* in this part of the country is nearly dry.'

On 1 October he reports to Bell '… heard that the Bugtis were assembling on the Northern edge of the desert, but were deterred from crossing owing to my presence at Mubarickpur with a detachment of the 3rd Auxiliary Horse' (which had lately been moved up to Upper Sind and placed under Amiel's command). 'On returning I left men to oppose them is certain villages. They came across on 30 September and drove off cattle from near Meerpur. Our men followed them over the desert to a watering place near Shahpur, where they left the cattle, which were recovered.'

The hot weather was now almost over. Who, among those who have served in Upper Sind, does not know the thrill of those October mornings and evenings when 'the breath of winter comes from far away?' And never was it more gladsome than in 1839, for men denied the laurels of Ghazni and the invigorating air of Afghanistan, who had dragged out a miserable existence in tents and sheds in the worst climate in the world, inglorious guardians of commissariat and communications, harassed not only by elusive enemies, but by impossible demands from the Advance, while Brigadier and Political Agent indulged in furious recriminations—to these the prospects of an expedition gave a piquant relish to the dawning season.

For Amiel, the first earnest of future activity was a requisition from Clibborn, the Brigadier Major at Sukkur, for 150 men to accompany the *dak* to Dhadar—the re-opening of the kafila line. But better things were in store. Before we turn to the next phase of the Levy's activities, it would be as well to pause and see in what estimation they were held by others, before the acid test of real conflict was applied.

Eastwick writes 'on 12 October a body of horse, called the Biluch Corps, arrived with their commander, Lieutenant Amiel. On the principle of *lucus a non lucendo* these men were called the Biluch Corps, they being Afghans, Pathans and Kahiris without one Biluch among them. Some of them were fine looking men: but they were in general mounted on raw nags that looked as if they had been fed on sand for the last year. Their pay was insufficient—for forage in the desert place where they were employed was dear and scanty—yet they were to pursue the hill robbers, men who pride themselves on the fleetness of their steeds.'

An official report on the Levy was written to Government by Ross Bell on the day following its appearance in Shikarpur, thus described by Eastwick. The plan of raising men through the local chiefs had not worked well, as all but the Khyris were found to be in league with the plunderers, and to be furnishing them with information. An attempt to enlist Afghans from the region of Dera Ghazi Khan had produced only twenty men. Meanwhile, Government camels grazing in the neighbourhood of Shikarpur were still being carried off. Amiel had not enough men to do more than protect the *daks* with escorts, and Government camels had to graze on the Sukkur side of Shikarpur.

Such as it was, however, the Levy was ordered to advance across the desert to clear the way for the regular troops, Postans having previously satisfied himself that supplies would be available as far as Khangarh. On 15 October Amiel received from Ross Bell orders to proceed from Shikarpur to Mubarakpur, Khangarh, Minuti and Shahpur, sinking wells for a large detachment: to take possession of Shahpur in the name of the British Government, to move on to Chattr and reconnoitre it. And, if a much inferior force was holding the plate to blow open the gates, take possession of it, and sink wells. Next day, he was furnished with a proclamation to be issued in the villages occupied by Jakhranis and Dombkis to band over their lands to Kamal Khan, the Khyrie chief and ci-devant owner of them, and letters addressed to Baloch Khan Dombki at Lahri, Bibrak Khan Bugti, and the Syeds of Shahpur.

The game was afoot. On 21 October Amiel was writing from Mubarakpur, and gives his opinion of the force necessary to extirpate the nest of plunderers in Chattr, Phulaji and the neighbourhood. One regiment of Native Infantry, one or two guns and some Irregular Horse would be quite sufficient. The guns were required as 'every village has a fort or walled enclosure: usually so badly built that the gateway is exposed and can easily be burst open.' He gives two alternative routes from Shikarpur to Shahpur with full details of water and other supplies available and continues 'Eighty Khyree foot in Khangarh will be useful in getting the guns across the desert. If some Irregular Horse could be assembled to the north of Phulajee and advance from thence, it would prevent the plunderers from fleeing in that direction. When the roads to the North and West are closed, the hills to the East where the Boogties reside cannot afford the shelter long, even supposing Beeburuk the Chief would so far incur the risk of two-fold vengeance from our Government as to give the plunderers an asylum within his territory. Of this there is little probability, the latest accounts stating that on Beeja

Khan's wishing to proceed in that direction he was not allowed to do so.'

> It is not to be expected that a band of plunderers will fight for the country they now have possession of, altho' the chief might wish to do so. His want of wealth and authority over the lawless set who have nominally acknowledged him as leader (from the situation of the country he at present possesses being, from its proximity to Sinde, the most eligible from which they might sally out to plunder the inhabitants dwelling on this side of the desert) will preclude his making any great resistance. This is supposing a Force marched against them. Against a detachment of Irregular Horse they might so far forget themselves as to retire to one of the numerous forts; in that case a blockade for a few days, or the arrival of a gun, would unkennel them.
>
> When the infantry have possession of Chuttur and Phulajee the Irregular Horse and Belooche Levy will have to rout them out of the hills and strongholds they will fly to. To do this effectually I would recommend that a galloper gun be attached to the Belooche Corps an outpost might be sent to Bagh, to close that way of escape. The Chandis and Mugsis might be made useful; it would put their friendship to the test, and they themselves at the same time prevented from plundering the country which I fear will be their principal occupation, and make their enmity towards the Jekranees and Doombkis increase as the opportunity of partaking largely of their plunder, without great danger to themselves, and at the same time being revenged on their enemies, presents itself should the first town we possess ourselves of be protected from plunder, the inhabitants will remain and others who have fled return; and no doubt the country will in a short time again become as flourishing and populous as it is represented to have been before the Jekranees and Doombkis obtained possession of it.

Here we have Amiel spreading himself in his quasi-political

capacity—sanguine, full of ideas based on imperfect knowledge, and jumping to conclusions. But he did not neglect the practical side of his duty, to prepare the route to be followed by the regular troops. In a letter written on the same day he reports having sent 28 cart-loads of flour to Khangarh, and the arrival of 29 in Mubarakpur. For 'kurbee', *juari* crops that had withered for want of water were being purchased. Wheels were needed to work the wells in these two places while he had cleaned out that in the fort at Mubarakpur, as the soil was such that '*kacha*' wells could not be dug in it.

Meanwhile, the enemy were not idle. Ross Bell, on his arrival at Shikarpur on the 22nd, was met with the news that Bijar Khan Dombki, with Darya Khan and Turk Ali Jakhranis, the robber triumvirate had crossed the desert from Phulaji via Barshori, north and west of Amiel's line of march, devastating the western and cultivated tracts of Kachhi, plundering the villages and destroying the wells as they went along; while the local authorities of Mehrab Khan of Kelat removed all the grain to the western hills, extorting money from the inhabitants and preparing to cut the green crops. Amiel was ordered to push on towards Phulaji, to attempt to cut off the raiders. But it was too late. On the 24th, he writes from Khangarh that Kamal Khan with his Khyeris and others, in all 287 strong, had started for Minuti, and that he was following next day. But the robbers had returned from the raid with their accustomed celerity and had partially filled up the wells at Minuti. He continues: 'Reports say that they are mustering at Shahpur; return we cannot, and all I require is the 6-pounder in front of the quarter-guard at Shikarpore. Down's men in the left flank (company) know how to use it, and the very knowledge of its having started will do more than Major Billamore bringing, slowly, 50 howitzers. With men like the plunderers, everything depends on advancing. If we remain in Shahpoor many days without any appearance of a Force coming from Shikarpore, report says they'll muster in force. I've a few locals, and altogether with me, with Khyheree horse and foot, 403. I care for the rascals, but neither water [n]or juaree is procurable at

Minoutee, so on we go. 24-pounders are difficult things to get over the desert: had a six-pounder been here this morning the Khyerees would have taken it on even if obliged to drag it themselves.'

Amiel duly pushed on from Minuti, after taking possession of the place in the name of the British Government and seeing that water for 500 men was available; and leaving Jemadar Alif Khan with a few men in Shahpur, was in Chattr on the 18th. He found the plunderers had retired on Phulaji, after failing in an attempt to destroy the wells at Chattr, and so determined to follow them up, after reassuring the inhabitants. He now was able to attend to his other instructions, and in a second letter reports that Baluch Khan, the Dombki Chief, had not yet made his appearance, though Inayat Shah (one of the Syeds of Shahpur) with Mir Hassan, later to earn notoriety, had been despatched 'So that Biburruk may be assured of one faith, a thing these men have not been accustomed to ... I made his minister a present of 100 Rupees which I hope you'll approve of; it may induce the Boogties to bring in provisions for our troops. The bazar at Shahpore is getting on famously, and I've no doubt in in a few days this will be a second Burlington Arcade.'

Ross Bell wrote back from his camp at Kunda, west of Barshori that no presents should be sent to any Bugti or Dombki—the British Government was not going to bribe these plunderers! They were being offered a pardon on terms, and Amiel was directed not to enter into any engagements with them.

The march of Major Billamore with the Force which had been detailed for the duty of suppressing or exterminating the robber tribes were delayed by lack of carriage, and Amiel's impatience daily grew. His letter to Bell dated 31 October, shows sign of having been written in great excitement.

Darya Khan Jakhrani and his freebooters had looted Phulaji presumably having given up hope of holding the place, made off on the appearance of the Levy. Amiel writes: 'until the infantry arrive they cannot be hunted out Itibah Khan and Abdul Hulleem had a skirmish at Phulajee with Darya Khan: the wounded were only two horses. The Jekranees are wandering about and come to the *nullah* for water. I took a sweep round the country this morning without being fortunate enough to come on any of the rascals ... Belooch Khan has not made his appearance, nor has our friend Biburuk. The fact is, Major Billamore and the guns are long on the road. Had I commanded the detachment every man should have carried two seers of flour and I'd have crossed the desert and pushed on. Our field-officers are mere old women, and I do not expect the *pultan* for week[s].'

This was coming in rather strong. Amiel's temperament was naturally self-confident, and from the beginning of his correspondence with Ross Bell he had been on terms of intimacy to which the Political Agent admitted few of his subordinates. He was riding for a fall. The delay was exasperating: but Billamore was not to blame. Amiel writes next day that Baluch Khan had appeared, and had been assured as to the maintenance of his position. He continues, 'I am going to Shahpore for the purpose of getting Major Billamore to leave 25 men at that place. Beeja Khan is piling up stores and making preparations: these infantry are very slow. Billamore halted at Minoutie in consequence of something going wrong among the guns. If they do not push on I shall try my fate alone: had the pultan been a little faster, Phulajee might have been in some measure saved.'

The Political Agent was just then making strenuous efforts to collect grain for the expedition. As already observed, the Khan of Kelat's minions in Kachhi were doing their best to remove the crops before the British could get at them. Ross Bell sent his Assistant, E. J. Brown, to stop this; and with a troop of the 1st Light Cavalry he surprised the Khan's naib, Mahamed Amin, and arrested him. This had a good effect: the crops were saved, though the stored grain had been removed. 'This country,' says Bell in his report to the Government of India, 'has been for years past in a state of anarchy, and latterly the tyranny of Mehrab Khan's naibs has been such that upwards of three-quarters of the population have migrated to Sind.'

Major Newport, who had remained in command of the depot of Dhadar after his desert ordeal in May and June, was also collecting supplies for the force.

Billamore at length arrived at Chattr and Amiel heard from him that he had asked for the services of Lieutenant Vardon and the detachment of Light Cavalry recently come to Upper Sind. This did not fall in with Amiel's views on the subject, and he writes to Bell: 'as the rascals would not face us in the plains in the first instance there's very little likelihood of their showing themselves in sufficient force to require regulars: they are never in that compact body that a charge would disperse them. What we require are a few infantry to knock them out of the hills. Vardon's horse among mountains would be useless, and only increase the quantity of commissariat stores should the detachment under Vardon join the head-quarters of the Regiment. I should feel obliged by your obtaining permission and allowing him to do duty with me. He is anxious to do so, and leaving the Regiment will be no loss as he has not charge of a troop. By having someone to look after accounts and other things I should have time to explore the country, find out and pursue plunderers, etc.'

This was written on 18 November, and it is amusing to read Billamore's view of the case. Jacob tells us that Billamore hated writing—to such an extent that his only report on his successful campaign was a verbal one. However, when he did write, it was to some purpose, as will be gathered from a letter addressed to Ross Bell from Phulaji *one* day after Amiel's.

'I beg to urge the necessity of Lieutenant Vardon's cavalry joining me as speedily as possible, as with them I can reconnoitre the country and obtain much better knowledge of it than from the Balooch Horse: indeed the only information I have as yet gained has been from the European Officers with me, who for two successive mornings have been to the hills to examine them and to report, as to the practicability of carrying guns amongst them; and the report, as far as they were able to go, was favourable for that purpose. With the Cavalry I can penetrate much further, and being under discipline they will be less likely to be observed than a set of men whose only object appears to be galloping about the country without bringing me any intelligence that I can rely on.'

Amiel, however, continued in his complacency. It is necessary to mention that his command was altogether independent of Billamore's; and this fact, coupled with a strong probability that their relations when serving with the regiment for both were officers of the 1st Grenadiers had not been of the best, explains the friction, which was soon to have an unfortunate effect. On the 10th, Amiel reports the country between the edge of the desert of the hills as quiet, though he suspected that the plunderers were lying tip in the *juari* fields by day. When the harvest came, they would have to leave the plains. Meanwhile Captain Raitt, Billamore's second in command, arrested Baluch Khan Dombki, presumably under the impression that he was connected with Bijar Khan; and Amiel had the satisfaction of correcting this error. Ahmed Khan, a son of Bibrak, the Bugti Chief, had come in and acknowledged himself the subject of the British Government, undertaking to seize the property and families of Jakhranis in Bugti territory, and treat the plunderers as enemies, and even offering to accompany Amiel with fifty horse men. Amiel does not vouchsafe an opinion on the value of these asseverations. Next day he writes '... I am continually wandering about between this (Chattr) and the hills, but have not been lucky enough to fall in with any of them. My own men as yet have not recovered the funk; the sight of a Jakranee puts them out. I should like to flesh them ... the only fear of the Doombkies and Jakranees escaping is their proceeding to Rojhan to the east of the hills into the Seik country: I shall write to Dost Khan Chief of the Muzzarees and likewise the Seik authorities ... Inayat Shah and Doulat Shah came here with Ahmed Khan Boogtie, the former having proceeded to Trukkee with Meer Hussan to satisfy Beeburuk regarding our good faith ... after Beeja Khan's flight people have come back to the country: I am making Kamal Khan make a list of them, disarming them for the present, they say they are cultivators, but probably many are plunderers ... I find great difficulty in obtaining information regarding the Murree country, few people having proceeded into a country where neither food nor habitation is procurable.'

And now at last the opportunity of 'fleshing' the Levy came. Amiel arrived on the morning of 13 November off Phulaji, where Billamore was encamped. What followed may be told in the words of his official report to Ross Bell.

About 11 o'clock intelligence was brought in that some camels were being driven off. I immediately mounted and went after the plunders. After going about a mile I was informed that infantry and horsemen were in my front. This was afterwards contradicted, only eight horsemen showing themselves. I continued to advance in the direction of the hills, the Khyerees having under Itbah Khan gone on in advance. I was to the right with the Russuladar, one duffadar and ten sowars of the 3rd Bengal Local Horse, and about 30 sowars under Duffadar Syed Ghoolam Shah.

Seeing some horsemen edging off to the right, I concluded them to be the horsemen supposed to have driven off the camels. I therefore moved at a quick pace to the right, and seeing the Khyerees draw up thought the horsemen had escaped into the hills, and went on: but I suddenly found myself within shot of at least 500 infantry and many horsemen. I called to the Khyerees to assemble round me and to open a fire retiring towards Phoolajee, as the Grenadiers and guns were coming up. The Khyerees from the quick pace they had come at once dispersed and I could not get them to assemble round me or open fire to stop the enemy, who continued to advance. I am sorry to say the Khyerees not behaving as I thought they would, I was obliged to retreat at a good pace towards Phoolajee, during which two of the Local Horse were killed and two wounded, 8 of Duffadar Ghoolam Shah's men, and I believe 15 Khyerees. I have now no reliance on the Khyerees and shall bring the detachment of the 3rd Local Horse on here.

I heard yesterday that Ahmed Khan Boogtie, dissatisfied with the manner I received him, had sent two men to Dodah Muree for the purpose of combining the Murees, Boogties and Jekranees to meet us. I therefore hope as these men have come into the plains and the Khyerees have behaved so ill, not having supported me in the least, you'll despatch Lieutenant Vardon with the Cavalry and a few Local Horse, if able to spare them, with the least possible delay.

Thus [says] Amiel in one of his rare official despatches to Bell. A demi-official written the same day is almost illegible. 'I am sorry to say the Khyerees unknowingly took me into a complete ambush, and my fellows have suffered in consequence. However, I cannot *rely* on my Levy. And therefore earnestly entreat that Vardon and cavalry and some local Horse may be sent—this cutting up my men will fill them with (illegible) that the camels will be the next they'll attack. I cannot from excitement write much, but of this be assured, that my Levy are useless, the Khyerees especially so—and should some Local Horse not come as soon as possible, the plunderers will cut up our line of communication. The ambush was well planned, I was close to the foot-men without seeing them—what could I do with ten locals?'

Alas, for Amiel and his fond hopes of hunting down by himself Bijar Khan and his rascals, thus showing the plodding Regulars the value of mobility! He had overtaken the infantry at a smart pace on his way out, but this had been nothing to the speed of his men on their return in full flight. Bitterly must he have regretted his easy resignation to the impossibility of instilling real discipline into the Levy: it was as though the six months of his command had gone for nothing, in spite of all his energy and care. Worst of all, his discomfiture had taken place under the eyes of brother officers of the 1st Grenadiers.

As to other narratives of the affair, Jacob is restrained if sardonic: Eastwick says, 'his (Amiel's) men at once turned bridle and rode for dear life. The enemy hotly chased them and slew more than a fourth of their number. One of Amiel's native ADC's caught his bridle and turned his horse round; the ten Puna horsemen kept close to him, and this small party retired with less precipitation, and in better order than the rest. 'Who was that on the white horse?' said Bijar, after the skirmish was over. On being told that it was the *Faringhi* officer, he observed 'Well for him that I knew it not, or his grey horse should not have saved him, fleet though it was.'

Two days later, the chastened commander of the Levy reports his loss as 21 men killed. There was in addition other matter to justify pessimism. Phulaji, after its partial destruction by Bijar Khan, could not be occupied in any strength. Amiel had failed to establish a bazaar there, and any Horse stationed in the place would have to be fed by the commissariat: on the other hand the Baluchis having swept the country of grain were living on 'juari, pounded gram, and other luxuries'. He recommends that posts of Native Infantry be established at Shahpur, Chattr, Phulaji and Lahri for their protection from plunderers if a Force proceeded into the hills.

He had, meanwhile, found out a little more about the Marri country and observes that, 'Kahun is spoken of as a town with a fort and bazar: should this prove to be the case, to effectually eradicate the marauders, a strong detachment of Native infantry must be stationed there, or the place destroyed.' He proceeds: 'I am informed by Eastwick in Hyderabad that Lieutenant Clarke is coming to join me with a detachment of the Kutch Horse. I believe Major Billamore intends remaining here until joined by Vardon and some local Horse. In fact, should these fellows continue there is no knowing the result. They are not sufficiently aware of the celerity a musket can be loaded with to fear a rush. Report says a night attack is their favourite plan. Two or three thousand making it upon as many hundreds is a ticklish affair. Major Billamore despises the idea. I however feel the sepoys may not be as steady as he imagines they will: his never having seen a shot fired has not added to his experience.'

Though all his confidence was gone, Amiel's spite against the man destined to avenge this and all the former insults and losses we had sustained at the hands of the marauders was inflamed and a few days later we find more than a glimmering of the reason. He writes from Phulaji on 20 November:

At present I am perfectly useless; my sowars are in the towns and villages for the protection of the inhabitants, and my force at present in Phulaji is 60 Khyerees and 80 Patans: these must remain for the protection of the place. To proceed with Major Billamore is quite impossible; not only has he told me to keep my cowardly rascals in the fort, but will not allow any of them to proceed with me should I go into the hills with him, altho' he wished for my only support, the 24 sowars of the 3rd Locals, Brown tells me it is your intention to continue my Corps, I would recommend that an alteration be commenced as soon as possible. The poneys on 15 rupees a month altho' adapted for convoys guards and daks are perfectly useless in war. In an advance they remain behind and in retreating they are cut up by the enemy.

I require for a commencement two or three from the Local Horse as jamadars and russuldars; they having been subject to discipline and knowing what is required from sowars will gradually instil a little discipline into the men under them. We cannot expect that those jemadars who have been in different service for years, in which running away or plundering were not considered crimes will be strict and look after their men.

He asks for the transfer of a son of the Rissaldar of the 3rd Locals and proceeds to other topics:

As it is your wish that the Murrees should be driven down from the north I should like for your permission to proceed to Seebee and collect a couple of hundred Kujuks. By all accounts these men are good irregular soldiers, and fear not my friends in the hills (the saying was *Marri mi nazed ba koh, wa kajjak ba maidan*—let the Marri go boast on his hills, the Kajjak will hold the plain country). [The] report says there are two roads from the north to Kahun, one from Lheree, the other further to the north. It is only by surrounding these brutes we can effectually exterminate them. Infantry, except by night, they'll not attack. Regular cavalry are not the thing for the hills, requiring too much commissariat stores. The Kujuks we might dismiss whenever the work was over; I might be useful collecting grain, etc., which I'm told is procurable from Seebee.

Meer Hussen, Biburuk's minister, is here and denies that any Boogties were present when my men were cut up ... I am much afraid the men in the hills will get grain from the Seik territories whenever pressure from the West and North is great: if I am to remain here I hope you will place 100 of Skinner's Horse under my command that I may make myself useful.

Next day Amiel received from Bell an official directing him, in view of his report of the uselessness of most of his men, to strike the Khyeris off the strength, now that their chief, Kamal Khan, had been restored to his lands. He was to select dependable men and give them to Billamore, while the remainder of the Levy could be disbanded at Shikarpur. These orders were rather more drastic than Amiel had bargained for. With regard to the Khyeris, he replies that they would be struck off the Baluch Levy from the 22nd but asks that four men should be retained. Two of them were wounded, and had killed two Jakhranis during his stay at Chattr. The third, Jan Mahomed, was the man who had come up and caught hold of his horse's head when the others ran away, entreating him not to remain as he was forsaken by the rest. Similarly, Itbar Khan had stood by him, and was well known as a brave man.

The upshot seems to have been that the Political Agent changed his mind and acquiesced in the continuance of the levy. He was, in fact, embarrassed by the difficulty of getting supplies for the Force, and by developments naturally following upon Amiel's failure, as is evident from a letter addressed to his Assistant, E. J. Brown, dated from Bagh, 19 November:

I have written letters to Dodah Murree and Beebuck Boogtie urging them to come and meet me; and have informed them that should they fail to do this five days after the receipt of my letter, and to disperse the large bands of their tribes which are in arms and ravaging the country, they will be treated as enemies. Should they themselves come or send messengers to you, be so good as to receive them with civility and request them to join my camp via Bagh. In this case you will send a letter and trustworthy person along with them. So long as the crops are not gathered in it is an object of the first importance to prevent them from being destroyed by the plundering tribes. It is also absolutely necessary that all the posts from Minoutee to Lehree should be held so as to secure the safety of the communication between Bagh and Rojhan.

I have just learned that a considerable body of well-armed Horse have passed this morning through Jhunoo, a village about half-way between Kasim-ka-Joke and Phoollajee. The marauders therefore besides getting in the rear of the post at Phoollajee are hovering near the highroad along which our convoys pass. Until the crops are cut I consider that it would be exceedingly inexpedient to have the posts of Lheree, Phoollajee, Chuttr, Shahpur and Minoutie without adequate protection. It will afterwards be more easy for cavalry to act with effect, and a more efficient body of Horse will be at Major Billamore's disposal. Two Rissallahs of Skinner's Horse may be expected at Sukkur every day, as well as the same number of Local Cavalry from Lower Sind. I shall write and request Brigadier Gordon to send I them to Major Billamore as soon as they arrive.

He proceeds to give in detail the arrangements he had made with the military authorities to secure Kachhi by cavalry posts, so as to allow Billamore to act with the whole of the infantry.

Amiel's next letter to Bell, dated from Chattr 23 November, gives his proposals for the future organization of the Baluch Levy. He advised that the material should be drawn from Afghans, Patans, Purdesees and Seiks, that a headquarter should be established and the men encamped in the plains and taught to move together and gradually assimilate discipline. He continues: 'I must here state my firm conviction of the inutility of employing Belooches; they appear to have no other thought except plundering. To discipline them would be impossible.' He suggests that the sawars' pay should be raised from Rs. 20 per mensem to Rs. 25, as the Bengal Local Horse (the Irregular Cavalry, a detachment of which were under his command, were paid at the rate of Rs. 30). As to their equipment, the Balooche Corps might be dressed in green ankrekahs, red turbans and waist-bands; the front rank armed with spears and swords, rear ranks swords and carbines. I recommend carbines from their being the most efficient weapon with which a horse man can be armed; in skirmishing, it is loaded with celerity; its range is quite sufficient and it is always ready ... a pistol ... would complete their efficiency.' He ends by urging that the corps be put on a proper Irregular Horse basis.

The main interest in these proposals is that once more Amiel is anticipating, even in some matters of detail, Jacob's organization of the force which was destined to succeed in the work in which the Baluch Levy failed—the Sind Irregular Horse. In regard to the composition of his regiments, indeed, Jacob, as we have already observed, rejected Afghans and Pathans as well as Baluchis, and after experimenting with Sikhs discarded them by degrees. He swore by the Hindustani Mussulman—the 'Purdesee' mentioned by Amiel. With regard to their equipment, Jacob writing in 1847 describes the dress of his Horse as 'a dark green "alkelug" (tunic), white drawers, jack boots, red pugree and "kumer bund".' While as to arms, he says, 'with regard to the arms of Irregular Cavalry, after many trials, I am certain that the native sword and a good percussion carbines are the only weapons for use save that the officers and *duffedars* may carry pistols—the lance is in my opinion (formed after considerable experience of its use both in the chase and in battle) useless for Light Cavalry.'

Amiel's reorganization scheme was pigeon-holed for the time being; 'a more efficient body of Horse being at Major Billamore's disposal.' This, was the detachment of the Cutch Horse—the nucleus of the Sind Irregular Horse—which under Lieutenant Walpole Clarke had been rushed up to Kachhi. Amiel writes to Bell in dudgeon that Clarke is serving directly under Major Billamore (he had hoped, as we have seen, that he would himself be placed in command of any cavalry detachment sent in support), while he had to remain in Shahpur to protect the inhabitants. He thus missed the brilliant affair in the Tegaf valley, in which Clarke, with greatly inferior numbers, succeeded in killing fifty of Bijar Khan's horsemen.

Preparations for the advance of the field-force were being hurried on, and on 24 November, Major Newport at Dhadar reported to Bell that he had collected the necessary supplies. Jacob, when writing the history of the campaign some twelve years later, says with regard to its commissariat with 'little or no assistance from either the Military or Civil authorities at headquarters these arrangements were admirably made by the officers of the force', which statement, doubtless made in good faith and in ignorance of the efforts made by Ross Bell in circumstances of great difficulty, does scant justice to the political officers. In fact though Jacob's Memoir, in view of the extreme paucity of other materials, must remain the authority for this campaign, it is inaccurate in several particulars; probably on account of its having been written from memory so long afterwards, when most of the officers who took part in it were dead. But we are at present concerned only with the events leading up to Billamore's operations in the hills.

Amiel, though relegated to Shahpur, was not confined to purely garrison duty. He writes to Billamore on the 25th that while in pursuit that morning of over a hundred Jakhranis and Dombkis he learned that they were assembling in strength, and had driven off some camels belonging to the Syed which were grazing near the town, the numbers of his force being known to them; and on these grounds asks for a reinforcement of 'at least 50 of the Kutch Horse'. Billamore took prompt action on this information, and the successful engagement at Uch was the sequel. But again Amiel and his men took no part in this affair. A few days later, he reports in a letter to Bell the return of a spy from the hills with the intelligence that Bijar Khan and Darya Khan were encamped at Sarab and that they intended paying him a visit when the dark nights set in and the Risala—the detachment of 250 of Skinner's Horse now under Amiel's command—had departed. Once more, he found himself exceedingly in want of flour; the Hindus told him that the hills were full of it, having been compelled by Bijar Khan to bring it there across the desert from Sind!

The politicals were still engaged in collecting supplies, and, as Jacob puts it, 'making up their minds as to what further should be done.' At last a decision was reached. On 28 November Ross Bell writes from Shikarpur to Lieutenant Postans, directing him to proceed to Phulaji and there take up the political duties of Northern Kachhi, enclosing his correspondence with Billamore, Amiel, and Erskine, with the first of whom Postans was to communicate! The Political Agent writes: 'As the time within which Dodah Murree and Beebruk had the option of joining me and professing submission to Shah Shoojah's authority, on condition of forgiveness for their past crimes, has expired, it will be proper that you should in concert with Major Billamore take measures for reducing both tribes to subjection. Any opposition will of course be forcibly suppressed by the military authorities, but should Dodah Murree and Beeburuk offer to place themselves in your hands, you are requested to suspend hostilities and merely to leave a sufficiently strong party at Kahun and Deyrah to keep possession of both places. In the event of Dodah and Beeburuk acting in the manner referred to, be so good as to send them to my camp under an escort sufficient to prevent their escape, though not nominally as prisoners.'

A further period of grace seems, however, to have been given; probably partly because the commissariat arrangements for the Force were still incomplete, while movement into the hills was scarcely practicable in uncertainty of the Bugti chief's intentions. Bibrak Khan's position was, in fact, critical. There might have been a possibility of avoiding or delaying by negotiations the political issue—his subjection to Shah Shuja—but this was only one of the objects which had brought the British Force to Phulaji. Bijar Khan, Darya Khan and Turk Ali had taken shelter in his country, and were playing a game of hide-and-seek with the cavalry on the border-line. To disown them, when the British had more than an inkling of his real relations with the predatory bands, was not enough: to get rid of them impossible. Many anxious Jirgas must have been held, and urgent messages passed to and fro, behind the curtain of the hills, before Bibrak decided to give in, which he did at length on 19 December.

Amiel, writing to Bell on that date, says: 'Postans has gone to Chuttuh where Beeburuk Boogtie has made his appearance. Major Billamore has not moved into the hills. Ere receiving the *hookum* he was all anxiety, yet immediately on receipt of it he finds himself deficient in grain … I heard this morning that Major Billamore leaves this for Sukkur on sick certificate. He wrote to Postans that the political bubble had at last burst. What he means, I know not: no doubt on his arrival he will make up some good story.' Amiel's old enmity against Billamore now appears in his willingness to believe any rumour to his discredit, and the immediate cause of this outburst seems to be explained in another letter written to Bell on the same day. He had heard that his own ill-success against the marauders had been canvassed in very equivocal terms over the whist-tables in Sukkur, and mentioning the imputation, he says truculently: 'Luckily some fellows are yet alive who know instead of not resenting an affront, I have generally, at least sometimes, asked for explanations when no affronts were intended'; and a few days later, 'I am glad you exonerated me from the charge of having quietly submitted to be insulted without demanding satisfaction.' When his own conduct in the presence of the enemy was the subject of mirth at Headquarters, the maiden success of the Commander of the Field Force at Uch must have rankled with double virulence. Ross Bell was naturally sympathetic on the question of honour: his own was so tender that six months previously he had challenged Brigadier Gordon to a duel.

The Baluch Levy continued its patrolling under difficulties and Amiel resumed the informal tone of his correspondence with his chief on every subject: 'Beer, the Parsee writes, is 'no go.' If such a thing was procurable my existence might be lengthened for some days ... I hear you have been kind enough to get the services of Vardon for 'naukeree' with me in this *nice* country. Should it be the case, do not allow him to get into the Shikarpore bazar, but despatch the boy to me under an escort. I assure you employment shall not be wanting for him.'

But he left Bibrak Khan awaiting the Sarcar's pleasure at Chattr, where Postans found him on 19 December. He writes to Bell on the 21st:

On my arrival at Chuttur on the 19th instant, I found the Boogtie Chief with the influential men of that tribe awaiting me and, in the course of a lengthened conference at which Meer Fatteh Khaun was present, I fully explained to Biburuk the terms on which alone he and his tribe could expect pardon from the British Government for their past offences, and its protection and countenance for the future. These have, hitherto, been fully acceded to. The Minister of the Chief, Meer Hussan, remains with me and under the guidance of a confidential agent, Sheer Mahomed, brother of Meer Hussan, a detachment will march on Deirah from this place tomorrow morning.

Ukhtar Khaun, a Vakeel from Dodah Khaun the Murree Chief arrived in my camp yesterday. The Chief himself is represented as too old and infirm to visit me but has delegated the above Vakeel with full powers to attend to any order he may receive from the servants of the British Government. A detachment will leave Fullajee for Kahun via Lehree tomorrow morning. Confidential agents from Dodah Khaun remain with me. I have directed Beburack to send one of his sons, Islam Khaun or Chandu Khaun, without any delay, in order that I may be enabled to depute a sufficiently confidential person from the Boogtie tribe to you, and have also called upon Dodah Khaun to lose no time in doing the same on the part of the Murrees.

But I beg leave to bring to your notice that the distrust and apprehension of these men is so great, that I find it most difficult to induce them to believe that we do not practise the same perfidy and treachery which distinguish their own intercourse on all occasions: my promises of safety when proceeding to and from Sukkur are evidently received with distrust, and the point is one that I shall have some difficulty in carrying; but the detachment in the heart of the hills cannot fail to have a salutary effect.

I have strictly enjoined on the Military authorities the necessity of inspiring these lawless tribes with all possible confidence in our good faith and moderation, by abstaining from the slightest approach to severity towards the two who now evince a friendly disposition; that supplies when furnished are to be scrupulously paid for, arid every conciliatory measure pursued towards a people, with whom we are now for the first time brought in contact, in order that their first impressions of us may be favourable, and induce a feeling of respect rather than fear. On the other hand I have fully explained to the Murree and Boogtie tribes that they may rest assured that in the occupation of their capitals no violence against the peaceably disposed of their subjects is in any way intended, and that the troops have orders only to offer resistance to those who may oppose them. The Vakeels themselves are security for the safe conduct to the detachments to Kahun and Deirah as far as the respective tribes are concerned; and that supplies according to the capabilities of the country are to be forth-coming, for which fair remuneration will be made.

I have verbally informed Major Billamore that he will use every exertion to destroy any parties of Doomkies or Jekhranees whom he may meet in the hills, providing at the same time for a strict espionage being kept between this place and Lehree over the passes to the hills from which it is more than probable the marauders will issue.

Duryah Khan has, I believe, presented himself at Shahpore, and Toorkali is on the point of coming in. I have directed Amiel to send them under a sufficient escort to me ... Bejar Khaun has made the most humble appeals through Meer Futteh Khaun to be allowed to come in, but I have replied that the same must be unconditional and that I had no power to offer terms.

The memorandum of instructions for Major Billamore reproduces the substance of this report. It also mentions that 'Abdullah Khyheree may be usefully employed in giving information respecting the haunts of the marauders'—one of Amiel's best men was thus lost to him.

The curtain now rose on the first and most successful campaign of the British in these hills. Its first-fruits were gathered in before it had really begun, as will be seen from Postans' next report, dated 23 December 1839:

The troops at this place marched yesterday morning upon Deirah and Kahun, the former accompanied by a gun and Irregular Horse and commanded by Major Billamore, the latter consisting of about 200 infantry and 50 Irregular Horse under Captain Raitt ... I myself accompanied Major Billamore's detachment for the first march and thus, have had an opportunity of observing how truly formidable the passes of these hills would have proved to our troops had the tribes who infest them continued hostile.

I beg leave also to report that Durya Khaun, Toorkali, Jaunee and all the noted leaders of the Kekhranees have thrown themselves unconditionally on the mercy of the British Government. Durya Khaun, Jaunee and some twelve of the heads of the robber bands are now in my camp; Toorkali is with Lieutenant Amiel at Shahpore. Durya Khaun is the acknowledged head of the Jekhranees, and confesses that he and Bejaur Khaun have been the greatest offenders against the peace of the country but that the Doombkies and Jekhranees were on all occasions assisted to a certain extent by the Murees and Boogties, who took their share in the spoil. That government property to a large amount has been sold out of the country and that portions only now remain in the hills.

The most active freebooter in the Jekranee tribe is Jaunee, noted throughout the country for his daring and the swiftness of his mare. It was this man who, I knew, had been annoying the country near Shahpore, whom we unsuccessfully pursued, and who confesses to have killed the three sowars reported in my private note of the 14th in retaliation for seven of his own band who fell to the swords of the Irregular Horse under Lieutenant Clarke at Goorgon. The whole amount of armed and mounted men under the Jekranee leaders is stated by Durya Khaun at one hundred and forty, and he has them completely under his direction.

On the occasion of these outlaws coming into my presence, I distinctly told them that I could only be answerable for their lives whilst in camp but that their persons must be considered in custody, and that their future disposal must depend on the pleasure of the Right Honourable the Governor-General of India at your orders; without recapitulation of the conference it is only necessary to observe that Durya Khaun on the part of himself, Toork Ali and the whole tribe acknowledged a long course of rapine and excess, but that in the power of the British Government alone would he have placed the disposal of his own and followers' lives, because he trusted in its mercy and hoped that notwithstanding the enormities he had committed, he might be allowed to become security for the future peaceable conduct of himself and his tribe and prove by their future acts their determination to abandon from henceforward their lawless practices and to be taken under any circumstances or restrictions into the service of the British Government; but that he well knew how little right he had to expect such clemency and whether his proposals were acceded to, or the lives of himself and followers demanded as an act of justice, he was prepared to submit to the will and pleasure of the British Government, as shown in his unconditional surrender.

My advice to these outlaws has been to lose no time in taking every possible opportunity of recovering government property from the hill-tribes; that the enormous amount of loss for which they were responsible stood as a formidable obstacle to their pardon; to call in, disarm and dismount their band, for any fresh instances of plunder by the Jekhranees would be visited on the leaders, and render their chances of escape still more distant: in short, to prove immediately as their only hope that they were sincere in their professions.

Durya Khaun has represented that he and Bejaur Khaun have been companions in guilt, so he would wish they should share in whatever may now befall him. That the Domkie Chief only asked for the safety of his life whilst in my camp, and his meeting no molestation in proceeding to it. His future disposal being left to your authority, I have granted my *purwanah* 'that the Domkie Chief's life if he surrenders is safe whilst with me, but that his doing so must be unconditional, and his future disposal left entirely to the pleasure of the Political Agent in Upper Sindh'. Bejar Khaun will be in my camp in the course of a day or two.

Referring to the correspondence between yourself and Brigadier Gordon which has been kindly forwarded for my perusal, and the statement put forth by me in my letters of the 16th and 17th instant, I beg leave to point out that late events have, I submit, proved the correctness of the opinions I advanced, on the advantage likely to arise from speedy operations, and the danger of the delay of two months which the want of supplies and commanding arrangements had occasioned. No sooner did the outlaws see our determination in spite of all opposition to enter the hills than they simultaneously surrendered to our terms. And the movement on Ouch, Deirah and Khaun (which getting supplies from Khangar we were enabled to make) have had the effect of at once bringing affairs to a favourable crisis in this direction. But for the causes before referred to, I have no hesitation in asserting that the same would have been the case a month earlier. Our remaining inactive has put the Government to unnecessary expense and public servants have incurred the risk of reprehension for a lack of activity which did not exist.

I will only add that the troops have now marched with the smallest possible amount of supplies, and are yet mainly dependent on what Deirah and Khaun may provide. I trust in my next to report favourably on the passage of the detachments through the defiles to Kahun and Deirah. I propose to see things on a secure footing in these districts and then to bring to you at Sukkur the Vakeels from the Murree and Boogties, with the Chiefs of the Doomkies and Jekranee tribes. Were I to send the latter prisoners now, I should incur the risk of unnecessarily alarming these outlaws, and it is of some moment at present to keep everything quiet, until our position shall have placed matters beyond a doubt of their stability.

The Force destined to achieve this end, and present the Politicals with a fair field for 1840, have vanished into the hills, and Amiel was left behind at Shahpur. He writes to Bell on 27 December: 'On the evening of the 24th the report of guns was heard, and no doubt the detachment under Major Billamore has had a skirmish. The report in the bazar is that Beeja Khan was at Derah when the detachment arrived, that they attacked and killed old Beeja, Beeburuk through fright has betaken himself to Trukkee … some time will elapse ere the true account reaches us.' The rumour was not true: Billamore did not reach Dera Bugti till the 31st; but we are not concerned with the history of the Hill campaign, and it is time to take leave of Amiel and his men.

The Baluch Levy continued under Amiel's command for more than a year but his scheme for reconstituting it on an Irregular Horse or regimental basis was dropped and its duties were restricted virtually to those of mounted police. For a striking-force, Amiel had detachments of regular and local cavalry acting under his directions. The famous Turk Ali was made a jemadar in the Levy, and a number of the freebooters enlisted: Turk Ali's grandson, Dad Muhamed, was later one of the most trusted of Jacob's Baluch Guides, into which body the Levy may be considered as eventually merging.

We have seen how Amiel's theories anticipated much of Jacob's practice. His failure in the face of the enemy must not blind us to the useful work he had done in opening up the country and proving—by bitter experience—the quality of our friends and enemies there. If we learn best by our own mistakes, the next best school is found in the mistakes of earlier actors in the same field.

Amiel's character and abilities can be fairly assessed from the many letters we have quoted. With abounding energy, and no small share of insight and imagination, he was lacking in the qualities of perseverance, concentration, and the practical adjustment of theory to fact. He was set to work with poor materials and without Walpole Clarke's gift of leadership, or John Jacob's powers of organization, he failed to improve them. So those who came after him were conscious of no obligation to Amiel, and his name is forgotten. Yet there may be some, to whom the history of Upper Sind is the history of Jacob, who may find some interest in the story of an obscure pioneer.

6

The Sind Battles, 1843
H. T. Lambrick

HYDERABAD

ON THE DAY THAT THE BATTLE OF MIANI WAS FOUGHT, MIR SHER
Mahomed Khan Talpur, the independent Prince of south-eastern
Sind, was only six miles away, with a force which amounted probably
to seven thousand or eight thousand men. It is unlikely that he had
any intention of joining his cousins of Upper and Lower Sind in
opposing Napier, who had no quarrel with him; and he was not on
good terms with any of the Hyderabad family except Mir Sobdar,
who on the advice of his minister, Munshi Awatrai, had determined
to adhere to his policy of non-resistance, having nothing to lose
by acceptance of the treaty but on the other hand, every hope of
being constituted Rais of Lower Sind. Early on the morning of 18
February, Sobdar sent Awatrai to Napier's camp to assure him of his
friendship and declared that he had taken no part in the hostilities.[1]
The General desired Sobdar's emissary to express his satisfaction
and to bring in all the belligerent Mirs to surrender in person before
noon, failing which Hyderabad itself would be attacked. Meanwhile,
a *vakil* arrived from Sher Mahomed desiring to be informed of the
General's intentions towards him. After consultation with Outram,
Napier wrote in reply: 'If you disperse your troops and keep no

119

one with you, I shall reckon you just the same as before.' The *vakil* was still in the camp when Mirs Nasir Khan, Shahdad Khan, and Hussein Ali Khan came in and surrendered, and witnessed the release of the last named by Sir Charles at Outram's instance.[2] He was also aware of the General's direction to Mir Sobdar, sent back with Awatrai, to be at his ease and look after the Fort and town of Hyderabad; and returned with this intelligence to his master. Sher Mahomed withdrew but decided to watch events a little longer before disbanding his levies.

On the 19th, the British army encamped at the ruined Residency and here Mir Rustom Khan, one of his sons, and his nephew, Mir Nasir Khan, also surrendered and were installed in a walled garden adjoining the ground occupied by the troops, entrenchment of which was immediately begun. Napier had for some time past intended to form a new base on the river Indus and on becoming assured that hostilities were inevitable, on 15 February, he had written to Colonel Roberts at Sukkur to send reinforcements and supplies down to him by water. On the 21st, immediately after Outram had left for Bombay, the General having ordered Mir Sobdar to send away all armed Balochis from the Fort, town and suburbs of Hyderabad, sent the 12th N. I. and Captain Hutt's battery, under the command of Colonel Pattle to occupy the Fort and unfurl the Standard of England on the round tower. This force was accompanied by Prize-Agents, who soon took possession of the Mir's treasures and proceeded also to lay hands on their personal household belongings; no distinction being made between State and private property. Under Napier's orders, however, the ladies were allowed three days and given facilities to remove themselves and such jewellery and private property as they could carry in palanquins, without search.

Evidence having been received from Karachi that Mir Mahomed Khan had joined with Mir Nasir Khan in ordering hostilities and as it was known that his men had fought in the battle, this Chief was also, on 23 February, 'invited to join his brethren in affliction in the garden'; and next day, the bedridden Sobdar was also conveyed thither, 'it appearing from records shown by the other Ameers, that 5,000 soldiers, under the orders of Meer Sobdar Khan, had been present in the fight at Meeanee.' Meanwhile, there was considerable looting going on, apart from the ordered proceedings in the Fort (by the beginning of March regular auctions were being held to convert its miscellaneous contents into cash) and on 9 March, Napier was compelled to issue orders that any soldier or camp follower found over a mile from the Camp without a pass would be apprehended and treated as a plunderer; observing that such conduct would 'not only prevent the Baloochees from becoming our friends but turn the Scindeans against us'.[3]

The fighting men among the Balochis had, in fact, been rallying to the standard of Mir Sher Mahomed ever since Miani and he was well informed as to the proceedings at Hyderabad. On hearing of the arrest of the Talpurs who had taken no part in the battle, particularly Mir Sobdar, his close friend, to whom a reassuring message had been sent by the General in the presence of his own *Vakil*, he felt little disposed to dismiss his followers and make his submission as ordered. Sir Charles had written to him on 3 March: 'you are rallying the defeated Baloochees: you have increased the number of your troops; and unless you come to my camp at Hyderabad and prove your innocence, I will march against you, and inflict a signal punishment on you.' But by this time, Sher Mahomed had heard of the seizure of the Mirs' private property, and the treatment meted out to their protesting servants; it must have seemed to him that surrender, and the tendering of innocence, were not likely to secure him from a similar fate. He, therefore, determined to make himself as strong as possible, and borrowed a lakh of rupees from Mir Nasir Khan's wife (that lady having turned to good account the three days' grace before she left the Fort) in the hope that a non-committal attitude, backed by an imposing force, would obtain for him better terms. The Baluchis were with him to a man, longing for a second trial of strength with the British, and the countryfolk his active sympathizers; for Sher Mahomed was the most popular prince in Sind. Bands of Balochis successfully attacked the steamer coaling station at Vikkar in the Delta, and the Agha Khan's camp at Jherruck.[4] This Dignitary, lately a guest of Mir Nasir Khan, having made friends with Napier, had been requested by him to secure the communications with Karachi.[5] These latter were, in fact, maintained by the agency of Seth Naomal, by a different route and Napier took occasion to summon from Karachi supplies and every detachment that could be spared.[6] The daks with Bombay via Cutch were however interrupted by Sher Mahomed's men: the Jokhio and Karmati Chiefs did their best to carry out the orders issued by the Hyderabad Mirs before Miani and a guerrilla warfare seemed likely to spread.

Napier's position was, in fact, very vulnerable at this time, had his enemies possessed military qualities beyond courage in actual hand to hand fighting. He had been forced to divide his little army in order to garrison the Fort; his camp was not fully entrenched and would need a further detachment to guard it if he left it to take the offensive, not only as being his base on the Indus, but owing to the presence of the captive Talpurs. On the other hand, the armed steamers of the Indian Navy secured him command of the River and he only had to wait for reinforcements from Sukkur and Karachi; having thrown away the opportunity of making use of HM's 41st Regiment, which Outram had halted for him on its way to Karachi, it was no longer within reach but Ellenborough, with equal foresight and promptitude, had sent troops from Ferozepur to Sukkur as soon as he heard of the outbreak of hostilities.

Sir Charles' chief anxiety was the daily increasing heat: this he had to balance against the advantages of playing the waiting game, which would bring him his reinforcements, exhaust Sher Mahomed's treasury, and encourage him to approach nearer to Hyderabad, when he would be easier to deal with. On 15 March, Sher Mahomed was in fact within twelve miles of the city, with a very large force: he sent a blustering message informing Napier that if he released his prisoners and disgorged his plunder, he would allow him to evacuate the country unmolested. The evening gun sounded at the moment the Mir's envoy had delivered his ultimatum, and the General told him that that was his answer.

In his anxiety, Napier was exasperated by the complaints of the captive Talpurs, against whom interested parties, seeing the lie of the land, worked upon his credulity with every conceivable allegation. He was led to believe that, though under the strictest surveillance, they were in constant communication with Sher Mahomed; and on the 18th threatened them in a savage letter that he would put them in irons on a steamer if they did not remain quiet. On the same day, he went out on a reconnaissance with the Scinde Horse and the Bengal Cavalry to divert Sher Mahomed's attention from the approaching reinforcements and to show him that he was not afraid of leaving his entrenched position—which, indeed, he had not regularly occupied, lest his army should lose confidence in themselves. He found signs that the Mir intended to give battle, and on the 20th again reconnoitred the position that he occupied at Tando Jam Ali, which he found very strong, and not unlike Miani. On his return, he received a message from Major Stack, who had reached Hala on his march down from Rohri with a small brigade consisting of the 1st Troop Bombay Horse Artillery, the 3rd Bombay Light Cavalry, and the 8th Bombay Native Infantry. Stack had been ordered to reach Hyderabad with all possible expedition, and had arrived unmolested at Hala when he received a note from Clibborn, Napier's Intelligence Officer, sent without the General's knowledge, 'Halt for God's sake! You will be attacked by at least forty thousand men tomorrow.' Stack sent the messenger back for further instructions. Napier was at dinner with his Staff when the letter arrived, and partly as a rebuke to Clibborn, partly to inspire confidence, scrawled a reply on it and passed it round the table, to the amusement of the company, 'Clibborn's men are all in buckram—come on.' Nevertheless, he thought it very probable that Sher Mahomed would attempt to intercept Stack, and gave orders for McMurdo to meet him at Matiari next day with a squadron of cavalry. That evening, he issued a General Order to the troops, announcing his intention to march against Sher Mahomed on the 24th.

On the morning of the 21st, McMurdo left with a squadron of the Poona Horse under Captain Tait. Napier had now almost given up hope of the other reinforcements summoned from Sukkur, and from Karachi, arriving in time; but that afternoon, to his surprise and delight, two fleets of boats came in sight, from up and down stream, almost simultaneously.[7] Those from Sukkur carried the 21st Bombay Native Infantry, with several guns, while from up the river came a reinforcement of Artillery Officers and men: exactly what he most wanted.

Meanwhile, McMurdo had joined Stack at Matiari, whence the column marched on the morning of the 22nd. In his anxiety to reach Napier, Stack outstripped his baggage: after passing the field of Miani Sher Mahomed's, Balochis were seen on the skirts of a *shikargah* to his left front, and subsequently advanced on the left rear of the column. McMurdo held them at bay with some of the Poona Horse and obtained the help of a troop of the 3rd Cavalry. The Balochis were eventually driven off by a sharp cannonade of Leslie's Artillery, which McMurdo had to call for from the head of the column for Stack still pressed onwards towards Hyderabad.[8] He had sent word to the General, who despatched Jacob with the Scinde Horse to reinforce him; they arrived about the time when the firing ceased, and formed the rear guard into camp. Napier himself met the column before it reached Hyderabad, with a troop of the 9th Cavalry and two nine-pounders, and the whole arrived safely in camp late that night.

Sir Charles gave the new arrivals a rest on the 23rd, which he employed in re-arranging his order of battle. He assigned the care of the Fort of Hyderabad to the recruits, and organized sailors and Marines from the Indian Navy ships, together with convalescent soldiers, some of Mir Ali Murad's men, and the Agha Khan's retainers who had survived their mishap at Jherruck, into a garrison about eight-hundred-strong, with two guns for the entrenched camp. The captive Talpurs were placed on board the armed steamers, in charge of the Indian Navy.

For his Field Force there remained at his disposal some 5,000 men, including about 1,100 cavalry, with seventeen guns. When the brigading of the troops was complete that evening, Napier drew up the whole in front of the camp, and put them through a few evolutions: While they were thus standing under arms, *vakils* from Sher Mahomed arrived, with a final summons to him to surrender. He led them along the line and bade them go and report to their master what they saw; but they sought a full hearing, and it was not till 2 a.m. that they were dismissed, with a letter to Sher Mahomed demanding his unconditional surrender if he chose to meet him as he advanced at the head of his army.

Already, on the evening of the 23rd, Napier had moved over the Fuleli an advanced force, consisting of the Madras Sappers and Miners, two regiments of Native Infantry, and two eight-inch howitzers; and they were joined by the General with the main body of the army before sunrise on the 24th.[9] He had just received despatches from Lord Ellenborough, announcing the annexation of Sind, and expressing his thanks to himself and the troops for the victory of Miani, sanctioning Regimental Honours, and promising them to individuals. Napier had the Governor-General's orders communicated to the troops, and felt the assurance of another victory in their cheers.

The troops now marched in order of battle, the Advance Guard; as before Miani, being led by the Scinde Horse. Behind them were the Madras Sappers, to cut down the banks of canals for the passage of the Artillery. Napier's last intelligence of Sher Mahomed's position was that he was either at Husri, Dubba, or Tando Jam Ali.[10] And the march was first directed on the last-named, nearly due-east of Hyderabad, all three places being within ten miles.[11] The country beyond the Fuleli was much interrupted by canal cuts from it, running with a general direction from north to south; and these had such high banks that a man on horse-back could not see over them. There were also numerous villages, groves, and gardens: the advance was therefore made with a screen of cavalry to the flanks, as well as in front, of the compact column of infantry and guns. After covering four miles, a peasant told them that the Balochis had shifted their position, and were some two miles to the northward. Sir Charles at once sent the Scinde Horse off to reconnoitre, ordered the rest of the Advance Guard to join the column, and changed its direction to the left. Jacob soon discovered Sher Mahomed's position which ran nearly north and south, and formed line within gun shot, sending back word to the General, who was close on his heels. The Baloch artillery now opened fire with eleven guns, and the Scinde Horse once more had to endure a constant cannonade while the rest of the army came up. The ordeal was not so protracted as at Miani: the head of the column was soon in sight, and Napier himself brought each corps into line, as (he says) even his Brigade commanders were officers of the rank of Major, with limited experience. The position first taken up was about 1,200 yards from that of the Balochis, and not quite parallel to their line; hardly was the dressing completed when the British left was found to be within range of their artillery and had to be withdrawn slightly, causing more delay. While thus employed, Sir Charles sent Major Waddington, with Lieutenants Brown and Hill, forward to examine the enemy's position and they coolly passed along the front from the centre towards the enemy's left, at 300 yards' distance, under matchlock fire. The General meanwhile gave orders for the Madras Sappers to facilitate the advance of his heavy battery for the ground, though level in the main, was broken by *nullahs* towards the left and subdivisions of the company were attached to each howitzer to assist in unlimbering and getting them into action.

The order in which the army was now drawn up from left to right, was as follows: the Poona Auxiliary Horse; the 9th Bengal Light

Cavalry; HM's 22nd Regiment; eleven guns, including the Heavy Battery; the 25th Bombay N.I.; the 21st N.I.; Captain Whitlie's battery; the 12th N. I.; the 8th N.I.; the 1st Grenadier N. I.; the Horse Artillery; the 3rd Bombay Light Cavalry; and on the right of the line, the Scinde Horse.

Napier being at length free to make a personal examination of the Baloch position, found it quite as baffling as Miani. The plain on which his army was drawn up was bounded on the left by the bed of the Fuleli, on the further, side of which appeared a thick grove of trees. He could also see the tops of some trees on its nearer bank, to his left front; but in front of them, and for more than a mile to the right, extended a high bank of heaped up earth, differing from the ordinary irrigation channels of the country only in the appearance above it of the heads and weapons of the Balochis, and the flashes and smoke of their cannon. It was clearly an entrenched position, offering no obvious weak spot: it was impossible to ascertain from the front in what strength it was occupied, though Waddington's reconnaissance had shown that the centre at least was held by numerous matchlockmen. One important fact noticed by that officer was the existence of several ramps, easing the steep slope of the bank. On the extreme right front, nearly two miles from the Fuleli, was a grove which Napier, on the report of his spies, suspected to be held by the Balochis with the object of turning his flank when he advanced. The extent of the Baloch line was in fact very ill-defined; but as a round shot whizzed past Napier's face, and into the breast of a soldier of the 22nd, he felt that further delay for reconnaissance would only cool the spirit of his troops. He, therefore, ordered the Artillery to open fire but the effect of the eight-inch howitzers did not equal his expectation, and he advanced the whole line about 500 yards in echelon formation, in which it was again halted, the right being thus still slightly refused. The Baloch guns kept up a smart fire, but now a heavy cannonade opened from each of the British batteries and continued for nearly an hour.[12] Several of the Baloch tumbrils of ammunition were exploded by the shells, and the dismembered bodies of men blown up with one of these could be seen hurled into the air.

There was yet nothing to show that Sher Mahomed had occupied the point opposite the British left near the Fuleli where the trees rising above the hight bank indicated, in Napier's view, the presence of a village like Sultan Shah at Miani; and he determined to launch his first attack here. He ordered the Horse Artillery from the right to the left of the line, supporting them with the Poona Horse and 9th Cavalry on their left, and on their right by the 22nd Queens', who at first were held somewhat retired. Leslie's troop advanced diagonally across the front by 'bounds', unlimbering at intervals and firing obliquely on the Baloch centre and left, while the British Artillery of the centre crossed their fire, playing on the Baloch line directly in front of them.[13] Sher Mahomed's men were now seen to move from their centre to their right, which confirmed Napier in his first belief that the point he menaced was not strongly held, and that he would be able to penetrate and turn the position by a speedy thrust. He, therefore, ordered the infantry attack to be launched in echelon from the left, adhering to this formation because he doubted the ability of his battalion commanders to move without confusion in a single line of such length, and also to provide against a counter attack from the wood to the southward. The Scinde Horse and 3rd Cavalry were told off to watch this, and attack the left flank of any body of men that might emerge from it.

As the Horse Artillery moved ahead, the 22nd advanced; but when within musket range of the bank, both came under a severe fire of matchlocks from the village of Nareja, which was among the trees as expected. But contrary to expectation, was occupied in strength. Half the Light Company of the Cheshires went down but there was no time to change the plan of attack; and just at this crisis, a breathless messenger came up to tell the General that the Cavalry of his right wing were charging. Napier instantly galloped across the front to see what had happened.

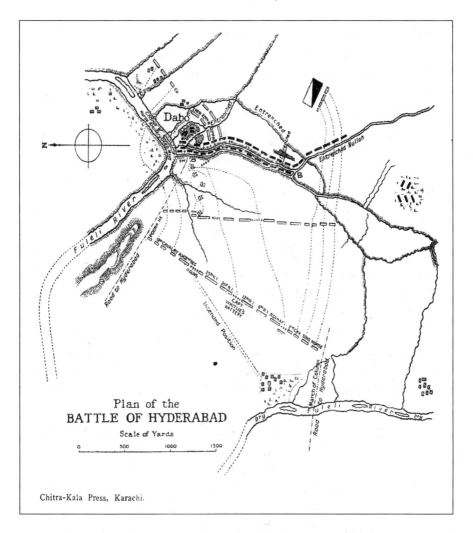

Plan of the
BATTLE OF HYDERABAD
Scale of Yards

0   500   1000   1500

Chitra-Kala Press, Karachi.

The absence of matchlock fire, and of any appearance of turbans
or flourished swords above the bank of the water channel where it
crossed the front of the ground which the Scinde Horse and 3rd
Cavalry had just taken up, had given their officers good reason to
suspect that this part of it was not occupied in continuation of the
Baloch position: their line could not, therefore, extend to the wood.
If so, it was a matter of small moment whether the latter was held by
the Balochis or not; for undisciplined warriors, once cut off from the

main body of their comrades, would never move far from such shelter to counter attack. Now, as Leslie's shrapnel began to enfilade their ranks, the tribesmen posted to the left front of the Cavalry Brigade began to waver and fell to their left. To a discerning eye, it was a perfect opportunity for throwing the Baloch array into confusion.

Major Stack, commanding the brigade, had in John Jacob and Captain Delamain, an impetuous officer who had seen hard service in Afghanistan, two cavalry commanders of no ordinary calibre. Which of the three saw and seized the critical moment for a charge is open to question, but in an instant it was done; done without reference to the General, who arrived only to see the two regiments irretrievably committed as they swept forward at speed, the fiery Delamain conspicuous at the head of the whole line which, like a wave, breasted the steep slope, crossed the 'karia', and poured over the further bank. Now they came in sight of the real left wing of the Mir's army, posted in and behind a second scarped and embanked channel running obliquely back from the first; and bearing slightly to the left, charged straight at it. The Balochis had hardly time to fire their matchlocks before the horsemen were in their midst, leaping the channel or crashing down into it, overturning the defenders right and left: in an instant, the tribesmen's formation was utterly destroyed and the two regiments fell on Sher Mahomed's horsemen, who were posted behind this wing in reserve.

The General's angry eye followed them through the dust: he recognized that the move was irretrievable; then, that it was likely to be successful, which put an end to his vexation and he could console himself as he spurred back to the left wing with the thought that his echelon attack from that flank was appropriate in the circumstances. Meanwhile, the Horse Artillery having reached the left of the infantry line, Lieutenant Smith spurred up the high parapet of the bank opposite Nareja village, to see where the guns could be brought to bear most effectively; his devotion was not in vain, for before he fell dead, he pointed the way for them to pass between the village and the Fuleli.

Sir Charles now galloped up from the right wing, just as Major
Poole, at the head of Her Majesty's 22nd, having fired a single
volley at forty yards distance, was on the point of storming the first
entrenchment. The General pressed his horse into the foremost
ranks with a shout and amid a hail of matchlock balls from the bank
beyond, they bore down into the canal, to be attacked in flank by
knots of swordsmen.[14] On the right of the 22nd, the 25th Bombay
Native Infantry followed their example; there was no hesitation, and
the issue of the hand to hand combat which ensued was not long
in doubt; for the striving masses of Balochis, penned in a trench
only six yards wide, and pressed back by the impetus of the charge,
lost the advantage of numbers: there was hardly room to wield a
sword, or parry with their shields the close line of bayonets springing
from that living wall of red-coats. Those that fell were trodden
under foot, and served to ease the ascent of the further bank for the
assailants, who struggled up it, contending every foot with a fresh
line of swordsmen, who slashed at them from above. Once more the
bayonet prevailed; and as the surviving Balochis fell back, pressed
on and down into a second far wider and deeper entrenched canal
in and behind which the defenders were massed in double strength.
Here, the fury of the combat reached a yet higher pitch: to the left
and right the Mir's guns continued to fire but everything depended
on the outcome of the struggle in the centre. The Balochis never
gained the upper hand, though the British line grew ever thinner:
now on the right of the 25th the artillery under Hutt advanced to
the edge of the first entrenchment, dealing fearful destruction at
point blank range among Sher Mahomed's reserves. But the Baloch
guns were not silenced till captured by the infantry. To Hutt's right
again, the Second Infantry Brigade came into action, supported by
Whitlie's battery. Those whose advance brought them opposite the
ramps left by the Balochis for the passage of their own guns soon
forced their way over them, penetrating the defenders' last line.

By this time Mir Sher Mahomed had left the field—to fight again
another day—on the advice of Hosh Mahomed Kambrani, who at

the head of a devoted band of fellow servants of Mir Sobdar Khan, yielded not an inch of ground, but fighting to the last man, died where they stood.

While this hand to hand struggle raged in the centre, the cavalry of the left wing were ordered by Napier to turn the village, and did so with comparatively little loss; they were followed by the Horse Artillery, for whom the indefatigable Henderson with his Sappers had cut a way down into the bed of the Fuleli.

Nareja Village remained unsubdued: behind breastworks, and in its loopholed houses, was a strong force of tribesmen on whom fell back many of those who had been dislodged from their entrenchments by the irresistable 22nd. The latter emerging on the plain, now brought up their right shoulders, and plunged into the village with undiminished resolution. The 25th N.I. conformed to their movement and on their right, again the 21st N.I. swept round in a vigorous charge, marked by heavy carnage.

The Mir's line was now entirely cut in two and the left offered little resistance to the advance of the 12th, 8th and 1st Grenadiers; but the latter had to hold their fire, as the British Cavalry of the right wing were seen immediately to their front, driving the retreating Balochis in front of them. For the same reason the Artillery, with the exception of Leslie's Troop on the extreme left flank, were now compelled to cease fire.

The combat in the village was fierce and confused: a magazine blew up close to Napier while he was endeavouring to reform the infantry; though several were killed around him, he was unscathed. At length the surviving Balochis were expelled, and fell back sullenly, before the wheeling advance of the 21st could completely surround Nareja. The General emerging at the head of the victorious infantry now put himself at the head of the Bengal Cavalry and Poona Horse and pursued the retreating masses for several miles, inflicting heavy punishment but not without loss to themselves; Captain Garrett of the Bengal Cavalry being among those killed. This pursuit prevented the defeated Balochis from gaining the line of the Indus, which they might have crossed to make head again with their brethren in the hill country: they were driven on to the swords of Stack's brigade which, after shattering Sher Mahomed's left wing by their charge, had then chased his horsemen, kept in reserve as at Miani, clean off the field. Two of the officers had actually sighted Mir Sher Mahomed himself in full flight, and could probably have captured him, when Colonel Pattle overtook them, and considering that the cavalry had become too dispersed, stopped their pursuit. The Balochis were by now scattered to the four winds, and Napier returned, to be greeted with three cheers, beginning from the sadly thinned ranks of the 22nd and taken up by the whole of the infantry, who were now drawn up in two lines south of Nareja village, at right angles to the original direction of the attack.

The General sent his wounded into Hyderabad and ordered injured Balochis also to be collected and given medical aid; then he sat down to write his despatch. Its last words read: 'I have every reason to believe that not another shot will be fire[d] in Scinde.' But he reckoned without the tenacity and popularity of Sher Mahomed.

Previous Accounts of the Battle

All accounts of the battle of Hyderabad, in the various *Lives of Sir Charles Napier*, and *Histories of Armies and Regiments*, follow more or less closely that given by Sir William Napier in *The Conquest of Scinde*; which, as far as it is possible to ascertain, is much more accurate than his description of Miani.

The battle aroused less interest than Napier's first victory, which had been won against much greater odds, when far more was at stake; and it is natural that there should be fewer first-hand accounts of Hyderabad. Major Waddington, for instance, does not seem to have thought it worthy of a companion-piece to his pamphlet on Miani. I have not been able to find any original sources worth mention beyond the following:

(a) Sir Charles Napier's despatch, and subsidiary returns (reproduced in *Records of the Scinde Irregular Horse*, Vol. I., 30–33).

(b) References in Sir Charles Napier's journal and letters, quoted in *The Life and Opinions of General Sir Charles James Napier* (Vol. II, 350–352, 356, 358–364, 371, Vol. III, 89, 110, 155, 169–170, 441, Vol. IV, 109–110, 304).

(c) Captain Henderson's account to the Adjutant Madras Sappers and Miners Bangalore, reproduced in *Madras Artillery records*, Vol. VII (Miscellaneous).

I should add that almost contemporary descriptions or critiques of the battles of Miani and Hyderabad appeared in the *Calcutta Review*: an article on Miani in 1844 (Vol. I., page 236) and another dealing both with Dubba and Miani some years later, in Vol. VI, page 604.[15]

I must admit, with great regret, that I have not seen these and do not know by whom they were written.

It is very disappointing that the letter in which John Jacob must have written a description of the battle to his father does not seem to have been preserved in the family papers. The late Major General A. Le G. Jacob indeed told me that such a letter had in fact survived, until some years ago he sent it in original to Jacob's Horse, unfortunately without keeping a copy, and that it had thereafter disappeared. Neither Colonel K. de L. Young or Colonel B. M. Mahon, who recently commanded the Scinde Horse, recollect having seen such a letter, and it is possible that the General was thinking of the holograph letter on Miani, presented by him and preserved in the Scinde Horse Mess.

In the absence of independent accounts, it is not possible to write decidedly certain details of the battle, though the general outline is clear enough.

William Napier and his successors all write as if Sir Charles launched his attack almost immediately after the reconnaissance, though between the two, there was a cannonade lasting nearly an hour.

SINDHI SOURCES

Baloch and Sindhi authors also seem to have taken less interest in the battle of Hyderabad than in Miani. Mir Yar Mahomed, the author of *Frere Namah*, must have been in confinement in the steamer on the Indus on the day of the fight: his mention is of the briefest.

Munshi Awatrai had no concern with events after his master Mir Sobdar had been imprisoned; however, after his description of Miani he added: 'In the battle with Sher Mahomed, the Mir had also posted his army in a canal bed, but the event was the same. At first he kept the English at bay with his powerful artillery, but after a time Napier treated about 500 of his soldiers to copious draughts of liquor, and ordered them to storm the guns. Fired by this, the men advanced fearlessly and routed Sher Mahomed's men and captured his artillery. This account of the battle was related to me by the sons of Seth Tindanmal Shikarpuri whom Napier Saheb took with him, and were eye witnesses.' This is an amusing counter-blast to Napier's assertions, that the Balochis screwed up their courage with bhang! Seth Naomal Hotchand dismisses the battle in a few words.

The poem on Dabba, given in سنڌ جا مير (Mirs of Sindh) was probably composed by the same blind minstrel who sang of Miani. On this occasion, however, the author has little good to say of any of the warriors except Sher Mahomed himself, and Hosh Mahomed. From internal evidence, the poem must have been composed in 1848. As it is a good example of a Sindhi satirical ballad, I will reproduce it here:

> The general was a brave soldier, and enlarged his camp. Hearing of Mir Sher Mahomed, he took his guns with him, and gave him battle in the Town of Nareja. Brave men came forth from Mirpur, heaving well considered the matter; the warlike Chiefs rode along with bold Sher Mahomed, they came to Nareja, and there they fought. Sher Mahomed was a rock, the Mir was a strong mountain! As soon as he came, he killed the English in heaps; he settled with the English,

did Mir Sher Mahomed. Clouds and waves of swords came on them from above, no one can deny that Sher Mahomed fought a fine battle. Ahdi, son of Ali Murad, who was always successful, was shouting out 'Kill them, O kill them.' Sher Mahomed overturned the big bed of the English, and the whole bank of the Fuleli ran red with blood. He escaped with his life; the Mir was always successful. Now came Hosh Mahomed the Kambrani, and made an attack; coming into the entrenchments this bridegroom dealt out wounds: the Shidi gave up his breath. The Shidi was killed with one hundred men; no blame can attach to him. Victory is in the hands of God, and he gives it to whom he wills. The heroes never yielded: well done, lords, well done!

(Mulraj the Mahtar did not fall short: he stood fast, a man roused to anger. He gave battle at Multan; no one will deny honour to him. Mulraj became famous in the land; and smiling enjoys his fame. I am making known these deeds of Mulraj at Hyderabad).

Here the Lagharis watched the struggle—observe the conduct of the Thoras! First the Thoro Nawab fled: the wretch's face turned green. He brought dishonour on all the Thoras, the idle evil doer! His effort was not worth a cowrie, though he swallowed the Mir's bounty in lakhs and thousands. As to Ahmed Khan Laghari's behaviour just ask me and I'll tell you. He had neither a moustache on his face nor one hair of a beard. The children of false Ali Murad were sold into the mountains; he had not a scrap of honour, listen to the deeds of this leper! He drove not only his brothers, but his children into exile. Poets will speak the truth, although people are moved to wrath.

That a man's promises should not be broken, let the ways of disgrace and dishonesty be exposed fully!

Ghulam Mahomed Laghari fled to Kahanbra. Let us give him a red petticoat, and a spotted head-sheet, and a set of ivory bracelets for his arms: let us give him two nose rings, large and small, for his nose. He had made a promise to Mir Nasir Khan, but the coward absented himself. I, the poet, am speaking the truth to my own Mir.

Khan Mahomed slinks away and flies, leaving his palace, paying, 'as long as God gives me life, may he preserve me from girding on the sword!' He jumped down into the tamarisk jungle, and never looked behind. Dost Ali got stuck in the mud, with drooping lop-ears he said to Ahmed Khan, 'Uncle, Friend, let us get away!' His mother was drowned in the Fuleli at that time.

Dost Mahomed Badhani fled: he floated away in the river. He made an oblation of half an anna, saying 'the river God will protect me.'

Jahan Khan son of Mahomed ran away. These cowards were useless. This crow hid himself and fled crouching; he did not set foot to the ground. He was as potbellied as a grain-bin; he overate, and wasted good food.

Ghulam Shah Khatian was in the fight at that time. This good man was with the army when it was broken; when it was carried away like dust.

Here, in the grove of date-palms, the Katanhar flower had opened. The tents pitched were worth seeing, and the garden of flowers. Let us stew the cooking pots, while the brave men tell of their deeds. The Khans take this food in comfort, and make merry.

The fair faced and valiant cavaliers rode their horses. In the camp of Shahdadpur twenty-one thousand men are heard of.

They bring Mir Sher Mahomed, and are taking their daily rations. Seeing the heat of the sword, the cowards are rubbing their noses on the bround. 'These men' says Ali, 'Why do they not drown themselves?'

For a well-bred filly, one stroke of the whip is enough; but the slow pony gets thirsty. Give praise to the brave, and leave talking of cowards.

God will bind on Sher Mahomed the turban of Sind.

Another ballad by a Manghanhar named Mihru, reproduced by Richard Burton in his *Scinde and the Races that Inhabit the Valley of the Indus*, which was sung throughout the country, invokes 'a hundred thousand curses on the Thoro who set fire to his own gunpowder'.[16] This refers to the universal belief of the Balochis that the explosion of the magazine at Nareja, in the earlier stages of the battle, was due to the treachery of Mahomed Khan Thoro, and not, as was almost certainly the case, to a lucky shell from the British Artillery.

The legend persists, for when I last visited the battle field in August 1942, the people of Nareja village said that some traitor in Sher Mahomed's camp had told the British where to direct their fire. Mir Ali Bakhsh Khan Talpur ascribed the disaster to Mir Bijar Khan. The local tradition is that the Baluchis ran out of gunpowder in consequence, whereupon Hosh Mahomed Shidi advised Sher Mahomed to secure his own retreat while he led the defence. The Shidis, Nuhanis, and Bhurgris are said to have fought well, but the others indifferently. Sir William Napier makes mention only of the Lagharis and Nizamanis, as being entrenched in the village.[17]

Sher Mahomed's *vakils*, who came to Napier to offer him the Mir's sword when he was on the march to Bahawalpur early in 1846, told him that the Mir had taken up his station near Nareja village, and that the movement noticed by the British early on in the battle, of crowds hurrying to their right, was of chiefs with their followers hastening to receive their last orders from him.

The *Sind Gazetteer* quotes a Persian manuscript by one of the retinue of the Aga Khan, in which the battle is thus mentioned, 'When they (the Baluchis) were hemmed in by the British soldiers on the one hand and cannonade on the other, they gave expression to words, of course in their own language, which distinctly hit off their character, when translated they stand as follows: 'these rascals do not give us time even to steam ourselves with the hookah'.[18]

INDIVIDUAL EXPLOITS

The undaunted courage of Hosh Mahomed Kambrani has already been mentioned. It was warmly-praised by Sir Charles Napier and his brother, who in his Life of Sir Charles Napier writes thus of him: 'Heroic in strength of body and mind this brave man and his brother slaves at Dubba, fighting with unbounded fury, fell to the last man under the bayonets of the 22nd Regiment.' Sir Charles also alluded to him in his despatch as 'the great promoter of this war'.

To another soldier of Sher Mahomed—an artillery man—was accorded the honour of being, for aught I know to the contrary, the first 'unknown warrior'. Napier ordered his body to be removed from the battle field to the Fort at Hyderabad and placed this inscription over his tomb: 'This monument marks the last resting place of one of the Ameer's soldiers who was killed in the battle of Hyderabad, whilst bravely fighting the gun placed over his tomb.'

On the British side, there were many gallant exploits. Mention has been made of Lt Smith's heroic devotion and Napier's despatch also recorded how the intrepid Lieutenant Coote, of Her Majesty's 22nd, 'first mounted the rampart, seized one of the enemy's standards, and was severely wounded while waving it and cheering on his men.' As to feats of swordsmanship, the encounter of Lt Nixon with a Baloch Chief, and MacMurdo's three successive triumphs in single combat, in the last of which he was wounded, are described with boyish gusto by Sir Charles. But for cool courage in the midst of the enemy, none surpassed the General himself. As has been seen, he was throughout the heat of the fight with the 22nd, who bore the brunt of it. His orderly dragoon's horse was cut down behind him, and the hilt of his sword struck by a ball; in Nareja village a magazine blew up close to him, bringing death to many, but left him untouched: no Baloch assailed him, though he was at times almost alone among them. The fortune of Miani followed him.

The best testimony to the magic of Napier's leadership, which bred heroes, was the fact that six men of the 22nd concealed the wounds they received in the battle, thinking there would be more fighting; they had to fall out in a long hot march, when two of them were found to have been shot through both legs.[19]

NUMBERS ENGAGED AND CASUALTIES ON EITHER SIDE

Napier's Army at the battle of Hyderabad numbered about 5,000, but so far as I am aware, no field-state for 24 March, giving the strength of the units engaged, is available; nor even such unofficial estimates as those of writers on Miani. I have been unable to ascertain even what troops were told off to guard the baggage, which Lt Leeson is commended for marshalling close-up to the line. Sir W. Napier states that of the 5,000, about 1,100 were cavalry. The newcomers, the 3rd Bombay Cavalry, numbered just under 300 sabres. Of the two infantry battalions that had joined since Miani, the 8th mustered 818 men, and the 21st must have been almost equally strong; it is also necessary to assume that, with the addition of Leslie's Troop and the 2nd Coy. 1st battalion, Bombay Artillery, the gunners were at least double the number present at Miani, to reach the combined total of five thousand. It is evident that Napier deserves great credit for bringing into the field every effective man he could find. One lesson of Miani he had learned: 'No general ought to detach even a tailor before a battle'.[20]

In passing, I must call attention to an error in dates by which the simultaneous arrival of the reinforcements from Karachi and Sukkur by river is assigned to 23 March. This originated with Sir Charles himself, in a letter to his brother dated 16 April 1843.[21] Sir William must not be blamed for making the most of this dramatic incident, according to which men, guns and stores were landed, organized, and brigaded, and launched against Sher Mahomed all within twenty four hours. But the same cannot be said for latter writers, such as Rice Holmes, for Napier's journal, embodied in the *Life* shows plainly that these reinforcements reached him on 21 March, when he was beginning to be anxious about the progress of Stack's Brigade.[22]

The strength of Sher Mahomed's army as stated in the despatch was 20,000. Napier wrote some days afterwards that he gave this figure 'to keep bounds' but that all his spies concurred in saying that the Mir had more than 26,000: and this figure was without more ado adopted by his brother.[23] Sir Patrick Cadell, in his *History of the Bombay Army*, says 'an estimate of 16,000 would seem more nearly correct'—I do not know on what this is based.

The total British casualties were a little higher than at Miani; but the killed numbered only 39, of whom two were officers, as compared with 62 including six officers in the former battle. Considerably over half the 270 casualties were sustained by Her Majesty's 22nd, which had 23 men killed, and five officers and 119 other ranks wounded. The 21st and 25th Bombay N.I. came next, with thirty and twenty-five casualties respectively, only seven being killed between them. Lt Burr, of the 21st, who was severely wounded, died some days after the battle and lies buried in Hyderabad Fort. Among the cavalry, the Poona Horse had three men killed and an officer and seventeen men wounded, with seven horses killed and eight wounded; the Scinde Horse had eighteen men wounded and thirteen horses killed. The Bengal and Bombay cavalry came off lightly, with more casualties among their horses than the men; and the losses among the other units were trifling. These figures sufficiently attest the part played by the Cheshires in the action.

Of the losses of Sher Mahomed's *lashkar*, it is difficult to speak. In his despatch, written on the day of the battle, Napier says: '500 bodies have been counted on the field of battle, and it is said that the neighbouring villages are filled with dead and wounded men.' Among the chiefs killed were Ghulam Ali Talpur, Ali Khan Talpur and Jaffar Khan Marri. The two Talpurs were, I think, collaterals of the main line of the Manikanis. Napier says that he learnt from Sher Mahomed's vakils on the occasion already mentioned, that 'five princes of the Talpur house fell at Dubba, with an immense number of minor chiefs'. Sir William, with his peculiar flair for improving on the truth, says, 'the vanquished lost about 5,000 … eight hundred bodies were lying in the *nullahs* and at Dubba, but all the villages and lanes beyond the latter place were so filled with dead and dying, that to avoid them the army was forced to encamp on the ground it occupied before the action commenced. All the fallen Baloochis were of mature age, grim visaged men of athletic forms, the carcass of a youth was not to be found.'

When some years later Sir William produced a further panegyric of his brother, entitled *The Administration of Scinde*, and again gave five thousand as the number of Sher Mahomed's army killed at Dubba, John Jacob, who wrote and published *Notes* corrective of the manifold errors in this work, writes laconically in reference to this 'more correctly, two thousand'. Sir John Fortescue, the Historian of the British Army, on the contrary writes that the Baluch losses at Dubba were twice as great as Miani; a most absurd statement which does not deserve discussion.[24] The duration of the close fighting was far shorter than at Miani, and it was really confined to only a part of their line. Among the Baluch losses, whatever they may have been, were 8 men taken prisoner: a matter of satisfaction to Napier, who was shocked by the mutual refusal of quarter at Miani.

QUESTIONS AND DISCREPANCIES CONNECTED WITH THE BATTLE AND NAPIER'S GENERALSHIP

The principal unsolved question of the battle of Hyderabad is the responsibility for the charge of the cavalry on the right wing, which, though not deciding the victory, undoubtedly opened the way to it. Writing in July 1843 to Sir George Arthur, Napier says: 'I am sadly vexed at having said in my despatch that Major Stack led the brilliant cavalry charge at Dubba: it was Captain Delamain, whose modesty is so great that he never said a word on the subject. I am not in charity with Stack for allowing me to mistake his report, if I did mistake, on that charge.'[25] This however does not touch the point, who gave the order?

As already observed, no letter of Jacob describing the battle appears to be in existence, nor have I knowledge of any other bearing on this particular question. In reporting Jacob's death, the 'Homeward Mail' of 4 January 1859, gives the credit of this brilliant movement to him: 'when large masses of the enemy showed an appearance of wavering, Lt Jacob seized the critical moment, and charged with such fury as to convert the enemy's movement into a flight, and the Scinde Horse and the rest of the cavalry sabred the fugitives for miles.'

Jacob, says Sir Charles, relying upon gossip at the time when they became estranged, used to say that he had done more for Napier than Napier had done for him; but Jacob's first public statement of their relations, in a letter to the *Bombay Times*, written after considerable provocation in October 1851, passes over the events of the war in Sind in a few words, seemingly taking it for granted that his services were too well known to need re-statement.[26]

For the present, then, though perhaps not for ever, this interesting detail must remain undecided.

Sir J. Fortescue, though stating that the details of the action are exceedingly obscure, curiously enough missed this point, simply giving the whole credit to Stack, while puzzling himself over a remark of Sir William Napier's that Leslie's Horse Artillery, on gaining the extreme left flank, were able to enfilade the Balochis' left wing, hitherto concealed 'from end to end'.

Fortescue says: 'if his account of the Baluchi line be correct, the range must have been very long for round shot, and impossible for grape. Possibly Leslie fired shrapnel, but for this he would need howitzers, and there was only one howitzer to each battery.' Two eight inch howitzers had in fact reached Napier with his reinforcements, and he had had two twenty-four pound and two twelve pound howitzers at Miani.

In sober fact, the range from Leslie's position opposite the right of the Baluch line to their extreme left would have been over a mile; and the obvious conclusion, is that Sir William Napier had permitted himself to exaggerate somewhat the effort of Leslie's fire.

Was Napier Aware of the Existence of Nareja Village Before He Attacked?

Rice Holmes draws attention to the discrepancy between two statements of Sir Charles on this point, in Appendix P of his book, *Sir Charles Napier*; he might have added a third.[27] He was fortunate in being able to consult a survivor of the battle on the point. Sir Montagu McMurdo replied 'When we formed up on the plain, we judged the situation of the village by the high trees about it (as Katri at Meeanee). But we could see little, if anything at all, of the low mud houses, because of the extraordinarily high bank thrown up in deepening and scarping the double canal.'

The strength and difficulty of these natural entrenchments struck Napier particularly on his last visit to the battle field, in 1851 although 'the ditches and their banks are lessened; they were made up and widened for the battle, and their slopes were steeper: I doubt my own resolution, had I been aware of their tremendous strength; but I was not, until my horse was on the edge and there was no choice but to shove him down. How we shoved down, or up again on the opposite banks, I know not.'[28]

Of his men, Napier wrote: 'At Meeanee they showed hesitation and wonder: at Dubba they were like cucumbers. As to myself, I felt a different man, my confidence in the soldiers and in myself being complete; I felt at ease, and could have changed my whole order of battle in the fight had it been wanted.'[29]

Fortescue considered that the storming of Nareja village (by him called Dabo) was 'quite unnecessary'. Napier himself felt that he might have done better, as he frankly admitted to his brother:

> I will answer your questions about Dubba, namely; could you have menaced Dubba with your left, and pushed the cavalry of your right, sustained with some guns and infantry, towards the wood where you suspected the ambush; then passing the *nullah* with your left (?) and centre have driven the enemy in a confused heap on Dubba, where your left was holding them in check?

This is nearly what did happen, but by accident, though I at first thought of it, for Blenheim came into my mind where something of the kind happened. While examining the enemy's line I was under fire of guns directed at my large staff, and one shot went close to my face and into the heart of a 22nd grenadier. This did not help thought, though it did not much disturb it; but what most annoyed me was that the men were under a cannonade the moment we formed line, and it would not have done to go back then, no, not for ten yards. Even a seeming hesitation would have been bad. All the houses of the village were loopholed and perfectly concealed in front, but were open to the river, and by a bold examination of their right, this would have been discovered; an ablerman would have done so. It was a fault that cost many lives, and would have given the deep regret had it arisen from carelessness; but it was only want of experience in command. Henceforth my care shall be to closely examine an enemy's flanks.

Such naiveté really disarms criticism and casualties at the rate of one in twenty are not a heavy price to pay for beating odds of four to one. A victory in which the enemy is scattered to the winds, after suffering severe casualties and losing the whole of his artillery, is ordinarily to be styled as crushing; and all the more honour is due to Mir Sher Mahomed and the Balochis who rallied to him thereafter, for continuing the struggle after such a lesson.

The guns taken numbered eleven, of which three were brass, and in good order.[30] One of these latter, nearly six feet in length, had from a good position on the right of the Baloch line, inflicted a good deal of loss on the British. The iron guns were all very inferior, uneven in bore, and much corroded; however, their carriages showed signs of recent repair, and they were fitted with elevating screws. Eight out of the eleven guns had a bore less than three inches, and the remaining three were under four inches.

Among other trophies of the fight, nineteen standards were taken, the majority of them by Her Majesty's 22nd; one is specially mentioned, a silver knobbed standard captured by Corporal Tim Kelly, who shot the defender.

TOPOGRAPHY OF THE FIELD OF HYDERABAD (DUBBA) A CENTURY AFTER THE BATTLE

Before entering upon a description of the ground where the battle was fought, a word is due to its name.

Sir William Napier says: 'This memorable battle, fought thirty-five days after Meeanee, and within a few miles from that field, bears three names, Dubba, Naraja, and Hyderabad: the first from the village, the second from the plain, the third from the city near which it was fought. The last is the one by which it must be known, being that which is inscribed on the colours and medals of the gallant soldiers by whom it was won.'[31]

In actual fact, Nareja is the name of the village, while the district is called Duabo *scilicet* two waters, from the streams of the Indus and Fuleli, once a natural branch of the Indus, which pass through it—this name appears to have been corrupted to Dubba by the earlier writers, but refined by Rice Holmes to Dabo. There is a place called Duabo, about three miles east-south-east from Nareja: it gets its name from two canals from the Fuleli between which it is situated. But it is some distance from the battlefield.

Sir Charles wrote 'We don't like to call our battle Dubba because the skins of grease in this country are called dubbas. All the boys were horrified at the name, and McMurdo rode about, bleeding like a pig from his wound, after the battle, to find another village to call after: Lord Ellenborough has settled it for us—*Hyderabad*.'[32] In truth, the village which was the key of the Baluch position was at the time, and still is, called, Nareja: there is no village of Dubba, and one wonders why the battle could not have been called by the obviously appropriate name. We call Marlborough's first great victory Blenheim, from the village which was included in the French line, though on the continent it is known as Hochstadt, from a town three miles from the field: an analogy for 'Hyderabad', but not for 'Dubba'. The people of Sind speak of the battle as 'Nareja' or perhaps more often 'Sher Mahomed's fight'.

Another perversion of terminology is that by which the entrenchments occupied by the Baloch army are styled, by all writers including Rice Holmes, as '*nullahs*'. Residents in India do not need to be informed that this word indicates a natural water-course, generally a broken and irregular gash in the soil, or the stony bed of an occasional torrent—with which the officers from the Deccan or Gujerat who formed the bulk of Napier's Army were familiar; but the extensive artificial irrigation of Sind being new to their experience, they loosely applied the word they knew best to what were nothing more or less than canals.

This criticism is not made in a spirit of pedantry, for Fortescue, rendering the word '*nullah*' correctly as 'ravine' in his description, innocently calls up an entirely erroneous picture of the field.[33]

General McMurdo, as we have seen, uses the correct English word for them; but if we must employ Indian nomenclature, let it be the appropriate Sindhi 'Wah' or '*Karia*'.

Since the canals in Sind are cut out of the dead level plain, the soil originally removed forms no inconsiderable bank on either side of them: but this is added to by the silt which, deposited in them with every inundation, has to be cleared out annually. The older the canal, the higher its banks will be above the general level. The artificial channels dug from the old Fuleli above Hyderabad, which in Napier's own words 'intercept the flat country for miles, and at every mile, like a grating' probably date, many of them, from the time of the Kalhoras. The traveller passing from Hyderabad to Mirpur Khas today will notice them: long embankments of white earth, rising to twelve or fifteen feet above the plain; doubtless higher than in 1843; the majority of them derelict, superseded by the new Barrage canals and water-courses, which are designed to flow on a gradient which keeps the deposit of silt to minimum, thus eliminating the need for annual clearance.

Another well-known feature of the old irrigation system of Sind arose from the insistence by large zemindars on having exclusive sources of water supply for their lands. Two or more 'karias' will be found running parallel and close together for miles, from the point where they take off from the main canal.

It was two of these that Mir Sher Mahomed selected for his position, the smaller one, known as Khair Wah, being occupied by the front line as far as the point marked B on Napier's map, and thereafter continuing unoccupied opposite the British right wing.[34] The first mile of Khair Wah was abandoned as a canal many years ago and now does duty as a cart track. The larger canal running behind it, up to this point B, sheltered the second line of the Balochis, and from thence bending away at an obtuse angle was held by their left wing: this is called Imam Wah Husri, and was in use until 1932. Even now, it presents much the same appearance as at the time of the battle, deep and wide, with steep banks inside. The country people told me its upper portion was called Sobdar Wah: perhaps in memory of the gallant servants of the Mir of that name who fell there.

The subsidiary defences of the position, mentioned by Sir William Napier, and shown on his map, were also improvised from smaller channels behind Nareja village, the names of two of them, Boledai Wah and Rind Wah, still surviving. The modern revenue survey map indeed shows a most remarkable resemblance to the contemporary plan: but changes are rapidly taking place. Year by year the local zemindars are cutting away more and more of the bank of these old channels, using the rich silt for levelling and improving their lands, so that identification of every part of the position may soon become impossible.

The field is also traversed by a new Barrage canal, the Husri Distributary, which cuts into the lower part of the Khair Wah and by the main North Western Railway line running West to East about two miles South of Nareja. This latter was about the line of the charge of the Cavalry of Napier's right wing.

The 'wood' on this side of the battle field which gave Napier so much anxiety no longer seems to exist: it must have been roughly where Tando Hyder village is now.

The northern end of the battlefield has retained its character almost unchanged. The bed of the Fuleli is partially cultivated near the village since its supersession by barrage canals, but is still well-marked and deep, and about 20 yards wide. There is however no trace of the Shikargah on its further bank, while on the nearer bank a mango grove occupies what was at the time of the battle open plain not far in front of Nareja.

The village itself is said to be smaller than it was a century ago. But there are the same low mud houses, interspersed with trees, tucked away behind the high banks of the double canal and invisible from in front of it, though open on the other three sides.

The banks and beds of the canals are much overgrown with jungle, but there are still portions which give a perfect idea of their state at the time of the battle. In one of these, about 400 yards south of the village, is situated the tomb of Hosh Mahomed Kambrani. It is on the further or eastern bank of the larger canal: a plain structure of yellow stone with no inscription, the plinth carved in simple designs. Close by are two tombs made of brick, where men of the Nuhani tribe who fell by Hosh Mahomed's side are buried.

Opposite this point, some three hundred yards in the direction from which Napier attacked is the British memorial of the battle. It is plain obelisk, surrounded by guns sunk in the ground.

The inscription reads:

To

The Memory

of those

who fell in the battle of Dubba on

24 March 1843, and who were buried

near this spot.

Lt J. C. Smith	Horse Artillery
Captain Garret	9th Bengal Cavalry
One drummer.	21st Regiment, N.I.

Rank and File

3rd Bombay Cavalry	1
Poona Horse	3
Her Majesty's 22nd Foot	23
1st Grenadier N.I.	2
12th Regiment N.I.	1
21st Regiment N.I.	3
25th Regiment N.I.	3

Close to the monument are two very large Kandi trees, which may well have been growing at the time of the battle.

CONCLUDING OBSERVATIONS

The present designations of the units which fought under Napier at Miani have been given in the first half of this paper.[35] Of those which took part only in the battle of Hyderabad, the 8th Bombay Native Infantry later served in the Afghan War of 1878, the Great War of 1914–1918 and the Arab Rebellion of 1920. In 1922 it was designated the 3rd battalion 4th Bombay Grenadiers. It was disbanded in 1930.

The 21st Bombay Native Infantry partially mutinied at Karachi in 1857—one of the very few Bombay Regiments to do so and was disbanded next year.

The 3rd Bombay Light Cavalry fought in Persia, the Mutiny, Abyssinia, Afghanistan, China, the Great War, and the Afghan War of 1919; and from 1921–22 were merged with their old comrades of Hyderabad as the 17th Q.V.O. Poona Horse.

The 1st Troop Bombay Horse Artillery is with us as N. Horse Battery R.A., and the 2nd Company First Battalion Bombay Artillery is now the 15th Field Battery R.A.

Those corps which under the Governor-General's Order of 5 March, had been permitted to bear the Word 'Hyderabad, 1843' on their appointments, Standards, and colours were now authorised to substitute 'Meanee'; 'Hyderabad' being granted to all who took part in the second battle, under a General Order of 11 April.

A special distinction was reserved for Leslie's Horse Battery. The Governor-General having taken into consideration the peculiar merits of the 1st troop of the Bombay Horse Artillery, under Major Leslie, which having participated in the distinguished services of the army of Candahar, under His Excellency Major-General Sir W. Nott, G.C.B., and having returned to India with the troops from Cabool, marched from the camp at Ferozepore early in January, and joined the Army of Scinde in time to decide, in conjunction with H.M.'s 22nd Regiment, the battle of Hyderabad, is pleased to order that the 1st Troop of the Bombay Horse Artillery shall hereafter for ever be denominated the 1st or 'Leslie's' Troop of Horse Artillery, and shall in addition to all other decorations or inscriptions upon its appointments, bear the 'Eagle'.

The Honours for individuals' services appeared in a gazette of 4 July 1843. Napier himself was advanced from a Knight Commander to the Grand Cross of the Order of the Bath.

Outram received the Companionship of the Order, and with him twenty four other officers; of the Staff, Lt Colonel Pattle, second-in-command; Majors McPherson and Waddington, Captains Green, Wyllie, and Blenkins; four of H.M.'s 22nd: Lt Col. Pennefather, Major Poole, Captains George and Conway; four of the artillery: Majors Lloyd and Leslie, Captains Whitlie and Willoughby; Major

Storey and Captain Tucker of the 9th Cavalry; Major Stack and Captain Delamain of the 3rd Cavalry; Major Browne commanding the 8th N.I.; Major Reid and Captain Fisher of the 12th N.I.; Major Stevens of the 21st N.I.; and Major Woodburn and Jackson of the 25th N.I. Most of these received brevet promotion at the same time.

It does not seem that these awards were entirely in accordance with Napier's recommendations: he says 'there are gross mistakes about the C.B., but it cannot be helped'.[36] It was also published in Orders that the conduct of Captains Jacob and Tait was considered to have entitled them to honorary distinction, which could not be conferred on them at the time on account of their want of rank. 'His Grace the Commander in Chief has however announced his intention of recommending both these officers for the brevet rank of Major and for the Companionship of the Order of the Bath, after they shall have been promoted to the regimental rank of Captain.'

Tait duly became C.B. in February 1846, and, in the same gazette, Captain Hutt of the Artillery and Captain Henderson of the Madras Sappers, who had been specially recommended by Napier in a letter to Lord Ellenborough, written in September 1843: but Jacob had to wait till 1850, for reasons which need not be entered into here.[37]

Taking a last view of the battle of Hyderabad, I am inclined to think that Mir Sher Mahomed, or his advisors, made the dispositions for battle in the light of the lessons of Miani, to avoid the faults of Nasir Khan's position. In the first, place, all the guns were placed behind the entrenchments instead of in the open in front of the line as at Miani. They could not, therefore, be put out of action in the preliminary bombardment, but as we know were served gallantly and continued to fire until the British had stormed the first entrenchments with the bayonet.

Secondly, the posting of the Mir's foot soldiers was a great improvement on Miani. At that battle, the Fuleli protected the Baluch host only until the British line reached its edge: thereafter they were completely open to the British musketry, and had to climb up the bank to counter attack. At the battle of Hyderabad, though men were posted in the bed of the first canal, it seems that they were a sort of 'forlorn hope' whose duty was to take in flank those who stormed it, the main strength was drawn up behind, so that Napier's men had to do the climbing to get at them.

In his despatch, Sir Charles wrote: 'The Baloochee infantry and artillery fought well; their cavalry made no stand, and 5,000 disciplined soldiers were not to be long resisted by a barbarian force, even though that force were nearly five to one.' This puts the business in a proper light. Sir William Napier's estimate of his brother's achievements is vitiated by his tendency to endow the Baloch tribesmen with all the qualities of Napoleon's 'grognards' and to put Sher Mahomed on a par with Masséna. Descending somewhat from this pitch of absurdity (under the influence of which Sir William seems to have speculated whether Hosh Mahomed could not have been a spiritual, if not a natural, descendant of the French Revolutionary General Hoche), it is a mistake as I have already pointed out, in writing on Miani, to compare Napier's battles with those won—sometimes the winning was doubtful—against European trained Marathas and Sikhs.[38] Once we turn to the pages of Orme, we find truer parallels: if it is suggested that the Balochis were tougher than the opponents of Clive, Stringer Lawrence, and Forde, we should remember that the hosts they rotated generally contained a nucleus of Frenchmen; and if we pass on to Cutwa and Buxar, we find that odds of seven to one, European artillery, positions of immense strength, and Rohilla cavalry who had the courage to charge home were of no avail against disciplined troops, led with the skill and determination of Adams and Hector Munro.

The truth is, that a Baloch Host in the plains was incapable of manoeuvring; but if Napier had chosen to lead his army round Sher Mahomed's left flank and fallen on their rear, he would have gained nothing but their artillery: the tribesmen would have dispersed, as soon as they saw their flank was turned, would have plundered the countryside, including perhaps the town of Hyderabad, and would have remained a thorn in Napier's flesh. Very properly, he seized the opportunity of attacking them in a position in which he could hope that they would wait for him, and be soundly beaten: and so it fell out; though as Sher Mahomed escaped, and there were among the Balochis men of remarkable tenacity and loyalty, the blow was not final.

Let Sir Charles Napier's own words close our account of his two splendid victories—the words of the speech he made when presenting new colours to his own Regiment, Her Majesty's 22nd Foot, at Ambala in November 1850:[39]

Shall I ever forget the strong and lofty entrenchments of Dubba— where the 22nd advanced in line unshaken, a living wall! and under a murderous fire stormed the works! There those honoured old colours of which we have just taken leave; bravely borne forward by their Ensigns Bowden and Blake, one of whom Lt Bowden I see before me bearing them this day, but in higher rank, were in a few minutes seen to wing triumphantly aloft amidst the combatants on the summit.

Men of Meeanee! you must remember with exultation and with pride what a view burst upon your sight when under a heavy fire you reached the bank of the river, a hurl of shields and Scindian capped and turbaned heads and flashing scimatars high brandished in the air, spread as a sea before you, and 35,000 valiant warriors of Baloochistan threatening you with destruction! Then the hostile armies closed and clashed together and desperate combats thickened along the line! The superb 9th Cavalry of Bengal and the renowned Sinde Horse—the dark chivalry of India burst as a thundercloud charging into the dry bed of the torrent, driving the foe before them! At that moment a terrible cry arose on the right! It was the dreadful British shout of battle! It began with the 22nd and was re-echoed from right to left from Regiment to Regiment along the line! Lines of levelled bayonets now gleamed charging through the smoke, and the well-fought field of Meeanee was your own!'

PIR ARI

Napier followed up the victory of Hyderabad by the bloodless capture of Sher Mahomed's capital, Mirpur, and the fort of Umarkot: but he was disappointed in his supposition that the Mir, being cut off from any 'base', in the Desert, would flee to the Panjab. The Mir kept the field, and though he had very little money to pay his men, the country people supplied him with grain of their own free will, and moreover kept him perfectly informed as to the proceedings of the British troops, from whom they concealed his plans and movements.[40]

Napier had been allowed to send the captive Talpurs out of the country, and they were removed to Bombay at the end of April, on the last day of which the General, leaving troops at Umarkot, Mirpur and Tando Allahyar, the whole under command of John Jacob, took up his quarters in the palace of Mir Nasir Khan. But with Sher Mahomed at large, the conquest of Sind was by no means complete: and on 1 May he was reported to have collected ten thousand men. He made several offers to come in, on such conditions as that his treasure would be spared; but Napier would hear of nothing but unconditional surrender: and his troops being for some time immobilised for want of camels, a deadlock set in. The General was also anxious lest his movements should thereafter be hampered by the inundation; and worse than all, the heat was becoming insupportable.

A further unpleasant possibility was that the tribes West of the Indus would cross the river and join Sher Mahomed. As early as 5 March, Napier had received information that the Chandias were crossing the river from Sehwan and Larkana to join the Mir, and he had given orders to Col. Roberts; in command at Sukkur, to 'stir up the Chandias at home' if he strong enough: while Ali Murad had his orders to plunder them.[41] Sometime afterwards Wali Mahomed, Chief of the who had been close on Napier's rear before Miani with a large lashkar, had been seized by Napier's dubious ally, Mir Ali Murad and by him sent prisoner to the General. To the disgust of

the Mir and the astonishment of Wali Mahomed, Napier told the old
Chief that he was free to go home; whereupon he made all speed
back to his country under the Western hills, vowing he would repay.
Napier's clemency with steady, loyalty to the British.[42] This could
not have happened at a more opportune time; Wali Mahomed was
by far the most influential Chief in North Western Sind, and many
who hitherto may have been inclined as a point of honour to strike
a blow against the Feringhi were disarmed by such generosity to a
faithful subject of the Talpurs, from the man who had treated the
rulers themselves with uncompromising sternness.

Napier says that Shah Mahomed, younger brother of Sher
Mahomed sent him a letter some time before the battle of Hyderabad
offering to assassinate Sher Mahomed, and that he forthwith
forwarded this letter to the intended victim, warning him to be on
his guard.[43]

There seems strong reason to doubt whether the letter was
authentic: for at some time after the battle, when Sher Mahomed's
cause was desperate, he committed his family to the care of Shah
Mahomed, who crossed the river and installed them in Rani Kot,
a remarkable fortress which Mir Karam Ali Khan had built some
thirty years before, in an inaccessible gorge in the Lakhi Hills. It
now became a first object to Napier to prevent Shah Mahomed
from raising the country on that side, as if he was able to gather a
strong force together and act in conjunction with his brother, even
if he were unable to cross the river to join him, the war might be
prolonged for months.

Napier therefore, at the beginning of May ordered Lt Col.
Roberts to move down the right bank from Sukkur to Sehwan with
a column of all arms, meanwhile sending an armed steamer of the
Indian Navy, under the command of Captain Nott, up stream to
Sehwan to chase away all boats that might be found, to prevent
the Balochis crossing to the left bank.[44] The General had hoped
to be able to move against Sher Mahomed by the 15th, but was
apprehensive of the inundation from the Indus, which he believed

would cut him off from his base: he was at a loss to procure camels to carry five months' provisions, which he thought would have to be taken with the troops.

Meanwhile intelligence was received of more boats being collected by the tribes of the Lakhi hills for their passage, and Napier sent the 'Satellite' steamer, with a detachment of sepoys under Lt Anderson to break up the 'concentration'. This, as described by Sir William Napier, was a smart little affair.[45]

The steamer reached the point where the river washes the base of a spur of the Lakhi range on 27 May. Three hundred Balochis opened matchlock fire on her from the cliff, wounding Commander Miller. The guns of the steamer replied, and a party of sepoys were landed and drove off the Balochis with heavy loss, at a trifling cost to themselves. The boats collected by the tribesmen for their crossing were destroyed, and Anderson proceeded to Sehwan, which Colonel Roberts reached on the 29th after an uneventful march, with nearly 1,500 men made up of Captain Blood's battery of four guns, a troop of the 3rd Bombay: light Cavalry under Captain Walter, and detachments from the 6th, 15th and 20th Bombay Native Infantry.

The blow at Lakhi seems to have caused Shah Mahomed to repent momentarily of his association with the irreconcilables: Napier records in his Journal of June 1st that he had written to ask forgiveness. Nevertheless the Mir decided to advance; whether from the impossibility of feeding two or three thousand men *in* the bearren fastnesses of the Lakhi hills, or to secure the support of the powerful Rind tribe, the hereditary enemies of the Chandias; or merely, as Napier thought, to see what Roberts is about and have credit for driving him away when he shall cross the river. Be this as it may, Shah Mohamed moved his lashkar down the valley of the Bandhni Nai and encamped at Pir Ari, within 15 miles of Sehwan. Nor was he inactive, for he had a successful skirmish with some horsemen of an adherent of Mir Ali Murad, who had been pacifying or taking charge of the country in their own fashion; several of them were made prisoners. But Shah Mahomed was now within Robert's reach.

Roberts' orders were to cross the Indus to the left bank on the night of 9 June, to take his part in Napier's enveloping movement against Mir Sher Mahomed. But on the 7th, information was brought in of Shah Mahomed's move to Pir Ari, and was verified by Alif Khan Tehrin, the well-known ex-Rissaldar of the Baluch Levy, who had accompanied the column from Sukkur. Roberts determined to surprise the Mir, and at midnight on 7–8 June marched out to attack Shah Mahomed with Blood's battery, the troop of cavalry, three companies of the 6th Bombay N.I., and two each of the 15th and 20th N.I., about 900 men in all. At daybreak the force was marching south beside the wide sandy bed of the Bandhni Nai, full of tamarisk jungle; to the left the craggy heights of the Lakhi range rose dark against the sun, covering with their shadow some smaller hills to the right, beyond which again swelled up the broad saddle-back of Badro, scarred with ravines. Soon they caught sight of the Mir's position, around a large oblong enclosure of line trees, surrounded by a thick and almost impenetrable hedge. The Balochis appeared to be retreating, and Roberts ordered Captain Walter to lead his troop to the left to head them off from their retreat southwards, and if possible drive them across to the right, to which side the artillery and infantry were directed. Walter, taking Alif Khan with him, advanced with his handful of horsemen, and noticing large bodies of the Balochis dispersing to right and left, turned on a party of horse and foot about 250 strong, who were drawn up in rear of two guns close to the southern end of the grove. Before the Balochi gunners fired, the speed of Walter's charge had carried him past them, and plying the sword with vigour the cavalry made havoc of the astonished tribesmen; about eighty of them were killed before the rest, completely dispersed, found shelter in the jungle.

Meanwhile on the right, the infantry advanced steadily in echelon, led by the Light Company of the 20th, then Blood's battery with the right wing of the 15th, the whole supported by the Grenadier Company of the 20th and two companies of the 8th. The Balochis did not stand, and on gaining their position Roberts halted his main body, only pushing on the light company of the 20th in a vain attempt to establish contact. Meanwhile he ordered a party of the Grenadier Company to search the grove, which was found to be a burial ground: and Mir Shah Mahomed himself was found concealed with three or four servants in some thick undergrowth. On seeing the sepoys he raised his gun, and one of his followers drew his sword: the sepoys were about to fire on them when Shah Mahomed called out that he was the Mir, and Captain Fraser coming up at the time, delivered up his sword to him. A few minutes earlier, after the firing had ceased, a Baloch had jumped out of a bush and severely wounded Lieutenant Lancaster in the arm, being promptly shot before he could do more damage.

Roberts having thus brilliantly achieved his objects, marched back to Sehwan, taking with him Mir Shah Mahomed, seventeen prisoners, two cannon, a standard, and some horsemen of Mir Ali Murad, who had been captured by Shah Mahomed's men two days previously. The heat was by this time fearful, and before the column regained the Camp at Sehwan, at 1 p.m., two European Artillerymen had succumbed to sun stroke. In the fight the losses of the victors were trifling, and apart from Lt Lancaster, fell entirely on the Troop of the 3rd Cavalry, who had two havildars and six troopers wounded, all but one severely, together with one horse killed and seven wounded. This gallant band in their charge inflicted the great majority of the casualties sustained by the Balochis, who left about 90 dead on the field. Four of them fell to the sword of Ali Khan Tehrin, who rode at Walter's side.

OBSERVATIONS

There is nothing obscure about this little affair, and its results were just what Napier required. The Western tribes were deterred from attempting to join Sher Mahomed, and from any hostile enterprises on their own side of the river.

It remains only to say something of the ground: but first a word as to its name. Sir William Napier writes of Peer Arres, Rice Holmes, Pir Awe, Sir Patrick Cadell, Pir Ares. Fortescue escapes the difficulty by making no mention of the action in his chapter on the War in Sind.[46]

Having more than once visited the site, I can affirm that the name of the place is as given in this paper: the revenue map of the District shows it correctly. The final S appended [sic] to their various combinations of letters by previous authors, originated simply in an error in transcription, probably of Roberts' actual despatch. The manuscript of the subsidiary casualty roll seems to have been clearer; for it was printed with the name correctly rendered, according to the spelling of the time, as Peer Aaree.[47]

The locality remains unaltered in all essentials by the passage of one hundred years. A grove of fine trees mingled with dense undergrowth, still covers the grave yard, and is still surrounded by 'an almost impenetrable hedge'. Just to the south of it, may be seen the rough graves of the Balochis killed in Walter's charge.

The grove is watered from a stream flowing from a hot spring in the low hills to the westward, which irrigates on its way lands owned by the Rind tribe. Here the traveller Masson camped with a kafila of merchants on their way from Kalat to Karachi in 1830.[48]

As to the subsequent history of the Units which took part in the engagement, the 6th and 15th Bombay Native Infantry were disbanded in 1882. The 20th is still with us, as the 2nd battalion (Prince of Wales' Own) 6th Rajputana Rifles. The 3rd Company 1st Battalion Bombay Foot Artillery has become the 30th Field Battery, R.A.

Pir Ari was of course too trifling an affair to be made a battle honour; and I have not ascertained whether the troops which took part in it received the Sind Medal. But Napier rightly made it clear, in his Farewell Orders, on the departure of the 20th, 15th and 6th Bombay Native Infantry from the province, in the course of 1844, that they were to be reckoned among the Conquerors of Sind.

SHAHDADPUR

On 1 June 1843, Napier's plans for the reduction of Mir Sher Mahomed were complete, after a month's preparation; they resembled on a small scale, the wide-flung net that Lord Moira spread for the rounding up of the Pindaris in 1817. The Mir was somewhat in the area between Sakrand and Kuhera on the north, and Hala and Shahdadpur on the south; generally keeping not far from the Indus, to the other side of which his family had been evacuated under the care of his brother.[49]

Napier's first care was to secure the river, by patrolling it with the armed steamers of the Indian Navy: not that Sher Mahomed was in a mood to escape to the right bank, but as long as he remained unsubdued, the tribes on that side were likely to cross to join him. We have seen how efficiently the Indian Navy performed its task.

Next, Napier had to provide against the Mir's retreating to the northward: and for this purpose Colonel Roberts was to cross the river opposite Sehwan, while Mir Ali Murad with his own forces operated somewhat further inland, both to move southward.

The General was even more concerned lest Sher Mahomed should break through to the south. He possessed considerable territories in the Delta of the Indus, and this region was so far quite unsubdued. Towards the end of April, Jacob had on his own initiative advanced with a squadron of his regiment from Mirpur to quell insurgents in the neighbourhood of Naukot, but had been recalled by an express from the General after making two marches.[50]

A similar movement of Police down the Indus without orders a month later had caused the General further vexation, for they had been attacked by the Balochis and lost six men killed. He wrote 'We had no business to poke our noses into this southern district of Meerpoor, all around which I had made friendly by negotiation— it was thus isolated and sure to fall without a life lost when Sher Mahomed is crushed. This disagreeable event has, or may, injure my plans much.'[51]

Napier reserved for himself the task of preventing the Mir, when pressed from the north, passing down southward 'to establish himself in the marshes of the Poorana river, whence it would be no easy job to dislodge him, even in cold weather.'

The last possibility was that Sher Mahomed might escape into the desert, north of the line Hyderabad—Tando Allahyar-Mirpur-Umarkot. The General could congratulate himself that he held the latter and had destroyed Kot Imamgarh, another place of refuge: but there remained Shahgarh, still held by adherents of Mir Mahomed Hussein, Rustom's son and it was essential to prevent Sher Mahomed from gaining the desert at all. For this John Jacob was made responsible.

Jacob had been left by Sir Charles to hold down the country east of Hyderabad, with Headquarters at Mirpur and detachments at Umarkot and Tando Allahyar. He was now cast for an offensive role, which the General communicated to him on the second of June; four companies of Infantry were to be sent to enable him to make a demonstration in Sher Mahomed's rear. Napier was concerned at the fearful heat; he had already been prostrated himself, and the troops in Hyderabad were suffering. What of those in the outposts—could not Jacob thatch his tents? Jacob wrote back cheerfully. 'We have no tents to thatch except a few belonging to some of the Native Officers, but I doubt not but that we shall weather it out.' He would be able to make a most effective demonstration against Sher Mahomed from Mirpur; if the General would give him two guns, besides the four companies of infantry he had suggested, the Mir's people would consider the force an army. Meanwhile he had heard that some of that Prince's agents, with a body of horsemen, were collecting men and grain some 25 miles to the north of Mirpur.

On 4 June, Napier noticed the beginning of the monsoon wind, which encouraged him to move: this date also marked the expiry of his ultimatum to Sher Mahomed. He wrote to Jacob:

You shall have two six-pounders, they and the four companies of infantry march this evening, and will be with you on the 7th; and on the 8th I wish you to march in the direction of Kohera, or Koonhera or whatever that rendezvous of the Ameer is called. My reason is this—Colonel Roberts will have the steamers and boats at Sehwan this evening—I think he will cross the river by the 7th bodily, arid land somewhere north of Sukkurund (say Doom), and I shall desire him to march against Sher Mahomed on the 8th if he is able to fight him. On the same day (8th) I shall push the 8th Native Infantry towards Aliar ke Tanda, to prevent Shere Mahomed crossing our line and getting down to the south—on the 9th I will move by the north east through Dubba towards Shah-i-Kaut, which is east of Muttaree, the 8th Native Infantry doing the same to join me: by this I shall be able perhaps to block him to the south, and you will act as you find best on the east.

Napier was anxious lest the movements of his troops should produce merely a dispersion of those of the Mir—'which is his game if he knows how to play it. I would much rather see him with 40,000 men in one point. I like this fellow for his resolute resistance: I will give him safe conduct if he will come and see me.'

Meanwhile intelligence as to Sher Mahomed's movements was perplexing; Napier heard he was making a demonstration towards the south, and halted the infantry and guns at Tando Allahyar, on their way to join Jacob, to whom he wrote on 6 June 'Do you also remain quiet till you hear from me. I want to see my board a little more clearly before I attack Sher Mahomed: it is no joke hunting him in this weather. I shall wait till I hear from Roberts that he is fairly across the river and on our side. Should anything you hear make you think it right to move, I leave the doing so to your own discretion, but in that case send to let me know as rapidly as you can. Every account I can get seems to say he has 1,200 people but not above 800 of these are fighting men.'

This estimate fell far short of the reality. Jacob knew for certain that 300 men had left Mirpur to join the Mir, and there was talk of five thousand with four guns proceeding to Sakrand.[52] The tale of 2,000 men at Nasarpur however proved false, and Napier gave orders for the guns and infantry to proceed. On the 9th they joined Jacob at Mirpur; four companies of sepoys and two guns, under the command of Lieutenant Sir Francis Ford, Bart., of the 20th Bombay N.I., the whole being placed under Jacob's orders.

The information now was that Sher Mahomed was at Hala and in a letter telling Jacob that he might now advance, Napier speculates on the reasons for his clinging to the river, and his probable reaction to the movement of the forces drawing in upon him. Jacob must prevent the Mir from escaping into the desert, from which he and his men might disperse and assemble elsewhere.

Before this letter was despatched Napier was able to add the welcome news of Colonel Roberts' exploit at Pir Ari: which arrived in a steamer bringing down Mir Shah Mahomed. He closed the letter 'Roberts will be across this evening and will bother brother Shere, I suspect … between you and Roberts, Shere Mahomed has a good chance of being picked up.' In his journal he wrote: 'His great object is to cross the Indus to his family, and he will not quit the water for two days; and then probably try to negotiate with Ali Moorad, who has my orders to keep him in play. I have every hope therefore of Jacob getting two day's start.'

Jacob marched from Mirpur on the night of the 10th, and Napier spent the next two days passing his own force over the Fuleli, which was now carrying a strong stream. He wrote:

However it is necessary for me to be a day or two in arrears or the Lion would bolt into his den before Roberts or Jacob could reach him. I now leave him quiet to *mamock* Ali Moorad, if he can: it will do Ali good thus to pull down his vanity. It is said the Lion has shut him up in the fort of Sukkurunda without any grub: I hope he will not get out until half-starved. Ali assured me, when I told him to be cautious as. Shere Mahomed was too strong, that he would capture or treat with him as I wished: that he could kill him, or make him prisoner, according to my wishes—anything I liked! If my own arrangements were not so far in blossom, Shere Mahomed should be left to thrash him for his vanity.

On the 13th, Jacob arrived at Shahdadpur with his force. According to information received by Napier that day, Sher Mahomed had moved south to Shah-i-Khaut, east of Matiari, and that evening Napier marched out to Nasarpur hoping to encounter him and end the war at a blow. Jacob's information was that the Mir had moved to a fort called Oocleyra, some 16–17 miles south east of Hala. Meanwhile the General's nephew, William Napier, wrote to him—'You have Sir Charles' permission to rob, murder, steal, hang and anything else to procure carriage; you may do anything if you can but catch Shere Mahomed: do this, and all your crimes will be pardoned. Roberts is at Sukkurund today or tomorrow. By tomorrow night you will be not far from Koheran. Shere Mahomed's followers have mostly abandoned him and he will try to bolt to the desert. He fears the river and Koheran, and I don't think he will venture South.' Jacob assumed that the Mir's movement southwards might well be the result of Roberts crossing the river in his rear; he had heard nothing from that Officer, but Shahdadpur seemed the best position from which to intercept the Mir should he move eastward.

He was not mistaken. At 11 p.m. on 13 June a Brahmin servant of Sher Mahomed came into his camp and told Jacob that his master was on the march to attack him with his whole force amounting, as he said, to 8,000 or 10,000 men. Jacob pushed his picquets forward, and about 3 a.m. they sent back word that the enemy was coming on in considerable force. He sent several parties to reconnoitre, and finding that the Balochis advanced very slowly, determined to attack them. Leaving a troop of the Scinde Horse and a company of Infantry to protect the camp, he marched with the remainder, about 800 men of all arms.

The Baloch Lashkar on becoming aware of his advance halted and formed on the bank of a *nullah*, horse, foot and artillery, in imposing numbers, and opened fire on Jacob's column with three guns: he in turn formed his line and replied with his artillery. Every movement on the powdery white soil raised volumes of dust; Sher Mahomed and his subordinate leaders seem to have lost contact with each other, add somehow a rumour spread that another British force was about to attack them in flank. A sudden panic seized the Balochis, who broke their ranks and began to withdraw from their position. Jacob seeing their irresolution advanced with the Scinde Horse, whereupon they dispersed and fled in every direction. The ground in their front was extremely rugged, intersected with deep ravines which prevented a charge by the time Jacob had found a way across these obstacles the Mir and his men were well on their way to safety, and among the jungle sandhills and canals running full of water effective pursuit was impracticable: but a few prisoners were taken.

The victory was all but bloodless: five or six Balochis had been killed by Jacob's artillery fire, and two of his horses by theirs. But the Mir left on the field several standards, and three well-equipped brass guns. The prisoners stated the number of their force actually present as 4,000, the remainder, with another gun, having remained behind or deserted. Among their Sardars were Mir Khan Mahomed, Sher Mahomed's younger brother: Mir Mahomed son of Mir Rustom Khan; and a brother in law of Mir Nasir Khan; proof enough that in this last attempt had lain the hopes of the Talpur race.

In his despatch Jacob added that Sher Mahomed had fled with ten horsemen in the direction of the river, and that he would attempt to cross it to reach his family in Rani Kot, and not fly to the desert without them. But in fact, the Mir seems to have fled to the Northward, for Roberts had not been able to cross the river to take part in the hunt. His force was in great distress owing to the appalling heat, and remained at Sehwan. The General, too, had intended to push onto Jacob's assistance with his cavalry and artillery, but on the morning of the 15th he was himself incapacitated by heat-stroke. He was lying half-conscious when Jacob's despatch arrived and this, in the words of his nephew William Napier, 'did him as much good as Doctor Gibbon.'

H.M.'s 28th Regiment, which formed part of his force, had meanwhile lost one officer and twentyone men dead from heat apoplexy, and eleven more died at Hyderabad. Thither Napier was carried in a palanquin, after recalling the whole of the force with which he had advanced. His recovery was rapid, and William Napier wrote to Jacob again 'Your defeat of Shere Mahomed cured him.'

In his despatch, Jacob had observed: 'The conduct of all officers and men under my command has been most steady and excellent throughout, but in an action such as that of this morning there is no room for the display of much military prowess.' But Napier recognized the value of the stroke at such a time. Mir Ali Murad's attitude had begun to arouse his suspicions, and no one knew better than himself that regular troops could not keep the field much longer without fearful losses from the heat. Three weeks later, when Jacob arrived in Hyderabad, after capturing two more of Sher Mahomed's guns, the General told him that at Shahdadpur he had prevented a Pindari war in Sind.[53]

OBSERVATIONS

The only first-hand account of the affair of Shahdadpur other than Jacob's despatch, is that of Mir Khan Mahomed, who shortly afterwards surrendered to Napier. The General asked him why they had not made a better fight of it, as they had twice opposed him stoutly.[54] Khan Mahomed replied: 'Why, General, it is just because you did fight us twice that we did not like the third time, we are afraid of you. But to tell you the truth I knew as little of Jacob's fight as you do. I commanded the right wing, the Ameer the left; he had the guns and I nearly all the cavalry; it was hardly light when I heard the Lion's guns and thought Jacob was upon him, as nothing could be distinguished in my front, therefore I rode full gallop expecting to charge Jacob's hand. You know our horrible dust, I thought I was followed, but when I reached the Ameer he was almost alone; then the dust cleared up and behold only twentyfive rascals had followed me. Had Jacob been there I should have been killed for all had run under cover of the dust: so the Lion and I ran too, that is all I know of the battle.'

The scene of the encounter is a little to the north west of the town of Shahdadpur, and presents much the same appearance now as it did a century ago, the ground being much broken and covered with sand hills. A dhoro, or bed of an old branch of the Indus and the pre-Barrage Marakh canal, which bifurcates close by, were probably the *nullah* and other obstacles mentioned by Jacob.

Shahdadpur, where the downfall of the Talpurs was thus consummated, had been the cradle of their power, and owes its name to the head of their House, who is buried not far away.

Mir Sher Mahomed's route after his discomfiture is still a matter for conjecture. Rathborne was informed that he had in fact doubled back to the desert, on finding that the Indus was too well guarded by the Indian Navy.[55]

Maulvi Abdullah Laghari, of Sanghar, whom I questioned on the subject, says that Sher Mahomed did in fact take refuge with the remnant of his men in the desert; and that if rain half not fallen they would have perished. They worked their gradually northward to the Registan of Mirpur Mathelo, and eventually crossed the Indus near Ghotki and entered the hills.

For some years Sher Mahomed remained in the Marri country inciting the predatory tribes to harass the Sind border: later he sent his sword to Napier, but would not surrender himself. For years he remained the hope of the diminishing party of irreconcilables, like Bonnie Prince Charlie to the Jacobites: the 'Manghanhars' sang that God would grant him the turban of Sind, and on the walls of the mosque at Wateji Richard Burton noted the couplet scrawled by a patriotic 'unemployed'.

O Shere Mahomed, turn the reins of thy steed towards Scinde,
And with one flash of thy brand consume 'Nupeer'.[56]

It remains to say something of the campaign as a whole. Napier was much censured at the time for persisting in his 'wild goose chase' against Sher Mahomed in the height of the hot weather, which cost so many lives. But the best answer to these critics was the complete success of his operations. Once he was committed to a war with Sher Mahomed, to have quitted the hold leaving the Mir with ten thousand men and some useful artillery intact, would have postponed the pacification of the country by six months at least. The most that might be urged is that Napier was unduly cautious, and slow in preparing the combination of converging Forces between which Sher Mahomed's power was finally broken. It must be admitted, incidently, as pointed out by Commander Merriman, that Napier never duly acknowledged the contribution of the Indian Navy to his success.[57] There are many who have been disgusted with William Napier's extravagant eulogies of his brother's skill, energy and foresight; they may point to the lack of military qualities, other than courage in actual combat, among the Balochis, in view of which Napier's elaborate calculation and coordination were uncalled for. His operations were, in fact, such that they would have accounted for a more formidable enemy—no bad criterion for generalship!

We may accept the conclusion of Sheppard that Napier's fame as a general may well be left to rest on this 'little masterpiece of War'.

Notes

1. Munshi Awatrai, *Sindh jo Mir* (Sindhi Mss.).
2. James Outram, *Commentary on the Conquest of Scinde*, 448.
3. Edward Green, *General Orders of Sir C. Napier* (Bombay: Times Press, 1850).
4. William Napier, *Conquest of Scinde*, 369.
5. William Napier, *Life and Opinions of General Sir Charles James Napier* (Vol. II), 342.
6. Seth Naomal, *Memoirs of Seth Naomal Hotchand*, 129, 132.
7. Napier, *Life* (II), 349.
8. Stack says that he halted the column (Miscellaneous, *S.I.H. Records* [Vol. 1], 28), but I have adopted Napier's version.
9. Henderson (*Madras Artillery Records*).
10. Napier to Ellenborough 23 March (*S.I.H. Records* [Vol. 1], 27)
11. Husri is six miles S.S.E. of Hyderabad. William Napier seems to make a mistake here (Napier, *Conquest of Scinde*, 375).
12. Henderson.
13. Napier, *Life* (II), 351.
14. Ibid.
15. Mentioned in the *Bibliography of Publications on Sind and Baluchistan* by N. M. Billimoria (1930).
16. Richard Burton, Scinde and the Races that Inhabit the Valley of the Indus, 84–5.
17. Napier, *Conquest*, 387.
18. Aitken, *Sind Gazetteer* (1907), 138.
19. Napier, *Life* (II), 371.
20. Ibid. 339.
21. Ibid. 362.
22. Ibid. 349.
23. Ibid. 364.
24. Fortescue, *Historian of the British Army* (XII), 299.
25. Napier, Life (II), 402.
26. Napier, *Life* (III), 456.
27. Ibid. 170.
28. Napier, *Life* (IV), 304.
29. Napier, *Life* (II), 352.
30. Miscellaneous, *S.I.H. Records* (Vol. I), 33.
31. Napier, *Conquest*, 391.
32. Napier, *Life* (III), 155.
33. Napier himself uses the word 'ravine' on one occasion (Napier, *Life* [II], 850).
34. The plan illustrating this paper is that given by Rice Holmes in his Life of Sir Charles Napier. The point B should be obvious from the description. Nareja village is shown as Dabo, another misleading feature is the indication of some hills to the N.W., copied from the earlier plan. These were at most sand hills.
35. Cadell, *History of the Bombay Army*, Appendix 11.
36. Napier, *Life* (II), 420.
37. Ibid. 437.
38. Napier, *Conquest*, 379.
39. John Mawson, *Records of the Indian Command of Sir Charles Napier*, Appendix.
40. John Jacob quoted by Outram, *Commentary*, 448.
41. Napier, *Life* (II), 343.
42. Ibid. 382.

43. Ibid. 368; Napier, *Conquest*, 426.

44. Napier, *Life* (II), 377.

45. Napier, *Conquest*, 431.

46. Ibid. 432; Rice Holmes, 95; Cadell, *History of British Army* (Vol. 12), chapter 30.

47. Miscellaneous, *S.I.H. Records* (Vol. I), 43.

48. Charles Mason, *Narrative of Various Journeys in Sinde, Balochistan, Afghanistan and the Panjab* (Vol. II), 148.

49. This place is a little to the west of Shahpur Chakar.

50. Miscellaneous, *S.I.H. Records* (Vol. I), 36.

51. Napier, *Life* (II), 383.

52. Outram, *Commentary*, 448 (footnote).

53. John Jacob's notes on William Napier's *Administration of Scinde*.

54. Napier, *Life* (II), 413.

55. Miscellaneous, *S.I.H. Records* (Vol. I), 44.

56. Richard Burton, *Scinde or the Unhappy Valley*, 80.

57. R. D. Merriman, *Journal Sind Historical Society* 6.3 (1943), 211–22.

7

Memorandum of Occurrences Which Took Place at Hyderabad in Sindh Between 14 and 18 February 1843

Dr Ramjee Gunnoojee

A Short Life of Dr Ramji

ON 15 FEBRUARY 1843, WHEN DR RAMJEE WAS SPECIALLY DEPUTED to quell the disturbance among the Beloochees at the time of the conquest of Sindh under General H. Pottinger and Colonel Green, C.B., he sustained a heavy and irreparable loss of his property and savings of 20 years' active service, that was plundered by the Beeloochees in the attack upon the British Residency at Hyderabad at the time of the said conquest. Yet Dr Ramjee did not care much about this as his important and urgent duties required him to remain even though he should lose his life in the service of the British Government, for he thought that by remaining at Hyderabad Sindh, he could from time to time give valuable and important information to General Sir Charles Napier about the proceedings of the late Ameers of Sindh and expected to receive a handsome reward and remuneration in lieu of his great losses. Although Dr Ramjee lost both his ancestral *Inam* as well as his self-acquired property yet he never complained about the heavy shocks which he received one after another in his old age.

He served as a Medical Adviser and Sindhee Interpreter to the late Ameers of Sindh for about 6 years, and during that time he acquired the entire confidence and goodwill of the Ameers as well as of the several chiefs and principal merchants of the town from his daily intercourse with them in his Medical Capacity and therefore was appointed Special Native Officer on behalf of the British Government for negotiating and assisting in quickly putting an end to the long standing hostilities in Sindh, under the late General Sir James Outram (then Major Outram) and the late Sir Charles Napier, subsequently Governor of Sind.

MEMORANDUM OF OCCURRENCES

The Ameers on assembling in the Kacheri on 14 February 1843, sent for Colonel J. Outram and Captain Brown in order to make a new treaty. While they were discussing my friend named Lowang, a camel driver, came to me and said that if arrangements were not amicably made with their Highnesses by the British Government, the Baloochees had declared that they would kill the above named officers for which purpose they were assembled at the Fort gate.

Finding that no treaty was made and the Kacheri having risen, I clandestinely informed Ameer Nusseerkhan of what the Beloochees intended to do, and if they killed the Government Officers they must bear the consequence and suffer as other Rajas had under similar circumstances. On hearing this, he ordered Ameer Johankhan to escort Colonel Outram and Captain Brown to their Camp safety lest the Beloochees should treacherously attack them.

Colonel Outram, as he was leaving the Kacheri, ordered me to remain there and communicate with him what might happen. When Colonel Outram and Captain Brown arrived at the Fort gate, the whole of the Beloochee advanced against them but Ameer Johankhan prevented them upon pain of severe punishment from doing anything hostile.

At that time I was employed as a Post officer writer at Hyderabad and on 15 February I learnt from a Cossid that an English Dawk from Sukkar and the one I had despatched from Bombay were plundered by the Beloochees on the previous night. I made the circumstance known to Major Outram through Dewjee Jamedar of the Government Dawk. Major Outram directed me to apprise Ameer Nusseerkhan of the loss and to request him to recover the Dawks and to put a stop to such practices as there existed great friendship between the Ameers of Hyderabad and the English Government, whatever might be the feeling of Ameer Roostum towards them. Ameer Nusseerkhan was not in the Fort when I called to see him with the above message but was said to have left the previous day and to have assembled a force in the garden of Ameer Curramally, to which place I proceeded to see the Ameer; but being informed near the Fullalee River that he had started for Meanee, after sending a large force in the direction of Major Outram, my endeavours to see and join Major Outram at this crisis were of no avail. However, I returned to Hyderabad and wrote a letter to Sir C. Napier in which I acquainted him of the attack about to be made on Colonel Outram and also of the preparation to make an attack on himself. I closed my letter and looked for the bearer to carry it to Sir C. Napier, but in attempting to do this I was twice seized and my life threatened by the Beloochees. At each time I was fortunately saved by the servants of Moonshee Chowtram and Moulvy Mohamad Ally.

I subsequently saw Aga Khan and expressed my anxiety that my letter should reach Sir C. Napier and asked him to get me someone who could take it to him. Aga Khan procured me a person to whom I delivered the letter with twenty rupees with a promise of twenty more if my letter reached Sir C. Napier first of all the letters that were sent to him.

Aga Khan informed me that my property was plundered by the Beloochees but that my wife and family had escaped. He advised me to accompany him to Jerruck rather than remain at Hyderabad and be ill-treated, if not murdered, by the Beloochees. This advice

I declined to follow, knowing my duty required me to remain even though I should lose my life in the service of my masters, as by remaining at Hyderabad, I could from time to time give valuable information to the General of the proceedings of the Ameers.

On 16 February, I addressed another letter to Sir C. Napier, G.C.B., acquainting him that there was not a fighting man in the Fort of Hyderabad, that its gate was always kept shut, the Chopdarkhan and Mohamedkhan were in the Fort, that near the quarters of the British Resident three guns and about one hundred Pathans were seen, that in Meanee, Ameer Nusseerkhan, Shahadadkhan and Hoossanally Khan had assembled about fourteen thousand Beloochees to oppose the General, and the Ameer Sher Mohamed was near Alleyar-ka-tanda with his force. I sent the above letter by the Jemadar. On the understanding that the British Government would not fail to remunerate me, I undertook the hazardous duty of negotiating with the Ameers, and at one time I was obliged to remain hidden in disguise in the enemy's Camp to give minute information to the General. A reference to Colonel Outram will procure testimony as to how I managed to render my services on that occasion.

On the 17th, [at] about 2 p.m., the Ameers returned to Hyderabad after the battle of 'Meanee'. I was in the house of Moulvi Mohamed Ally, at the time. I there learnt from a barber that the Ameers were about to evacuate the Fort and to send their families and property to the hills, and to prepare for a siege; that Ameer Nusseerkhan had contemplated to fall suddenly on the British force in conjunction with Mohamed Khan and Cahdhuja Beloochee. On hearing this, I proceeded with Moulvi Mohamed Ally to the Fort to ascertain the truth of their assertions. I saw Ameer Nusseer Khan and Shadad Khan who were sitting together conversing. On entering their presence I related what I had heard and asked them if such was true. Ameer Nusseer Khan answered that he had been deceived, that Major Outram told him that the army under General Napier would not move further than Suckrani and advised him to disperse the large force he had gathered with the assurance that everything would terminate amicably. The General, he said, daily advanced on Hyderabad leaving him in doubt and fear that he had no alternative but to meet and know what course was left to him. On hearing this, I reasoned with the Ameers and told them that it would be madness to make any further attempt to oppose the British. I cited instances of how the great sovereigns of Delhi, Poonah, Sirungapatum, Kabool, and other princes had each in his turn succumbed to the British power. I told them that all India was now under British subjugation and it ought to be their interest meet the British as friends instead of enemies; Moulvi Mohamed Ally entreated the Ameers to consider the folly of resistance and used such persuasion in bringing them to a sense of the danger of persisting in such views.

The Ameers lent an attentive ear to what was said and after I had done speaking, asked who would make their peace with General Napier. I told [them] that I would carry their message and that if they trusted me I would not deceive them. I further requested of the Ameers that while negotiations were pending, they should keep quiet or else it would prevent any good understanding being come to.

It is proper here to explain that a period of upwards of six years from daily intercourse in my medical capacity, I had gained the confidence and goodwill of the Ameers and was aware that, dictating to them in the manner I had done, would not be thought presumptuous. A *mooktiarnama* was then written in the Persian language and signed by the Ameer Nusseerkhan and Shahadadkhan, giving me power to negotiate and they said that they would accede to whatever arrangement I might make with the General to secure the peace of the country. I told them that until they received a letter either from Major Outram, myself or the General on the subject, they should not evacuate the Fort and send away their families and property and that they should not organize any force.

Having informed the Ameers of the above, I left the place accompanied by two Beloochee *sawars* with the *mukhtiarnama* in my hand, and on arriving at the Fort Gate, I saw several chiefs and principal merchants consulting together with regard to the removal of all the families and all the property from the Fort in order to oppose the British Force. I told them of what I had arranged with the Ameers and remonstrated against their proceedings and advised them to remain quiet until I communicated to the Ameers the result of my visit to the General. Finding that they consented to my desire, I started for Meeanee and reached the General's Camp at 3 p.m. on the same day.

Having presented the *mookhtiarnama* to the General, I related the whole of the circumstances which had occurred and sent a message with the two Beloochees that the Ameers should come and meet the General and that they need not be afraid as everything would be amicably settled. Ameer Nusseerkhan and Shahadadkhan, on receiving this message, presented themselves before the General the next day.

8

General John Jacob's Notes on Sir William Napier's
'Sir Charles Napier's Administration of Scinde and
Campaign in the Cutchee Hills'
(with Foreword by Patrick Cadell)
John Jacob

IT IS WELL KNOWN TO ALL STUDENTS OF SIND HISTORY THAT
Sir Charles Napier and John Jacob were alike in being men of
striking personality and vigorous opinions, which they did not
hesitate to express in strong and even violent language. In the days
of the Conquest and in the years that immediately followed it, the
relations between the two were very friendly. Napier recognized
Jacob's exceptional qualities as a leader and organizer. One proof
of this is the flattering manner in which he entrusted Jacob with
the task of raising a second regiment of the Scinde Irregular Horse
and of commanding both regiments. But their relations afterwards
became less cordial. Probably, this would have occurred in any case.
Jacob was a severe and sometimes intolerant critic of other people;
and the element of rodomontade and Gasconade in Napier's words
and actions must have been irritating to the accurate mind and
strong common sense of Jacob. Probably, however, the chief cause
of estrangement was, as Jacob himself suggests, his sympathy with
James Outram in his disputes with Charles Napier and the latter's

historian brother William. Jacob was not merely a friend of Outram; he was frequently his counsellor; and the trend of his sympathies must have been known to the Governor of Sind. As we know from the evidence of Crawford Chamberlain and others, Charles Napier could not tolerate any support of Outram. When, therefore, Sir William Napier's book on the administration of Scinde appeared in 1851, with many errors of fact, (doubtless in many cases due to the author's ignorance of India), with many inflated claims on behalf of Sir Charles and, above all, with a persistent silence regarding Jacob himself and his undoubted achievements both in the Hill Expedition of 1845 and in the guarding of the Sind frontier, it is not a matter of surprise that Jacob covered the pages of his copy of the book with a series of notes, often violent, sometimes unjust to Sir Charles Napier but marked generally by superior knowledge. It is with these notes, and the different forms in which they have arrived, that this article proposes to deal.

In the old Library of the Commissioner in Sind, there is a copy of Sir William Napier's book, with the loan of which I have been favoured, with the following inscription: 'This book with marginal notes in the handwriting of General John Jacob is presented to the Library of the Commissioner in Sind by H. Evan M. James, *olim* Commissioner in Sind, 11 November 1914.' The inscription is in Sir Evan James' own handwriting. Nothing is known of the provenance of the volume, but the well-known bookseller, Mr Francis Edwards, informs me that he can tell by a mark in the book that Sir Evan obtained it from him. I shall refer to it hereafter as the James copy.

In spite of Sir Evan James' statement, made of course in absolute good faith, it at pace appeared to me very unlikely that the notes in the book were (with a few exceptions) in John Jacob's handwriting, which I had seen elsewhere, particularly in one of his diaries once lent [to] me by one of his relatives. The bulk of the notes was in a clear handwriting, almost copperplate. To four of these notes a few words had been added, and on two pages there was a separate note in another hand. These only appeared to be in John Jacob's distinctive handwriting, in addition to the heading on page one, 'Notes by John'. A short time ago, I was able to procure from Mr Edwards another copy of the *History*, also believed to have notes in John Jacob's handwriting. An examination of these showed that they were certainly not in his own script. They were written in a minute handwriting and were often shown in inverted commas. Obviously, these were copied from some other book. On the other hand, examination showed with equal certainty that the notes thus copied were much fuller than those in the James copy, and were also much less guarded in their tone, particularly in the remarks referring to Sir Charles Napier. They were, in fact, unexpurgated and beside them the notes as they appeared in the James copy were sometimes almost anaemic. It may be noted that this second volume appears from a name in it to have belonged once to Mr J. P. (afterwards Sir John) Willoughby (1798–1866). This is not without interest as Mr Willoughby (as he then was) was a Member of the Bombay Government and was one of those whom both Sir William and Sir Charles Napier constantly vilified without either justification or moderation. Further and, I think, decisive light on Jacob's notes is however obtainable from an examination of yet another copy of the *History*. This is none other than John Jacob's own copy, now in the possession of his grand-nephew, Major General A. le G. Jacob, C.B., C.M.G., C.I.E., C.B.E., D.S.O., who has been good enough to let me examine it. This copy is headed by the note: 'The marginal notes etc. are written by me John Jacob', and this is undoubtedly the case. They are written, often scrawled, all over the pages, with numerous letters and extracts from orders inserted. A comparison with what I may call the Willoughby copy shows that the latter contains a copy of all Jacob's notes *verbatim*, and of nearly all the extracts. These notes are, however, written minutely in an orderly manner on each page. In the James copy, on the other hand, the notes are considerably altered and as I have already remarked, chastened down in many cases, though still strong enough in all conscience. They are, moreover, spread over the pages in the same places so far as possible as the original notes in

Jacob's own copy. A further examination of the original notes shows that the amendments and omissions in the James copy were made or indicated by Jacob himself. In some cases, though not in all, the changes to be made are shown in pencil in the original copy, and, where new words have been substituted, these are written in pencil in Jacob's handwriting. For example, the note between pages 14 and 15 in the Jacob copy ran as follows: 'The wretched people were undoubtedly frightened for they knew the power of the British and the General conducted himself like a madman and a mountebank.' Jacob has himself corrected this in pencil so that the last clause runs, and appears in the James copy, as follows: 'and the General so conducted himself that they were in the greatest alarm at what might next happen.' Another alteration to be observed is that all references to Jacob himself are changed from the first to the third. Where, for example, in the original notes he wrote 'I', the James copy invariably substitutes 'Major Jacob'.

The conclusion as regards the notes in the three copies of the book appears therefore to be as follows:

A. The notes in the Jacob copy are Jacob's own, made, if not in the heat of the moment, at least *curtente calamo*.

B. The notes in the Willoughby copy must have been made from Jacob's own copy. If it could be shown that the copy was in the possession of Mr J. P. Willoughby, we might presume that the notes, which must have been of the highest interest to him, were copied for his benefit, by some friend who was also a friend of Jacob.

C. The notes in the James Copy were made from Jacob's copy, with the amendments and omissions made or indicated by Jacob himself; Jacob must indeed have supervised them, and seen them after they had been entered in the James copy, because as already indicated there are additions to four notes and two new notes, all in Jacob's own handwriting which do not appear in the original or Jacob volume.

The question of the notes having been, one may venture to assume, solved, there still remains the problem why Jacob should have troubled to tone down the notes, and to supervise the copying of them in another volume. If he had been merely supplying a copy of the notes for a friend, we would not have expected him to amend them and to supervise such amendment. The most probable solution would appear to be that he intended the notes to be published, or at least to be prepared for publication. We know that Jacob was not averse from the publication of his notes and opinions, whatever the storm of opposition the latter might be likely to arouse. We have only to refer for this to his *Tracts on the native Army of India* and to Pelly's volume *The Views and Opinions of General Jacob*. I cannot, however, find that these notes on Sir William Napier's book ever were published; and if they were intended for publication, it would appear a somewhat roundabout way to re-write them into another copy of the same book. The only other explanation that suggests itself is that Jacob desired, or was asked, to let some distinguished person have a copy of the notes, and thought it advisable to tone them down and make them more impersonal. It may be noted that both the Jacob and the Willoughby copies are in their original binding, while the James copy has been somewhat handsomely rebound.

The old controversies have died down, and both Charles Napier and John Jacob rest securely in the niches of fame which they so fully earned. Their swords are not yet rusty because three of Jacob's and one of Sir Charles' are, to my knowledge, piously preserved. But the rest of the poet's lines are applicable to them:

Their bones are dust
Their souls are with the saints, we trust.

August 1937   **P. R. C.**

General John Jacob's Notes on Sir William Napier's
*Sir Charles Napier's Administration of Scinde and the Campaign
in the Cutchee Hills*

A	B
Jacob's Copy (All Notes in Jacob's Handwriting).	**James' Copy**
p. 1 The marginal notes, etc., are written by me, John Jacob.	p. 1 [In Jacob's handwriting] Notes by John Jacob.
p. 2 How childish are these nicknames. All this is grossly misrepresented. The Ameers etc.	p. 2 This is a mere nickname. How childish are such nicknames. The Ameers etc.
p. 3 Sir C. Napier's accomplice Meer Ali Morad having been allowed and encouraged to seize on their private estates—The Meer was indeed it seems ordered by Sir C. Napier to turn them out of the country.	p. 3 Meer Ali Moorad having seized on their private estates. The Meer was indeed it seems ordered to turn them out of the country.
p. 3 Totally untrue.	p. 3 Untrue.
p. 5 Is this indeed all! Sir W. and Sir C. Napier, the breath of whose nostrils appears to be evil speaking lying and slandering may foolishly think thus; but he etc.	p. 5 Is this indeed all! Sir W. and Sir C. Napier may think thus but he etc.
p. 12 Grossly and absurdly false—this could only have been written by one utterly ignorant of or regardless of the truth.	p. 12 Absurdly false—this could only have been written by one utterly ignorant of the truth.
p. 13 Sir C. Napier told me that I had prevented etc.	p. 13 Sir C. Napier told Major Jacob that he had prevented etc.
p. 14–15 And the General conducted himself like a madman and a mountebank.	p. 14–15 and the General so conducted himself that they were in the greatest alarm at what might next happen.

A	B
Jacob's Copy (All Notes in Jacob's Handwriting).	James' Copy
p. 15 (across third paragraph) This is mere drivel.	
p. 16 (after 'military commissions') I have sat on scores of them and have repeatedly been compelled to swear on the Gospels that I would adjudicate and decide on disputed titles to lands 'according to the custom of war in such eases.' The thing was a pernicious farce.	
p. 18 Driveling absurdity.	p. 18 Absurdity.
p. 18 All this is purely imaginary and was never said or written by anyone but the Napiers.	p. 18 All this is purely imaginary and was never said or written by anyone but the author
p. 19 The Governor expended about two and sixpence a day	p. 19 The Governor expended about sixpence a day.
p. 19 (opposite third para) Contemptible and ludicrous. The abuse and thwarting were all imaginary—everyone was ready to afford aid.	p. 19 The abuse and thwarting were all imaginary, contemptible and ludicrous. Everyone was ready to afford aid.
	p. 20 After 'were kept' in note, the words [in Jacob's handwriting] 'to the great annoyance of his successors.'
p. 21 I have no doubt but; that fifty Mr Richardsons or fifty thousand if necessary could be found ready and willing to undertake the duties of Lord Chancellor for 500 a year—but what then?	

A	B
Jacob's Copy (All Notes in Jacob's Handwriting).	**James' Copy**
p. 25 (penultimate para): 'drivel.'	
p. 29 False and absurd. All pure invention of the Conqueror's.	p. 29 Not so and absurd. All pure invention
p. 36 I travelled about Sinde ... I positively declare etc.	p. 36 Those who travelled about Sinde ... can positively declare etc.
p. 40 Not true.	p. 40 Incorrect.
p. 42 It might have been as well to have said.	p. 42 It might have been as well said.
p. 55 Exactly contrary to the truth ... the very Courtesans of Hyderabad paid a part of their earnings to the Collector.	p. 55 This is contrary to the truth.
p. 58 I paid 250 Rupees a month for permission etc.	p. 58 250 Rupees were paid for permission etc.
p. 65 I might as well give Sir C. N. permission to plunder Portsmouth.	p. 65 Sir C. Napier might as well have asked permission to plunder Portsmouth.
p. 67 This is like chalking the size of the little man on the large one, shots outside the mark not to count. What is the use etc.	p. 67 What is the use etc.
p. 69 Perhaps the Cutchee Hill men were expected to attack the Forts!!	
p. 70 This is false. Malcolm had ... than any of my subalterns, and the historian well knew this—vide letters attached.	p. 70 Captain M. had ... than any of the other subalterns of the Corps and the Historian might have known this.
p. 73 Silly falsehood. Our author presumes etc.	p. 73 Our author presumes etc.

A	B
Jacob's Copy (All Notes in Jacob's Handwriting).	**James' Copy**
p. 75 This imbecile vanity was so lauded at the time that Sir C. said he should give it a dispatch to itself.	p. 75 This 'imbecile vanity' was so lauded at the time that a dispatch to itself was talked of for itself.
p. 76 Ali Akbar … and Sir C. was completely his dupe.	p. 76 Ali Akbar … and Sir C. Napier was duped by him.
p. 76 Shaikh Ali Hoossein was a most diabolical scoundrel as has now been legally proved.	p. 76 Ali Hoossein was a great scoundrel.
p. 79 Impertinent nonsense.	p. 79 Nonsense.
p. 80 But what right in law reason justice or decency had Sir C. to force a minister on Ali Morad.	p. 80 But by what right in law reason or justice could a Minister be forced on Ali Moorad.
p. 81 Though a great scoundrel the man was and is … an enthusiastic sportsman—his debauchery exists in the imagination of the Napiers.	p. 81 The man was and is … an enthusiastic sportsman.
p. 81 A deliberate falsehood. The detachment etc.	p. 81 The detachment etc.
p. 83 This is mere impertinence.	p. 83 What reason etc.
p. 85 This is directly contrary to the fact. The greatest danger was from Sir C. Napier's entire ignorance etc.	p. 85 This is not the fact. The greatest anger was from the entire ignorance etc.
p. 92 I have had considerable trouble—but have at last settled it.	p. 92 There was considerable trouble—but it has at last been settled.
p. 97 Gammon.	p. 97 Nonsense.

A	B
Jacob's Copy (All Notes in Jacob's Handwriting).	**James' Copy**
p. 98 This was a little display of Charlatanism in poor Sir Harry Smith's style ... without effort at display on your part.	p. 98 This was a little display of folly ... without effort on your part.
p. 101 Which is the mountebank here, and which the General?	p. 101 Which is the mountebank here?
p. 103–4 Served as one of my Jemadars etc.	p. 103 Served as one of the Jemadars etc.
p. 107 When I took command I found.	p. 107 When Major Jacob took command—he found. p. 107 [Jacob's handwriting] 'Who was their old master, the 'Luon'! The Chandias and Mugzees might as correctly be described as subjects of France as of Shere Mahomed of Meerpoor.
p. 119 This is a most disgraceful misstatement.	p. 119 This is a misstatement.
p. 121 (after the-words Bengal Army) Sir Charles knew nothing of the native Indian troops.	
p. 122 Are now in my service and have related to me all its details.	p. 122 Are now in the service of Major Jacob.
p. 123 Sir C.N. was well acquainted with the truth, the circumstances having been brought to his notice by me before he left Sinde.	p. 123 The circumstances were brought to the notice of Sir C. Napier by Major Jacob before Sir C. N. left Sinde!
p. 124 (Long extracts from| Sir C.N.'s orders re. McKenzie Affair, and slaughter of villagers).	

A	B
Jacob's Copy (All Notes in Jacob's Handwriting).	James' Copy
p. 128 This is most true. It is delightful target one word of truth at the last.	p. 128 This is most true [added in Jacob's handwriting]. But there was plenty of time.
p. 135 This is most amusing! Seldom was a more avaricious old gentleman ever seen in India. Some most amusing and characteristic scenes occurred at Government House Kurrachee illustrative of this part of the Conqueror's character.	p. 135 This is most amusing!
p. 143 This is all ignorant impertinence.	p. 143 This is ignorance.
p. 145 This is mere drivel. Nothing of the kind ever occurred.	p. 145 Nothing of the kind occurred.
p. 149 Sir C. Napier called them Jacob's Horse, vide p. 70, but Jacob having stood by Outram and truth his name is not now to be mentioned. This is very ridiculous and contemptible.	p. 149 Sir C. Napier called them Jacob's Horse, see p. 70.
p. 149 Nonsensical impertinence. The men of the S.I.H. etc.	p. 149 The men of the S.I.H. etc.
p. 152 Gammon! ... this could not deeply have affected the Chandia Chief.	p. 152 Nonsense! ... this could not possibly have affected the Chandia Chief.
p. 155 These are mere words! Sir C. Napier throughout encouraged robbery and murder on the borders of Sinde by his own showing. It was only stopped when etc.	p. 155 The robbery and murder were only stopped when etc.

A	B
Jacob's Copy (All Notes in Jacob's Handwriting).	James' Copy
p. 155 This is mere cant and hypocrisy.	p. 155 This is cant.
	p. 156 [at the end of note, in Jacob's handwriting] but the buildings now existing are all quite modern.
p. 157 Poor Preedy is of course abused because he was too conscientious to bow down and worship the Conqueror. All this is incorrect.	p. 157 This is incorrect.
p. 160 This is totally untrue	p. 160 This is untrue.
p. 162 Sir C N. said it was made from bhang which was made from the date tree! But in truth etc.	p. 162 In truth etc.
p. 167 Gammon. The swords are—Shikarpore. I have beaten many thousands of them into horseshoes, and they are of iron, not steel.	p. 167 The swords are ... Shikarpore.
p. 168 The border tribes were almost totally irreligious like William of Deloraine.	p. 168 The border tribes were almost totally irreligious.
p. 168–9 The truth of McKenzie's affair was reported by me to Sir C. Napier before he left Sinde so that the statements in the text are willful falsehoods.	p. 168–9 The truth of the affair was reported by Major Jacob to Sir C. Napier before he left Sinde.
p. 173 Notoriously the most blackguard paper in India.	p. 173 Notoriously the worst-paper in India

A	B
Jacob's Copy (All Notes in Jacob's Handwriting).	**James' Copy**
p. 185 This is totally false. Fitzgerald ... were all placed under my orders and all marched under my orders.	p. 185 This is not true. Fitzgerald ... were all placed under Major Jacob's orders and all marched under his orders.
p. 194 All false or highly exaggerated.	p. 194 All this is highly exaggerated.
p. 195 (after 'Wounded on our service') But Sir C. trusted the greatest scoundrels among the natives because they spoke English and suspected honest men. Ali Akbar and Shaikh All Hoosein led the Governor by the nose, and made the Conqueror their tool.	
	p. 199 [added in Jacob's handwriting] The place appears in Arrowsmith's Map of Asia, published in 1842.
p. 210 Not true! McMurdo informed me by letter.	p. 210 Not so! Capt. McMurdo informed Major Jacob by letter.
p. 211 All totally false. Silly empty swagger.	p. 211 Not true. Empty swagger.
p. 220 All this is ignorant impertinence.	p. 220 All this is ignorance.
p. 236 Totally false.	p. 236 Quite untrue.
p. 237 (first note) This is completely misrepresented. The Murrees alone prevented Beejar's escape and long before this time I was directed to make the offer to the Murrees here mentioned.	

A	B
Jacob's Copy (All Notes in Jacob's Handwriting).	James' Copy
p. 237 (third note) They were probably more influenced by that scoundrel 'Punch' whose book is extensively circulated in the Murree Hills!	
p. 245 (end of note) Was solely due to the gross ignorance and mismanagement of Sir C. Napier. Like Sir H. Smith he attempted to frighten the border tribes by empty swagger.	p. 245 Was solely owing to mismanagement.
p. 252 (after 'terrible place Trukkee') About which so much fuss is made in this volume.	
p. 255 Grossly untrue.	p. 255 Quite incorrect.
p. 262 The Baggage Corps was one of the greatest absurdities ever perpetrated by man.	p. 262 The Baggage Corps was a great absurdity.
	p. 264 [In Willoughby copy, in pencil, perhaps written by Willoughby 'not a particle of truth in this truly Napierian effusion.']
p. 268 (after words 'useless to allude to') When the actor is one who might well read a lesson to Nicolao Machiavelii!	
p. 269 This is grossly false.	p. 269 This is not true.
p. 330 It is one continued falsehood. There is hardly a word of truth in the whole statement.	p. 330 Not so. There is no truth in the statement.

A	B
Jacob's Copy (All Notes in Jacob's Handwriting).	**James' Copy**
p. 332–3 The story about Young-husband etc., was one of Sir C.s most gross exaggerations.	p. 332 The story about Young-husband was a gross exaggeration.
p. 333 (at the end of note) Lt. Holbrow of the 12th Bn., N.I. told me that when he was on guard at the gate of the Fort of Hyderabad there were thus taken from the persons of the Ameers' women more than 50,000 Rs. worth of jewellery in one day.	
p. 342 Sir Charles Napier en-couraged predatory habits etc.	p. 342 The predatory habits … were encouraged.
p. 353 Sir C. is very right about this water etc., but why did he not order the work to be done on his own authority? He threw away thrice the amount on his absurd Shikarpore band without the sanction of higher authority. Why not take upon himself a really useful work.	
p. 355 Sir C.s oriental lore is peculiar.	p. 355 The oriental lore is peculiar.
p. 369 A deliberate falsehood. There was no risk.	p. 369 Not true. There was no risk.
p. 370 What is the use of all this nonsense?	p. 370 What is the use of all this?

A	B
Jacob's Copy (All Notes in Jacob's Handwriting).	**James' Copy**
	p. 407 [In Jacob's handwriting] None but the most consummate Griffin would have looked for distinguishing marks or attended to such nonsense as puggrees. To the experienced eye there is as much difference between a Belooche of Cutchee and one of Sinde as between a horse and a cow.
p. 409 Major Jacob (thank God!) had nothing etc.	p. 409 Major Jacob had nothing etc.

9

Letters Received by John Jacob, 1840–1858 and Sir Bartle Frere's Letters to John Jacob (with Foreword by H. T. Lambrick)

Patrick Cadell

The private and demi-official correspondence of James Outram, Bartle Frere, and other prominent public men with John Jacob, preserved by the latter, would seem to have passed on his death, to his elder brother George, whose grandson, the late Major General A. Le G. Jacob, C.B., C.M.G., C.I.E., D.S.O., was in possession of the papers in 1936, and allowed me to make copies for use in my *Life of John Jacob*, then recently begun, and now on the verge of completion.

I have drawn upon them to a much greater extent than Innes Shand, John Jacob's previous biographer.

Members of the Society will find two of Outram's letters quoted in an article of mine in No. I of Volume IV of the Society's Journal for May 1939.

While on leave in England that year, I was on the point, of obtaining access to the other half of the Jacob-Frere correspondence, which had been used by Martineau in his life of Sir Bartle Frere, and was similarly about to approach the Outram family for a sight of any of Jacob's letters preserved in Sir James Outram's papers, when the War supervened.

I have no comment to make on Sir Patrick Cadell's able articles on the letters; my own incidental comments on them, which figure in the *Life* which I hope to get published in England this year, or in 1947, will be found to correspond closely with his conclusions.

I may also add that I have made copious use of Jacob's letters to his father and other relatives and friends, which are of almost equal historical interest: one of these is referred to in my monograph on the Battle of Miani, in Volume VI, No. 3, of the Society's Journal, for February 1943.

H. T. Lambrick

A VALUABLE SERIES OF LETTERS ADDRESSED TO JACOB BY different correspondents is still in the possession of his family. The larger number of them are from his great friend James Outram. If these letters do not add much to our knowledge of historical events they at least reveal Outram's character; too occupied with day dreams, mostly of military glory; too liable to alternating fits of gloom and over optimism, but also generous and quixotic, and marked by an unfailing admiration of his friend Jacob. The next most important set of letters are those from Bartle Frere, when Commissioner in Sind. These deal more closely with Jacob's administrative work than Outram's do, but they show equal appreciation of his value. There is an interesting set of letters from Lord Elphinstone, Governor of Bombay, and several from the Governor General, Lord Canning. It may seem surprising that these high dignitaries should have written personally to one who was a subordinate officer of a Government itself subordinate.[1] Officers on the Sind Frontier were then, however, in a different position from that held by their successors. This frontier was still the furthest limit of India on the north west. Even after the annexation of the Punjab in 1849, it was the easiest route for communication with much of Afghanistan.

---

1 At the time when they corresponded with Jacob he was Acting Commissioner-in-Sind (in Bartle Frere's place).

After the departure of Sir Charles Napier, however, the Province ceased to be a governorship, and, in the language of one letter 'sank into being a commissionership of Bombay'. Communications concerning political relations on the Frontier had therefore, to go to the Government of India through Bombay. The delay caused by the devious journey and the processes of the Bombay Secretariat as compared with the easy intercourse with the Punjab Government, rendered the retention of political power in the hands of the Military Commandant at Jacobabad impossible as a permanent measure. So long as Jacob lived, however, the Frontier was under his control. These letters indicate the exceptional position and character of the man.

Outram wrote with carelessness and haste and many of his letters have no indication of the year or even of the month. They begin in 1840 when Outram and Jacob were already well known to each other. A copy exists of a letter from Jacob to his father, dated 20 July 1840 in which while enclosing the letters of praise he had received for his share in Billamore's expedition, he writes: 'Outram's praise at least is valuable. He is the most valuable statesman and the best soldier in India.' These laudatory terms are singularly similar to those which Outram was frequently to apply to Jacob. When the letters begin, Jacob was employed, at Outram's suggestion, in surveying the land route from Cutch to Hyderabad. Outram was Chief Political Officer in Sind, with the difficult duty of preventing interruption to the communications of the British army in Afghanistan. The first letter dated 19 September 1840, gives the news of Clibborn's disastrous repulse at Nafoosk. Outram blames as did Clibborn, the political officers for not ascertaining details of the route to be followed. Outram anticipated much trouble and wrote to Jacob, 'Come along, old boy, we'll have no mere promenade, like last year.' He proposed to serve in a military capacity, the first in these letters of the many instances of his anxiety, to leave political work for fighting; in his next letter of 2 November he anticipates war with the Sikhs. '50,000 Sikh infantry and 20 guns against a combined Bengal and Bombay

Force, about 15,000 infantry and 20 guns.' That trouble blew over, and by October 1841 Jacob was doing survey work on the Frontier but had already been marked by Outram for command of the Sind Irregular Horse, with political work. The time was indeed an anxious one; it was already due to these two men that the country remained so quiet in spite of the bad news from Afghanistan.

It is interesting to note that Outram, afterwards so enthusiastic a supporter of the Sind Mirs, suspected at this time that they were intriguing with Sawan Mal, the Governor of Multan. Intrigue was inevitable at such a time, and, from the absence of complaint in Outram's letters, the Mirs must have given very little trouble.

Outram is more occupied with the demands of Jacob for establishment to perform his new duties. He addresses a letter to Messrs Jacob and Stanley, Border Reivers (Stanley was Jacob's adjutant): 'Dear Gents, really I cannot apply for this additional Moonshee. I think you should have more bowels for me.' When Jacob made a modest request for Packalis, or water-carriers, Outram writes' 'Have some consideration for me in your propositions. I expect to get some pretty hard raps over the knuckles for the expenditure, I have incurred.'

Outram, however, gave Jacob all the help he could, especially in recruiting his regiment up to strength. Nothing outward happened till General England was repulsed at Haikalzai, when marching to Kandahar. The repulse could easily have been restored if England had shown any determination. He chose, however, to retire and to throw the blame on the young Political Officer, Lieutenant Hammersley, who ought, the General said, to have warned him of the collection of the hostile force. Hammersley was an assistant to Outram who took up his cause with his usual generosity. He writes to Jacob on 7 May 1842: 'I am shocked and disgusted at Hammersley's summary dismissal on England's recommendation. Surely His Lordship (the Governor General, Lord Ellenborough) should have allowed Hammersley an opportunity to defend himself.' Outram's advocacy did no good to Hammersley, who died in August, but had serious consequences for himself. He writes on 30 October: 'The Lord is so huffed at my standing up for Hammersley that rather than fix on me as Envoy with three Secretaries of Legation, a Private Secretary and a Commandant of Escort, which he had officially announced to his intention, he has had recourse in preference to abolish the whole Political Department slapdash. All is to be managed by a General Officer and his A.D.C.s. So long as Sir Charles will remain it will be done well, but after that I question whether the system will work well left to every chance Senior Officer. I am not at all sorry for thus being cut adrift rather than making it my own act by resigning as otherwise I should have done. I am happy to tell you that Sir Charles is determined to keep on your corps whether Shikarpur is retained or not, and that he has strongly advocated the appropriation of Shikarpur as I have done.' A few days afterwards, on 12 November, Outram writes, 'Good bye and God bless you, old boy. I trust we may some day serve together again.'

It is well known how Napier recalled Outram from Bombay to serve with him; how the Governor General's plan of leaving all power in the hands of the General, which Outram had anticipated would work badly with any other General than Napier, was not justified even with him. Outram was unable to prevent the General from being fooled by Mir Ali Murad. The war which Outram, if he had been allowed, would have prevented, became inevitable.

No further letters from Outram are preserved till he had returned from England and wrote, on 29 February 1844, on his way to Gwalior: 'You are a good honest fellow for writing to a discarded and (apparently) discomfited and degraded man. Sir Charles has thought it proper to cut me for acting as he or any other man of honour would have done under like circumstances, advocating the restoration of these unfortunate Ameers to their Estates at least if not their sovereignty.' After gloomy and as it proved, incorrect, prophecies about probable trouble in Sind, he states that he had come out in expectation of war in the Punjab with letters from the Duke of Wellington to the Commander-in-Chief. There was as yet no war and Lord Ellenborough refused to see Outram when he visited the Governor General's camp. Outram had accepted a comparatively unimportant post in Nimach. 'I have to begin again, and am prepared to vegetate at Mandlesaur.' From that place he wrote on 25 June 1844 in a state of even deeper despondency caused by the publication of the *Sind Blue Book* with its reflection on his policy and conduct. 'I have discontinued correspondence with friends in Scinde, because I feared it might hurt the parties who addressed me, having heard of the surveillance exercised over correspondence in Scinde.' Jacob notes against this: 'I told Outram two days back that this was an error.' Outram continues, 'I am undaunted though, like unlucky Joe in Hood's novel, ready to face the gallows as trumps.' He soon after resolved to return to England, to complete the leave which he had interrupted. Fortunately, he was detained in Bombay and thus had the opportunity of serving in the Southern Maratha Country. The disturbances there gave full scope to Outram's talents for personal leadership in fighting and foe political ability in inducing the insurgents to surrender. This was perhaps the most successful episode, in Outram's career, though not of the first importance. It gave the Bombay Government the opportunity to restore him to official favour. Though he first refused the political charge of Sawantwadi, the Southern Maratha Country, because of the treatment he had received on the Sind question, he later accepted the Residentship at Satara, then an Indian State. Thus he writes from Sawantwadi on 2 May 1845: 'Neither absence of time, or self-interest has diminished your kind feelings towards me. I have scrupled to write to you lest the knowledge might lose you the favour of Sir Charles Napier. Sir Charles, really thinking, as he repeatedly assured Lord Ellenborough, that the course he pursued would peaceably settle Sinde, has been compelled to uphold his error by unblushing falsehood.' He goes on, however, to mention Napier's praise of Jacob: 'Whatever else Sir Charles may be, he is the best soldier, next to the Duke, of modern times. His praise is sincere and most highly valuable.'

Sir William Napier's *Conquest of Scinde* had now appeared with its many inaccuracies, and its detraction of Outram. The latter was eager to make his rejoinder and his light duties at Satara gave him plenty of time to do so. This task, however legitimate, distorted his outlook and involved Jacob in the controversy that followed, very much against the latter's will, as Napier had shown him much kindness. Outram, in asking information from him, is careful to say that he has no intention of compromising him, and rather naively suggests that Sir Charles could not object to Jacob's answering specific questions. He admits that Jacob had dissuaded him from criticising Sir Charles' generalship in his battle as: 'unnecessary to my own defence to which you always inculcated I should strictly confine myself. Your generous sympathy with Sir Charles, now that he is in distress, is worthy of you though he is so little worthy of it after the cruel disregard he has shown for the distress of others.' From other letters it is clear that Jacob had warned Outram against personalities and had objected to giving information which might be used 'against his friend Sir Charles'. Outram at first wrote with some pity for Sir Charles as 'a poor old General. I really believe he was misled at the outset'. If he afterwards wrote with excessive bitterness, he had the excuse of the personal attacks made on him in the Karachi newspapers which must have had the approval of Sir Charles. Referring to these attacks he writes: 'Never was a human being so crucified as I have been for years past, and now to swallow the vinegar without complaining would be a blasphemous attempt to copy our Saviour.'

Although Jacob had protested against Outram's eagerness to incriminate Sir Charles, the latter soon suspected Jacob of disloyalty to him. Outram argued that Jacob could be loyal to him without being disloyal to Sir Charles, but this view would hardly appeal to the General. It is fair to the latter to point out that for a long time he continued his friendly relations with Jacob, and in January 1847 gave him that control over the Frontier which was to prove so beneficent. Before Sir Charles left Sind, however, he regarded

Jacob with hostility which could only have been due to the latter's friendship with Outram. Soon Jacob was involved in controversies with Sir William Napier and with the papers under the influence of the brothers, which continued over a number of years.

The letters of 1846 are mostly occupied with the publication of Outram's Rejoinder. After it had been printed in India and circulated among his friends, including Jacob, the sheets were sent to England and there published. From a fear that Napier's friends might prevent its publication, it was issued in two portions. Outram complains that this fear had prevented proper revision and that much that was damnatory of Sir Charles had been left out. It is unnecessary now to discuss the book. Jacob seems to have approved of it, and it served its immediate purpose. As usual Outram passed from despondency to extreme optimism. In March, he hears that Sir Charles has obtained a copy of the Indian Edition through the dishonesty of the Press underlings. 'Thus, in every way, am I sacrificed in the cause of truth and honour.' In May, when he sends his second Indian volume to Jacob, he expects that Sir Charles will be impeached, and in October, when the second portion had been published without hindrance in England, he believes that Sir Charles will not continue in Sind for three months longer, and that the Mirs will be restored.

Outram had, however, another disappointment in 1846. When the first Sikh war began, he had hoped to join the Commander-in-Chief, Sir Hugh Gough, as an aide-de-camp, but the march of Sir Charles with an army from Sind compelled Gough to withdraw his consent as a meeting between Napier and Outram would have been embarrassing. Outram accordingly writes on 8 March: 'This is the most bitter disappointment I have ever suffered in the whole of my life and well nigh drove me mad.'

In March 1847, Outram was still gloomy lest Lord Ellenborough and the Napiers should contrive to procure his dismissal but, as he states that the Court of Directors was unanimously in his favour, he could have had little real fear; and he still clung to the belief that the Mirs would be restored. With his usual partnership he was indignant that the grant of the Companionship of the Bath to Jacob was postponed; 'Devil take them for a Majority and C.B.-ship to the man who has done more than any other soldier in Scinde (after *he* who got K.C.B., a Regiment, a Government and £70,000) and I say even more than the big marauder himself, for *you* put an end to the war when he could do nothing.' This seems to put much too high a value of Jacob's bloodless success at Shahdadpur, but it is likely enough that Jacob's friendship with Outram did him no good officially.

Outram could not be expected to refrain from dwelling upon what was officially called 'a discrepancy caused by a trifling error', whereby Napier's Report showed an annual revenue from Sind of 44 lakhs with only 16 or 17 lakhs expenditure, which was later proved to be a Revenue of 30 lakhs with a civil expenditure of 31 lakhs, without inclusion of the heavy military charges.

In May 1847, Outram was appointed Resident at Baroda, a post with much heavy duties. With Sir Charles Napier's approaching departure from Sind, Jacob seems, curiously enough, to have suggested or believed that Outram would be appointed in his place. Outram sensibly replied that this could never be, as everything he did would be attributed to *zid*. It was Colonel John Sutherland, a well-known Political Officer of the Bombay Army, whose name had also been mentioned for the post, who wrote, 'Scinde will quietly sink into a Commissionership of the Bombay Government', and so the event proved.

Although Outram had published his rejoinder, he continued to criticize Napier and two of his comments on the Battle of Miani have some interest. 'Sir Charles might have won Mianee without the loss of a man scarcely, had he turned his guns down the Fulailee, as he might have done with a little management, and then, slipped his cavalry at them when cannonaded out of their position.'

In another letter he writes 'At Mianee Sir C. Napier was opposed to little numerical superiority for the rabble looking on from the other side of the Fulailee ought not to be counted; only the Luggarees and the few others who occupied the Fulailee who alone fought as did every man of the Bhoogties' (against Merewether in 1847). This, it may be observed, is not a fair criticism; there were a considerable number of mercenary soldiers in the Mir's army and thc Balochis fought bravely enough, if unskilfully.

Outram was highly indignant with the new Commissioner in Sind, Mr Pringle, who, he thought, wanted to take away Jacob's powers upon the Frontier. He wrote to Willoughby, a member of the Bombay Government and a firm friend of both Outram and Jacob 'I hope you will exert your influence to prevent the most suicidal measure which Mr Pringle has ordered in placing the control of the Frontier tribes under the Collector of Shikarpur, or indeed under any civil authority.' The private Secretary to the Governor of Bombay pointed out that Jacob had never been given any definite political powers by Napier. He had managed the Frontier by his position, probably without fully understanding it. Jacob was soon given the powers which enabled him to execute so many useful works though his position *vis-a-vis* the Shikarpur Collector was not defined till Bartle Frere's time.

In 1848, Outram was fully engaged with the problem of corruption, or 'Khatpat' at Baroda but his thoughts still ran on war and in April he wrote on the likelihood of hostilities in Egypt on which country he was sure that the French had designs. The Sind Horse under Jacob were, of course, to take part in the imagined campaign. The outbreak of Mulraj, the deposed Governor of Multan, in May, brought real war nearer. Outram's invariable anxiety for active service was accentuated by the fact that one of the two officers murdered at Multan was his own brother-in-law. He suggested to Jacob that they two should operate against Multan from Bhawalpur, and repeated the proposal to Sir F. Currie, the Acting Resident in the Punjab. He was very sanguine about his plan because 'the fact is we both enjoy the Bombay Government's entire confidence'. He suggested that he and Jacob should be joint commanders, and rightly anticipated that Jacob would 'laugh at such castles in the air'. When he received the replies of Jacob and Currie, he realized that his proposals must be 'considered to be wild speculations'. His health had deteriorated, partly as he believed, from attempts to poison or drug him at Baroda, and partly owing to his having adopted sedentary habits for his laborious work. He had to, therefore, consider taking furlough but determined to spend it in Egypt in order to obtain military knowledge of that country and the adjoining regions. A final unsuccessful effort to get to the second Sikh war instead of taking leave made Outram write on 7 November 1848: 'I thought at last I had the chance of serving with you, which has been my hope by duty and my dream by night, for many years, but it is not to be. There is some underhand machinery to prevent it. The chief took advantage of the order against volunteering to oppose my being employed.' It must to us seem unreasonable that Outram should have resented the application to his own case of a perfectly proper general order.

To Egypt, therefore, he went but even then the severe battles in the Punjab led him to return to Aden in case a chance of military service should offer. On 28 March 1849, he writes from that place: 'How mortifying to be cut out of every chance of seeing military service for the remainder of my life.'

The appointment of Sir C. Napier as Commander-in-Chief in India was a further blow. He writes from Cairo on 16 April vexed at 'the dastardly manner in which our Honourable Masters have succumbed to the Duke. Chiefly thro' [sic] their enormous influence with the Home Press and the cunningly reiterated praise of Sir Charles by the pens of both brothers, though apparently from disinterested sources, the British public have been brought to believe that Sir Charles is the only man to command an Indian Army.' Outram was at this time in very poor health, reduced in weight from nearly 14 to about 9 stone, with recurrence of his head attacks. Notwithstanding, he completed his report on Egypt, and returned to his post at Baroda, reaching Bombay in March 1850. Jacob had been appointed a member of the commission to enquire into the forgery whereby Mir Ali Murad of Khairpur had obtained at the conquest more territory than was properly due. Outram thought this a great opportunity to enquire into the whole of what was called the Mir's rascality, in order that something might be done for his victims, the other Mirs, and he was greatly disappointed when Jacob pointed out that the Commission could only enquire into the specific matter for which it had been constituted. In the next year, 1851, Outram had fresh trouble over the famous Khatpat report. He wrote to Jacob in severe terms about the weakness of the Bombay Government and his letters to that Government were not worded in ordinary official language. As a result, Lord Falkland's Government ordered his transfer from Baroda. He writes to Jacob on 18 October that he was turned out of office. Jacob made a generous offer of financial assistance to which Outram replied on 18 January 1852, 'your most kind offer has affected me more than anything that has happened since I left home, a boy, even to tears. I see no future outside Military Service.' As usual, Outram indulged in gloomy forebodings without sufficient reason. His case against the Bombay Government was unanswerable, and the Directors, though they disapproved of the tone of the letters, approved of his action. The Governor General, Lord Dalhousie, also supported him strongly and insisted that he should return to Baroda, the political charge of which was transferred to the Supreme Government. At the request of the new Governor of Bombay, Lord Elphinstone, Outram went for a time to Aden as Resident, thus again placing himself under the Government of Bombay of which he had so low an opinion. The reason for taking thus a less desirable post was the hope that he might get to the scene of war with Russia. When it became obvious that there was no chance of this, he returned to India and Lord Dalhousie sent him to the important post of Resident at Lucknow. He never lost any opportunity of bringing the value of Jacob to notice and characteristically suggested that he should be sent with his Sind Horse to assist the Turks; but Dalhousie would have none of this. Outram still in bad health went on furlough, and the fortune of which he had been dreaming for so many years at last came in reality. He was appointed to command the army sent to Persia and at once asked for the services of Jacob, now acting as Commissioner in Sind, and a regiment of his Sind Horse. Naturally, there are no letters between the two for the period of the campaign but we know from other sources that there was some friction between them. Jacob records in his private diary that Outram was not the man he used to be, and Bartle Frere, in a letter to Jacob, refers to the estrangement and blames Outram for it. Whatever the disagreement, Outram bore no ill will. Recalled to India by the Military of the Bengal Army and given a high command, he writes on 6 August 1857 from Calcutta that he has urged the Governor General to give to Jacob the command of the army which was proposed to send from Bombay side to Central India. He points out to Jacob that this will be the second most important army in India and writes of his own position with singular modesty, 'My part in the campaign will be very secondary. I shall merely preserve the country up to Cawnpore, and maintain the Commander-in-Chiefs communications.'

As it turned out, Outram earned undying remembrance by his generous, if incorrect, abnegation in allowing Havelock to retain command while accompanying him in the first relief of the beleaguered garrison of Lucknow. Afterwards, Outram assumed his proper command and conducted his operations with credit. Meanwhile, Jacob had been detained at Bushire in command of the remnant of the Persian force till it was too late for him to assume the command in Central India. His presence, moreover, was required on the Sind Frontier and thither he returned without complaint. Only one more letter to Jacob from Outram survives but it is characteristic. Outram, who had become Military Member of the Government of India, writes on 2 July 1858 that he may have to go on leave, owing to bad health and has recommended the Government to appoint Jacob as Military Member in his place, and offers to vacate for him immediately. The offer was in keeping with Outram's generous character, though it is unlikely that Jacob, whose iron frame was wearing out, would have accepted the post if it had been offered to him.

Thus ends the series of letters, which present both correspondents in a favourable light. Outram was too much obsessed by the fixed idea, whether it was the wrongs of the Mirs, his own quarrel with the Napiers, or his dispute with the Bombay Government over Baroda affairs. He was too restless and over anxious for military distinction. But he was generous and loyal with a real hatred of injustice. Jacob was the saner, sounder man, a good fighter, but loyal to his friends, even when such loyalty seemed likely to endanger his own career.

SIR BARTLE FRERE'S LETTERS TO JOHN JACOB

Bartle Frere's letters to Jacob form an even more valuable series than Outram's, and a better proof of Jacob's exceptional qualities. Frere could have had little previous acquaintance with Jacob, nor any military prejudices in his favour. Yet we find him almost immediately treating Jacob with the utmost confidence in all matters of administration and classing him far above his other District Officers. In political matters he trusted Jacob entirely. As a soldier he placed Jacob on almost as high a pedestal as Outram did, and even indulged in one of the day dreams of which Outram was so fond, in which he saw Jacob leading his men in the war against Russia. At the same time he held to his own opinion on the few occasions on which it differed from Jacob's, and did not fail to regret the intemperate expressions [of] Jacob in his pamphlets and letters, in a manner which Outram never attempted.

Frere found Jacob's position ill defined, and indeed a good deal of regularization in the affairs of Sind was necessary. Although Jacob's control of affairs with the Frontier tribesman had been left unimpaired after Mr Pringle's attempt to give the Collector of Shikarpur jurisdiction over the Frontier District, the division of charges between the Collector and Jacob had never been defined. Although he had much political authority and work, he received no pay or allowances for this work for many years.

In his letter of 14 September 1851 Frere, writing about Kelat affairs, remarks on the total absence of recorded information from the time that Outram left Sind till Pringle's arrival. This seems to have been the case about most of the civil work. Nor did the military officers introduced to civil duties reach in most cases a high standard of efficiency. Frere writes in November 1852 'There is nothing I should like better than to pay a 3 months' visit to your frontier, but it is one of the few places in Scinde where I feel there is very little for me to do, whereas elsewhere there is the less agreeable but more necessary task of stirring up men to do what the country requires, and teaching them how to do it.' Again he writes on 12 September

1854 that he wished Jacob could 'cut himself into two or three pieces, a bit for each collectorate'.

Frere's greatest difficulty however came from the processes of the various Governments above him. That of Bombay was still suspicious that something remained of the elements of Napier's military despotism. They tried, moreover, to apply the principles and system prevailing in the long settled Divisions of the Presidency. They were also hampered by the fact that Sind was what is now called a deficit Province, and that all excess expenditure had to be sanctioned by the Government of India. Even the cautious Pringle had been unable to satisfy the Bombay Government's desire for economy. Frere writing to Jacob on 21 April 1853 complains greatly of the remarks of the Government on his establishment proposals 'as if they wanted me to follow Pringle's example and resign'. If the Bombay Government was thus reluctant to agree to any increase in establishment, it was still more unwilling to approve of the large capital expenditure for canals and roads which both Frere and Jacob desired. We find Frere informing Jacob on 14 September 1853 of the Bombay Government's opinion that 'with the silent highway of the Indus, we wanted no roads in Sind'. This view persisted for many years and was one of the reasons why Sind so long continued to be the Province of India worst supplied with roads. Fortunately the Government of India, at least while Dalhousie was Governor General, took a wider view. In the letter in which he mentions the Bombay Government's opinion about the Indus, Frere reports the 'glorious decision of the Government of India about roads', and in the next year they granted a further considerable sum for the Burdika Road. They also approved of expenditure on Jacob's favourite projects, the Begari, Nur, and Desert Canals. Even when the hurdle of the Government of India had been surmounted, there remained the Court of Directors and the Board of Control in London, which did not hesitate to reverse the decision of the Governor General to make grants to Sind. The Directors also, as Frere found when he went on leave in 1856, were anxious to reduce the allowances in

Sind to the level of those drawn, under very different circumstances, in other Provinces. The Board of Control was anxious to exercise the increased powers given them under the recent Act. One cannot but sympathise with Frere when he writes on 23 April 1856 of 'the wretched system of double Government'. He must, of course, be remembered [*sic*] that this machinery of Government, however, clogged and creaking, tended to economy and enabled the system to function with a minimum of taxation. There was little in the way of customs duties. Municipal rates and income tax were unknown and the land assessment was moderate. But certainly the system contrasts strangely with present day ideas of lavish planning, heavy expenditure and inevitably high taxation.

The difficulties of administration in Sind were doubtless increased by the uncertain future of the Province. The union with Bombay was still uneasy, and difficult in those days of poor communication. It was natural that union with the neighbouring Punjab should be suggested. Frere first mentions this on 23 July 1853 when he says that he has not heard a word beyond what was in the papers. He writes, however, from England on 24 August 1856 that the Government of India recommended that the Punjab should be made a Lieutenant Governorship, and that Sind should be added to it. Frere gave his opinion that, while the Punjab should certainly have a Lieutenant Governor, he would have enough to do without having Sind to look after. The correctness of his view was proved during the Bengal Army Mutiny of the next year. The Punjab, while saving the North of India, could hardly save itself and received her greatest assistance from Sind which remained perfectly quiet and orderly. Even before the rising of the Bengal Army, however, Frere had written from England on 9 December 1856: 'We are especially struck with your account of the Punjab administration. After wishing to absorb you and one and all Scinde, they are forced to take your road and use your men and your influence to get money and arms to Dost Mahomed' (the Amir of Afghanistan). Frere complained particularly of the unfavourable attitude of the Board of Control towards Sind, and the unfair system of accounts: 'If they were made out in the same way as in the Punjab, Scinde also would show a surplus.'

The fact that the Punjab and Sind administrations dealt in different ways with the tribes on their frontier, some of whom were common to both, undoubtedly led to a certain amount of friction. We find Bruce of the Punjab complaining of Jacob's unfriendliness in May 1855, while Jacob about the same time complains of the attacks made upon him in a paper of the Punjab Government. Jacob's policy had always been to support the Khan of Kalat in his supremacy over the Murrees and the other Baluch tribes, and to give him an annual cash contribution. Finally, the Government of India agreed to this. Jacob's proposal that Quetta above the passes should be held by a strong garrison was not to be finally adopted for another twenty-five years.

It is indeed surprising that Frere and Jacob should have been able to do so much in the face of such difficulties. In Frere's first year, on 28 October 1851, he was able to inform Jacob that the Governor General had warmly taken up his scheme for the Begari. Frere adds: 'I hope that it is in fair train to be another memorial of your good will to Cutchee which men will not willingly let die.' On 14 February 1852, Frere was able to propose that the colonies of reformed Lootoos (plunderers) should be included in the area under Jacob's control. On 6 August 1853 Frere writes, 'I have asked Government for money for the Noorwah, these, the Begari and the Noor, will be great works and, please God, if they succeed as we hope, will create a new Province and a new Era in these wilds.' On 2 June 1855 Frere writes: 'We will, please God, have the great Desert Canal yet, though this kind of work often puts me in mind of Robert Bruce and the spider.'

These works changed the whole character of the Frontier district, and of its population. They remain, after nearly a century, the greatest memorial of Jacob's activities.

Frere, with an unbounded belief in Jacob as a Political Officer, supported him in all his proposals and sought to have the range of his authority extended, in spite of the fact that, he writes on 23 November 1854: 'The Governor General has Punjabee objections to your being supreme on the Frontier'. Finally, Frere writes from England on 25 July 1856: 'In any matter between the Caucasus and the Sea, the English Government would never go far wrong if they left matters *entirely* to the judgement of one John Jacob who for some five generations of Governor Generals has dealt with our neighbours in the North West, and never once blundered nor been unsuccessful.'

His opinion of Jacob as a soldier was equally high, though here, perhaps, Frere had less opportunity for judging. At the height of the Crimean War, on 8 February 1855, he writes, 'Unless the Czar gives in, I fully expect to see you with your Scinde Irregular Horse on the plains of Russia.' Frere suggests that they should go up the Euphrates, and march by land to Beirut, and thence go by steamer to the Crimea. This was a day dream worthy of Outram, but no one can doubt Frere's sincerity when he writes on 25 November 1856, on hearing that Jacob is to go to Persia, as Second in Command to Outram, that Jacob is 'the best soldier in India'.

The admiration which Frere felt for Jacob as an administrator and as a man, did not prevent him from regretting the unnecessarily trenchant language of some portions of Jacob's pamphlets, and the tone of some of his letters to the military authorities, which brought down on him the rebuke of the Commander-in-Chief in Bombay and the Governor General. Nor did Frere hesitate to combat Jacob's opinion on occasion, though he always did so tactfully. Jacob, for example, wanted the much needed Railway for Upper Sind to be made in a direct line from Karachi to Sehwan over difficult and hilly country. Frere wished it to be made to the nearest convenient point on the river, such as Kotri. He rightly anticipated that ultimately the line would run from there on both sides of the river. Jacob wanted a canal to be taken from the river to Karachi which would serve for traffic till a railway was built, and also would bring fresh water to the Port. Frere points out that a drinking supply from the Malir or Habb rivers would be much safer.

Jacob considered that English, and not Sindhi, should be the official language of the Courts and Records. Richard Burton, in his *Sind Revisited* unkindly suggests that this was due to Jacob being himself a poor linguist. Burton, however, curiously for such a student of languages, holds that Jacob had hit upon the right principle, that everyone should learn English. Frere's answer seems conclusively correct: 'You know that I do not agree with you about Sindee, for I hold it to be one of the first duties of a Government to keep its records fiscal and judicial, in the tongue of the people. I hold that, however barbarous a jargon Sindee may be, we are bound to receive petitions, and record depositions and accounts in Sindee, so long as it is the only language spoken and understood by the majority of the people. Would not your arguments have condemned Petrarch and Chaucer for using Italian and English instead of Latin?' It took some time to realize that Sindhi was not a 'barbarous jargon', but a language of great philological interest, with a literature of its own.

Frere's letters of 1857 were written when Jacob was in the Persian Gulf with the Expeditionary Force. Those of them which were written during the Mutiny of the Bengal Army form a valuable record of the action taken by Frere, and of the quiet and good order that prevailed throughout Sind. He faced the crisis with his usual calmness and good sense. He sent every man that could be spared to assist, in the first place John Lawrence in the Punjab, and later to the disturbed areas in Rajputana. Frere has perfect confidence in the staunchness of the Bombay troops in the Province, and thought there need be no outbreak unless there was military mismanagement. He was handicapped by the brigadier commanding in Sind being old and incompetent, and there were in fact minor outbreaks among troops at Karachi, Hyderabad and Shikarpur but they were easily suppressed and Frere records that these were practically confined to the Oude Brahmins in the different units. Among the people of Sind there was no unrest whatsoever, the best tribute possible to the administration since the Conquest. All this time Jacob was in Persia, and his return was anxiously awaited by Frere. He was designated for the very important command of the Army which was to march from Bombay to Central India. He was able to send most of his troops, including the Sind Horse, back to India, but was himself detained so long that the command of that army had to be given to Hugh Rose. Moreover, as appears from a letter from the Governor of Bombay to Jacob, unrest had appeared among the Frontier tribes, and Jacob's presence was required at his old post. He accepted the great disappointment, for such it must have been, with philosophy and there is no mention of it in the few letters from Frere after his return. The letters from Frere during the last months of Jacob's life have not been preserved, but the collection, as it stands, is valuable evidence of the worth of both men and of the work they did for Sind.

Another series of interesting letters are those from Lord Elphinstone, Governor of Bombay. These begin in July 1856 when Jacob was acting as Commissioner in Frere's absence, and continue till Jacob's arrival at Bombay from the Persian Gulf in October 1858. The first letters refer to a correspondence between the Governor General, Lord Canning, and Jacob regarding the latter's advocacy of an advance to Quetta and the establishment of a Cantonment there. Lord Elphinstone, while admitting the soundness of the move, was doubtful of its immediate necessity or wisdom, as it would arouse suspicion in Afghanistan and would give an excuse to Russia for the course of aggression which she was already following in Central Asia. At this time, Jacob had entire control of political relations with Baluchistan, and was even authorized by Lord Elphinstone to write direct to the Amirs of Afghanistan, though the Governor pointed out that the Chief Commissioner of the Punjab must be the ordinary channel of communication if the Amir, Dost Mahomed, continued to make Kabul his capital.

The letters written by Lord Elphinstone during the mutiny of the Bengal Army show the calmness with which he met the crisis, and sent all possible aid to Upper India. With the exception of one outbreak at Kolhapur, the Bombay soldiers showed themselves absolutely staunch, and the local population nowhere showed any sympathy with the Mutiny to make some trouble. It was, however, with evident relief that Lord Elphinstone hailed the return of Jacob, to resume charge of the Sind Frontier and control the restlessness that there existed.

Jacob had been in touch with a previous Governor of Bombay, Mr George Clerk, through the latter's private Secretary French, who had served in Sind and was a friend of Jacob. At French's request Jacob sent on 4 December 1847 a statement which sets out his policy and difficulties. He says that the Frontier business is the simplest thing in the world to arrange. The difficulty was the ignorance and prejudice of the new Commissioner, Mr Pringle, because Jacob had been trusted by Sir Charles Napier, and everything done 'under a military despotism' must be wrong. Thus, the Commissioner wished to make Jacob responsible for all Napier's policy, with the propriety of which Jacob had little or nothing to do. He goes on to say that some of what he writes may appear to be due to silly personal vanity, but he cannot help that. He continues: 'I am not speculating. I deal with facts and from the nature of my mind disposition and training. I always find it more easy to *do* than to explain, and am quite conscious of want of ability as a writer and speaker which is an immense disadvantage in discussing these things. The previous robbers are now digging merrily at a canal, and are cultivating their fields, awkwardly enough, but with good will. This has been done by making the business of a "lootoo" disreputable and unlucky, as well as dangerous. The alteration in the country is marvellous; everyone is looking *khoosh*. The voice of the people is loud in my praise. Every child knows the value of what I have done, and all are thankful accordingly. This may well be set off against the persecution of the Commissioner.'

There are also half a dozen letters from Lord Canning, to the Governor General, from June 1856 to January 1857. These are noticeable especially for the length and freedom with which the Governor General writes to a comparatively subordinate officer on a distant frontier. He does not hesitate to find fault with Jacob's brusque and not altogether respectful manner of writing, and he does not agree with the proposal for an advance to Quetta. But he expresses his high sense of Jacob's worth, and his entire confidence in him. As an example of this, he authorizes Jacob to correspond direct with the Amirs of Afghanistan.

A further set of letters worth noticing are those from the Hon. Henry Dundas, who commanded the troops in Sind in 1848, and, later in that year led the Bombay column which was much of value in the second Punjab war. He succeeded his father as third Viscount Melville in 1851. His letters are naturally concerned with military matters, but they supply strong testimony to the qualities of Jacob as a soldier. Dundas was an officer of the Queen's army in the days when the sympathy between the officers of that army and the Company's officers was not invariable, and he had only recently come to India. He was not an old friend, as Outram was, nor an experienced official like Frere. Being himself a very competent commander, his opinion of Jacob as a soldier and military organizer has much weight. If Jacob could win the friendship and respect of such a man he could not have been the difficult and pugnacious person that some episodes might lead one to suppose. We find Dundas, after a visit to the Frontier, approving of Jacob's arrangements for its control and anxious to facilitate them, even to the extent of freeing his military command from subordination to the senior military officer in Upper Sind, though this afterwards proved to be impossible. When the dispatch of a force to the Punjab, including some squadrons of the Sind Horse, had been decided upon, we find Dundas writing: 'It is my anxious wish that you should accompany them.' He says, however, that Jacob must himself decide whether he can safely leave the Frontier, and adds that the Commissioner, Pringle, was doubtful about this. Finally, the higher authorities decided that Jacob could not be spared and, to his bitter disappointment, he was not with his men when they earned such renown in the Punjab. Those acquainted with the history the war and with Herbert Edwards' somewhat flamboyant account of the operation around Multan in his *A Year on the Punjab Frontier*, will find some amusement in the view of an orthodox soldier like Dundas. He wishes that WHISH [*sic*], the General at Multan would put Edwards into Quarter Guard to prevent his writing his Don Quixote sort of letters, and talks of the difficulties caused by Edwards' crusades. When the war had been brought to a successful conclusion, Dundas writes 'You will have heard of the immense renown the Scinde Horse gained by the only charge made by the cavalry, and which was complete and successful at the battle of Goojerat. Your men's conduct has been admirable on that and every other occasion. Their discipline and equipment is the envy and admiration of all Bengalees whose irregular Cavalry show in sad contrast to your fine fellow.'

In November 1853, when Lord Melville, as he had now become, had no official connection with Jacob, he writes from Jullundur: 'The organisation and equipment of the Sinde Horse may be said to have introduced a new era in the organisation of Irregular Cavalry for, in imitation of your system, the grotesque appearance which the Irregular Regiments presented in this Presidency (Bengal) armed with their spears and match-locks is gradually yielding to the same armament and system which you were the first to introduce.'

The spirit of the Bengal Army, however, did not change for the better. After the outbreak of Mutiny in that army, Melville writes on 18 November 1857: 'Bad as I always considered the system and discipline of the Bengal Army, I never contemplated the commission of such atrocities as have disgraced this Mutiny. That the Bengal Army would be the means of losing India, I, in 1849, took the liberty of stating to some Bengal officers who were excessively offended at my remarks on their bad discipline.' Melville also approved of Jacob's proposals for the reorganization of the Indian Army. He writes on 23 March 1858: 'I cannot understand the infatuation of the Bengal Government with their infamous military system. They would do well to adopt your system by which they may hope to obtain an efficient cavalry force, which they never will if they adhere to the old system.'

No better tribute to Jacob as a military organizer could be paid.

10

Observations on Baloch Poetry of the Sind Border
H. T. Lambrick

LONGWORTH DAMES' *POPULAR POETRY OF THE BALOCHES*
contains the fruit of many years' gathering, in inquiry and study by
an authority, whose knowledge of the subject, and of Baloch tribal
history and sociology, is not likely ever to be equalled in depth or
extent. Yet in one respect the collection must be deemed deficient.
The 'more recent war-ballads', which form the second category in
Dames' classification, and which he notes as 'mainly accounts of
inter-tribal wars during the past hundred and fifty years' (he writes
about 1900) are drawn almost exclusively from among the tribes
which inhabit the Derajat.

This seems to have been due mainly to the accident that Dames'
service as a District Officer began in Dera Ghazi Khan—it is noted
of many of these poems that they were recorded by him there in
the seventies—and he does not seem ever to have acquired an equal
knowledge of the Baloch tribes of Kachhi and the Sind Border
Country. His selection was evidently not confined to the former area
on the ground of the superior intrinsic merit of the poetry associated
with it, for he speaks disparagingly of the obscurity, tediousness, and
copious admixture of non-Baloch words in several of the ballads
he includes.

The only poems of this 'later war ballad' class in Dames' book, originating among other than Derajat tribes, come from their immediate neighbours in the Suleiman Hills: one records a fight between the Bugtis and the Drishaks, and another, a raid by the Marris on the Musa Khel Pathans. There is only one poem in this collection concerned with events which seem to have taken place towards the Sind border of Balochistan.

Considering the number and importance of the Baloch tribes located in Kachhi and Upper Sind, it is hardly to be supposed that their feuds should not have been chronicled in heroic verse by their bards. Many such ballads do in fact exist: but there is a much stronger ground for holding the group 'later war ballads and other tribal poems' given by Dames, to be insufficiently representative of Baloch poetry of the period.

By a coincidence, only the three individual lays already mentioned can definitely be held to have been composed in the nineteenth century, apart from the two ballads on Sandeman's expedition and the elegy on the death of Nawab Jamal Khan. The Bugti-Drishak fight, and that between the Mazaris and the Brahuis, seem to have taken place at the beginning of the century. But the fifty years or thereabouts which followed, up till Sandeman's march in 1867, are represented only by a single ballad, dealing with a petty and unsuccessful raid.[1]

Now let us consider what was going forward in Balochistan during these fifty years, for which Dames has produced a single ballad, not altogether devoid of intrinsic merit, but recording an unimportant and uninteresting foray.

Is it conceivable that Baloch bards, who could draw inspiration from such affairs, failed to celebrate worthily the events which made this half century the most stirring period in the whole history of their race since the golden age of Mir Chakar? Could they have neglected the novel and heroic theme of their collisions with the British power?

Did no poet sing of Jaro and Darya Khan, the Jakhrani horsemen whose swords reaped a harvest of loot from the clumsy columns of the Company's Army, in the days when Bijar Khan Dombki contemptuously refused to enter service with the Faringhi with a monthly salary of three thousand rupees? When Amiel's Pathans were routed, and the Sind Horse foiled in the quicksands of Uch? True, fortune is fickle: Walpole Clarke rides down the tribesmen in the Tegaf valley, and the old fox Bijar surrenders when Billamore stops the earths of the hill country. Released, he returns to Phulaji, and now serves the Sarkar faithfully, even in the days when its *Iqbal* seems to sink under the clouds of Kabul. But Jacob's strong hand, that held him fast, is removed for a while: the Jemadar of Guides once more becomes the Robber Baron, and sends fire and sword into Sind. His men sack Kambar under the eyes of the 'Shutar Sawars', the Bengal Cavalry flee before them, the Faringhis who come to storm Phulaji go back in disgrace.

Napier rouses himself, thirsting for Bijar's blood: yet, when he has him in his power, he relents, and hands the Chief over to Mir Ali Murad. So Bijar Khan dies at Khairpur, and his old comrades in arms, settled at Janidero, beat their swords into reaping hooks, under the magical influence of Jacob.

Nay, the twenty years immediately before the appearance of the Feringhi in the land make a prelude crowded with romantic incident: the stage is already held by figures whose names were to find in the printed page of the English a fame far wider than their household minstrel's proudest boast.

Here is Wali Mahomed the Chandia Tumandar, who helped the Talpurs to their throne and defeated all his neighbours, the Magsis, his bitter rivals, and the Marris and Khidrani Brahuis, in their own hills.[2] To him at Ghaibidero rides young Ahmed Khan Magsi, at night, alone.[3] The Rinds in overwhelming numbers threaten to exterminate his tribe. He has come to absolve the Chandia Sardar of his father's blood and craves his alliance. Wali Mahomed recalls how years before, in the days of Mir Nasir Khan, Sobha Chandio fell by the side of the Magsi Chief Bhut at Shoran, under the swords of the Rinds. Generously he forgets the later feuds, and marches with Ahmed Khan; the tide is turned and the Rinds are beaten: they renew the attack with overwhelming numbers: seven thousand, led by Sardar Khan and his brother Sher Mahomed, meet less than two thousand Magsis and Chandias. That day is remembered as 'Sher Mahomed Rosh'.[4] Seven hundred Rinds are slain, and only eighteen on the other side, among the water channels of Bhunga, in sight of the walls of Jhal. The Magsis proceed to the attack of Shoran: the Khan himself applauds the chastisement of Rind arrogance, and their sardars seek safety in Sind.

What of the Bugtis? The Sikhs, who took Multan in 1818 have penetrated southward along the Indus. The Governor of the Khan of Kalat in Harrand Dajil, Syed Mahomed Sharif, betrays the country into the hands of the unbeliever. The Sikhs stir up the Mazaris against their ancient foes, the Bugtis, and march with them into the hills. But Bibarak Khan routs them at Drinak, and the Khalsa kettle drums are hung in the inviolable shrine of Pir Sohri. Again the Mazaris invade, but are worsted, and the long jezail that bears the name of Mir Bahram is added to the trophies at Bibarak Dera.[5]

Meanwhile the Kalpar section of the tribe takes to plundering in Kachhi. Mehrab Khan of Kelat determines to assert his authority by force of arms, and marches six thousand Brahuis into the hills. With them are Dombkis, and Turk Ali Jakhrani. Bibarak Khan sends his Begum to the camp to ask for terms.[6] She is told that in acknowledgment of this sign of submission, the Brahuis will marry the Bugti women instead of enslaving them. Bibarak retires to the hills above Marava. Slave or free, the women of the Zarkani shall never sit in Brahui houses.

They are placed in a sangar on the edge of a precipice, and to each is given a knife. Their husbands and sons and fathers are to fight for them before their eyes, and if the tribe is broken they must not survive. But there may be those among them who will hesitate to strike home. Four old men with drawn swords are posted to slay the faint hearted, and throw their bodies over the cliff. Now the Brahui host is coming up the Siahan incline, between two ravines. In the narrowest place the Bugtis have built a sangar, where matchlockmen are stationed. The swordsmen massed behind them are strictly ordered not to charge before the enemy shall have advanced within the range of stones which they have piled up as missiles. But Bahram Mundrani and another hero brook no restraint, and rush sword in hand upon the foe. Their comrades pour after them: the foremost Brahuis turn to fly, but those behind are pressing on. The weight of numbers is their destruction on such confined ground. The whole mass is thrown into confusion: on either hand the ravines hem them in. They begin to stream backward down the hill in utter rout. The pursuit and slaughter continues down to Marwar in the Siahaf Valley. That day, it is said, Brahuis were seen to kneel down with grass in their mouths: they were as sheep and oxen before the Bugti warriors, the victors of Siahan![7]

The Kalpars turn to harrying the Buledhis, once the lords of the hill country, but now settled in Upper Sind under the rule of Khairpur.

Mir Sohrab Khan vows that the men of the plains shall carry off an even greater booty from the hills, and sends six thousand men under Gole Shah Khyheri. Jalal Khan Dombki, Turk Ali Jakhrani, and Masti Khan Marri march with the Mir's lashkar. Bibarak ensconces himself in the stronghold of Traki, and plays for time by negotiations. The Khairpur army, camped at their ease in Siahaf, are lulled into a false security—success seems certain. Suddenly the Bugtis launch an impetuous attack. The Mir's forces are broken: several chiefs are among those left dead on the field, and Gole Shah, escaping with the loss of an arm, flies back to Sind with the discomfited survivors.[8]

Now the British make their appearance, and Bibarak's star begins to wane. Major Billamore puts an end to the Bugti boast, that even God could not touch their Khan in Dera: the Chief is haled before the Great sahib, and is immured in the island fortress of Bukkur; yet fortune smiles again, and he is allowed to end his days in the halls of his fathers, his tribe still unsubdued.[9] Islam Khan, whom he has ever refused to summon into Sukkur at the behest of his captors, succeeds to the 'Pag'; secure in his hills he sees the new Faringhi General conquer Sind. Soon comes Shaitan-ka-Bhai northwards, with an army ten times as numerous as Billamore's. The Chief bows before the storm—he will not resist, neither will he surrender. He finds asylum with Mir Haji Khetran, and the General departs perforce, but ill-contented with a lesser prey. Ere long comes the opportunity for revenge, and the Bugtis plunder almost up to the walls of Shikarpur: 10,000 cattle are driven before them back to the hills. The Feringi Rasala follows them, and the tribesmen prepare to fight a rear guard action at Hudu. But the Company's men only stand looking at them. A single Bugti is killed by a long-range matchlock ball. Then the pursuers turn their horses' heads towards Sind, and the hills resound with Baloch laughter.

But soon there is talk of another Sahed, another Rissala, another *bandobast* at Khangarh. The *rahzans* who ride into the plains do not return. The harvest has failed in Siahaf and Marava, but is abundant in Sind and Kachhi. Every man who can wield a sword must go: the hated Khyheris, the spies of the British, shall supply the granaries of Dera. Who could have foreseen the disaster of Ambu's day, when they fell like corn under the sickle at Zamani, where Merewether rode like Azrail? The young men gave up their lives, but held fast the honour of their tribe, even though its power is broken.

But Jekam is not satisfied: he plans to take the Chief prisoner. Islam Khan swears that if he must surrender, it shall not be to him. He rides to Kashmor to Rassaldar Alif Khan, who brings him before Major Goldney. And so the exile at Mahmud Dero begins. By the muddy waters of the Ghar the Chief sighs for sparkling Siahaf: after the air of Pir Koh he cannot breathe the stifling heat of the Sind bazars. Alif Khan whispers that the British intend to turn the Bugti captives into sepoys, drill them and send them to fight the men of Kandahar.[10] And Ghulam Murtaza sends word that the remnant of the tribe is being overwhelmed by the Marris and Mazaris: his father must return, and he is willing to take his place.[11]

And so the Chief steals away, with valiant Alim Khan Kalpar: even the sleepless Jacob is outwitted, and finds his work undone. The Kalpar Sardar rides again.

Yet the success of old days evades Alim Khan: the stern horsemen of Hindustan baffle him at every point. Islam Khan learns the lessons of adversity. Half of his best men are still in Sind, with his Begum, Mai Mahindi: how can he resist the Marris and Mazaris with but half a tribe? The women murmur, and Jacob's voice is heard: 'The Sarkar is generous; but you must submit to it, and obey my orders.' Islam Khan makes overtures through the Khan's Wazir, Baloch Khan Dombki, who has prospered by friendship with the British, will be his *zamin*. All three wait upon Jacob at Khangarh, and the Bugti Chief makes his peace: his wife and the men settled at Mahmud Dero are allowed to return to him, and Alim Khan, the prince of freebooters, is persuaded to take service with the Faringi!

And so prosperity returns to the hills, and the tribe regains its strength: though they raid no more into Sind, they will tolerate no insults from their neighbours. Witness the day of Chambari, when eighty mares, and the arms of one hundred and thirty Marris, left dead on the Sham plain, were added to a booty of fifteen thousand head of cattle! All Balochistan owns that the pattern of strength and bravery is Ghulam Murtaza Khan.

In forty years, what people have experienced more dramatic vicissitudes? Here was a rich field for the labours of Baloch bards; but if the blood of heroes, the prices of valour, be their argument, what of the day when one tribe measured its strength against the Sarcar—the Company Bahadur in full force of infantry, horsemen and artillery—and prevailed? When the spoil was not a parcel of sheep or goats, but cannon, chests of silver, tents, horses, camels and pack-bullocks, small arms, gunpowder, and ammunition; all the panoply of the regular troops of the Faringi defeated at Naffusk?

To celebrate such a triumph, a poet was not wanting; indeed, two have claimed the authorship of the stirring verses which have survived, transmitted from mouth to mouth for a hundred years, to find now, as I believe for the first time, the wider currency that print can give.

The first mention of a Baloch poem on the battle of Naffusk occurs in a letter from Captain French, Assistant Political Agent, Sibi, at the time to C. R. Williams, whose brother was killed in the action: 'I was on outpost duty at Lehree, in Cutchee, near the Murree hills soon after the defeat of Major Clibborn's force, and frequently had the wandering bards of the country to chaunt of an evening their historical ballads. They extemporized and introduced the names of those who fell at Naffoosk and Surtoof, and with great praise of their gallantry.' This letter is quoted in *The Defence of Kahun* by C. R. Williams and those who wish to know why the British fought the Marri tribe cannot do better than read this little book but, in view of the fact that it is scarce, I may be permitted to refer them to an article in the Society's journal for May 1936, entitled 'The Marri Rising, 1840'.

But here we are concerned with the other side of the medal: let us lay aside for a while the Report of the Clibborn Commission, and 'Kahun' Brown's journal, and E. B. Eastwick, and the Regimental Histories; and let Meski son of Haren, Ramezai Bugti, take up the tale.

A Baloch ballad is always prefixed by a few phrases in prose, giving the name of its author and the subject of the poem. These are sung by the minstrel on the key note of the chant to which the ballad itself is to be recited.

The version which I have attempted to translate is the fullest and best of three which I have obtained, and was taken down from the lips of an aged bard in Upper Sind Frontier District. The late Tumandar of the Bugti tribe and his cousin, the late Sardar Islam Khan, gave me great assistance in writing it out, as the bard recited line by line, and were able to correct him here and there. They assured me that the result is the authentic poem, with which they had long been acquainted.

A shorter version, containing many of the same lines, is ascribed to one Jam Khudadad, but is considered plagiaristic.

———

Meski son of Heren sings: of the battle of Naffusk he sings:
of the victory of the Marris over the unbelievers he sings.

———————

I call to mind God, the maker of the earth; the beauteous Prophet, with the blessed rider: the generous Suhri comes to the help of all.

Fiery Dost Mahomed with his green-flashing blade, routed Shah Shuja from Kandahar. He went to Calcutta, bag and baggage, and immediately complained to the Sahebs. The countless army of the Company was set in motion: who can withstand the 'Sahibs' order? A Crore of men were assembled, lakhs added to thousands; the far-smiting musketeers could not be reckoned for number, with helmets on their heads, and feet shod with shoes; and thousands of horses were caparisoned for war.

They crossed the river, and came over to this side: the world, deceived, was taken to be shared out as spoil. A thousand praises to that Turk's son, generous Mehrab, the sword-wielder, who bound men to resistance in the game of war! He did not deliver his city into the hands of the white men, but gave his life in defence of his women-folk. Nasir Khan, thou art like a rose in a rich garden; thy name and fame spread all around, to far-off Delhi and verdant Kandahar: that thou mayest sit in thy country and ancestral lands, may Kelat be granted to thee for thy whole life!

Noble Bijar, and the lion-like Bibarak Khan cherished hope, and waited on the Saheb. They were imprisoned for a year, across the River.

Khans and Sardars were affrighted: they went to the white rulers with folded hands; taking rewards and pensions, they returned home pleased at heart.

The storm clouds burst over the land of Siahaf, and floods came down to Chattar anti the gates of Lahri. A thousand praises to the Marris of Kahan, the Balochis that stood firm in the land of the Prophet! Doda Marri sent back this reply: 'neither will I be tributary, nor will I sit among the unbelievers. I will thrash their heads and skulls with the sword!'

This news soon spread about the land; the foreigners' horsemen were made ready, and the cruel tribe of unbelievers mounted. With them were thousands of blacksmiths and syces; two lakhs of camels and a lakh of soldiers; men and beasts of burden of every sort together. They did not invoke God's name, that he should bring them to Karan, nor did the unbelievers think of war or battle. But we called to our Pir, that he should save us, and prepared to give battle at the pass of Naffusk.

The foreigners' kafila of camels wended its slow way: they went for two calls' distance and took their ease. They set up their engines of war and cannon and tents, drinking wine and fierce intoxicants. The cowards were spitting at the skies; the unbelievers made a thousand boasts—'we shall capture the Sardar of Kahan and make him our vassal.'

The Marris girt on them Indian sword-belts, over their lordly silken robes, and swore to devote their heads to death. First rode Bin Mahomed on his hawk-swift filly: the whole of the Gazanis were with the Khan. Karam Khan came, the Sherari wise in council: Haibat Khan roared like a tiger 'I shall smite their kafila, and loot their treasure, strike off their heads, and cut out their tongues: the cowards shah go back feeding on their shame.'

The night gave place today as the dawn appeared, and the Marris began the fight with the foreigners: the deadly muskets and cannon roared out. As the morning drew on towards noon, the bold men of the foreigners gave up hope of an easy victory. They decided to charge, and came clambering up the hill; a precipice fell upon their heads; from the summit it rolled them down the slope. The world quivered at the cannon's voice; the ground was hidden by the smoke of the musketry: but the tigers of the hills swept and drove them back! Their leaders fell back on to the level plain, and considered where to take up their position: the guns that had failed once more roared out again, flashing forth amid hot smoke. The Marris divided their front into two columns; Karam Khan fell with eighty four men. Mura Khan passed through the cannon's thunder bolts; Qatal escapes the death-dealing guns; the Merciful One preserved them in his strength.

They will drink the cups of God's grace with the Friends. There, where the Lord's drums sounded, the unbelievers fell, removed from his Presence.

There, too, fell as martyrs youths of high descent: in a moment four-score were wedded to death. I know not the name of all the heroes. The lordly Haibat, with his mare, beyond price; Mura Khan, the most beauteous of his generation: Lion-like Shahali, a paragon of strength and swiftness, with shining blade, handed down from his ancestors—the sword-cuts on the cannon are his witnesses!

Where was Lunar, the stalwart of the Muhammedanis, who ate his lawful produce on the high hills? The good Jarwars, with Mir Shahali, went as one man among the swords! They have sat down in Paradise before the Prophet: but the foreigners lay scattered, one upon the other. The Marris trod them under with their swords, and the bodies of the unbelievers lie like reaped *karbi*. For two years the hyenas of the ravines were filled, and the ravenous kites and vultures of the sky: the door was thrown open, to the hungry, and many obscure animals waxed fat upon them.

Generous Doda, valiant Sardar! Ali came to thy aid with his holy power. In this battle that was joined with the unbelievers, the Marris won by stroke of sword. Do not then make plans to fight with us; the Quran is between us, and Sohri on his chestnut horse. As two brothers we have sat next to each other—do not come treacherously across our border! You have wielded your swords with your own hearts' strength: the peoples near and far are thankful. Holy Ali gave you the victory, and all should repeat the 'kalima' of the Prophet.

Notes

Lines 1–3: A Baloch heroic poem always opens with an invocation of this kind. The 'Blessed Rider' is Hazrat Ali, who had a famous mare, Dul-Dul. Ali is held in particular veneration by the Balochis: they consider themselves to descend from Mir Hamza, who was Ali's uncle. The mention of Pir Sohri, the saint of the Bugti hill country, naturally follows, as the bard is a Bugti.

Lines 4–7: The poet alludes to Shah Shuja's defeat in his expedition to regain his lost throne in the year 1834. The British did not in fact decide to restore him till 1838.

Lines 8–9: E. B. Eastwick gives us a specimen of the Balochis' habitual exaggeration of numbers in assuming 'three lakhs' as the total of the Army of the Indus which marched to restore Shah Shuja. It was in fact about 25,000 strong; but five times that number of followers accompanied it.

Lines 15–25: The attack of the British on Mehrab Khana and the storming of Kalat were, in reality, unjust, as it was not the Khana but his treacherous Wazir who had directed hostilities against the army in the Bolan Pass. This passage shows that the poem was written before the autumn of 1841, when the British Government attempted to repair some of the injury they had inflicted, by recognizing Mir Nasir Khan, son of Mehrab, as Khan, in place of Shah Nawaz, whom they had elevated to the masnad.

Lines 26–28: The poet naturally makes no mention of the fact that the authorities in Upper Sind had made friendly advances to Bijar, and offered him a substantial consideration if he would refrain from harassing them, in vain. His surrender, after Major Billamore's force had more than once cut up his men, and made his position untenable, was unconditional.

Bibarak Khan, the Bugti Tumandar, had not personally engaged in hostilities against the British—but his tribe had done so.

Lines 37–40: Doda Khan, the Marri Tumandar, in fact wished to avoid having anything to do with the British. When first invited to pay his respects to the political agent he avoided doing so on the score of old age. But he put no obstacles in the way of the Column of Billamore's force which marched to Kahan, and seems to have done his best then, and thereafter, to restrain his unruly clans. When the bolder spirits of the tribe annihilated Walpole Clarke's detachment he said, 'There you go, selling your country for a few camels', and his conduct to Lewis Brown left nothing to be desired.

It will be observed that the poet says nothing of the presence, for over three months, of a British Force in the Marris' capital.

Line 44: Again poetic exaggeration. Clibborn's relieving column numbered about 1,000 fighting men, with 1,100 camels and 600 pack-bullocks.

Line 52: The progress of the British Force was in fact very slow. They had great difficulty in finding water for men and animals, and the latter were so exhausted that the steep ascent of Sartaf took many hours.

Line 61: Sardar Din Mahomed was son of Doda Khan, and apparently directed the defence of the Naffusk Pass. Doda Khan himself sat under a *khabar* tree in a sheltered place in the pass, from which he could see the fight.

Lines 68–84: The description of the engagement accords with the British version. Vide—a private letter of Lieutenant Fanning, quoted in the 'Defence of Kahun' by Williams, and Clibborn's official report, reproduced in 'the Marri Rising', by the present author.

Lines 85–102: The eulogies of individual heroes are a regular feature of Baloch (and most other) war ballads. Karam Khan and Haibat Khan are both mentioned by Brown in his Kahan Journal. Eastwick mentions a 'most distinguished chief' who 'actually thrust his shield against the mouth of a gun as it was about to be fired, and was blown away from it'.

I was informed by the late Sardar Islam Khan Bugti that this hero's name was Tota Sherani, who thrust his 'guri' or coat into the muzzle of the gun. He also told me that Shahali, who is mentioned as having left sword-cuts on the gun (they are still visible) killed an artillery man with an axe just as he was firing.

Lines 106–107: Captain Brown states, in a note to his journal, that he managed to have the dead of the British force, over whose bodies he had to pick his way down the pass of Nuffusk, buried by Mundu Khan Dombki and some of the Marris who took part in the fight. This seems to have been in January 1841 (*vide* Postans' account of affairs in Upper Sind and Kachhi in 1839–1841). The Marris themselves honoured their opponents for the dauntless courage they showed in the fight, and Din Mahomed returned the sword of Ensign Williams, who was killed among the foremost, with an encomium on his bravery.

Line 115: The poet is a Bugti. The two tribes were and are great rivals, but on this occasion the Bugtis could not but be delighted by their neighbours' triumph over the Faringi, from whom they had suffered themselves severally a few months before.

Line 116: The shrine of Pir Sohri is on the hill (Pir Koh) which divides the Bugti from the Marri country. Red is the colour associated with Sohri, who is thus represented as riding a chestnut horse.

1. *Illahi yad kharan kar dighara*
2. *Nabi sohanrava gon sagh zawara*
3. *Sakhi Suhri madaten karkasara.*
4. *Jaren Dost Mahomed wa savzen saghara*
5. *Sijawal thelithi zha Qandhara*
6. *Shutha dan Kalkate gon lad wa bara*
7. *Shitabi danh dathi Sahebara.*
8. *Charitha urd Kampani be-shumara,*
9. *Hukum Sahave sahen khyara?*
10. *Karor melithant, lakh gon hazara,*
11. *Niya jagh janokhen tuparaka*
12. *Sarena hol, jhala phazguzara,*
13. *Hazaren markhavo poshezghara.*
14. *Darya langho khutha gwast zha para*
15. *Jahan pharampto giptia pa bahara.*
16. *Hazar shahbashen ba Turk bachwara*
17. *Sakhi Mehrab mian wa zualifqara*
18. *Muhada bastaghanti jang dahara!*
19. *Na dathi shahar pa dasta sahevara,*
20. *Sire dathi pa la jane guzara.*
21. *Nasir Khan gulen chun bagh wa bahara*
22. *Thai namuz wa nam chodahara*
23. *Mozhen Dilhi dan baghen Qandhara,*
24. *Ba ninde phiruke zezo dawara*
25. *Qalat bashken thara sare jamara!*
26. *Wali Bijar wa Bibrak Han mazara*
27. *Kutha liai milithant sahevara*
28. *Nazarband bithaghant sale dan para.*
29. *Mudama, Han, sardar jhaktagiya*
30. *Shutha dan hakima dast bastaghiya;*
31. *Inam wa wajibian giptaghiya*
32. *Phadha hand gartaghan wazh diliya.*
33. *Samenan gware Siahaf zamina*
34. *Buna Chhattra dan Lahria giliya;*
35. *Hazar shahbashen Kahane Maria*
36. *Baloch oshtataghant peghambaria.*
37. *Jawab tharetagha Doda Maria*
38. *'Nawan ail wa na nindan Qafiriya*
39. *Na ziran shahadaghen zar bahria*
40. *Sara katami zaham koparia.'*
41. *Hame ahwal shuthaghant pa guzari*
42. *Jahude ghorava bitha tiari;*
43. *Charitha Qafire qom quhari,*
44. *Hazar gone lohar wa gani,*
45. *Du lakhe lerav wa lakh sipahi,*
46. *Hamon sahedar gone ba khudahi;*
47. *Khuda nyama niarath Kahan dahi*
48. *Na sujhi Qafira jang wa lirahi.*

49. *Manan Pir gwankh da Shah bhirahi*
50. *Naffusk khandaghe kiti lirahi.*
51. *Faringi sath karwane bihana,*
52. *Du gwankh mizila velho girana;*
53. *Jazar, top, tambuan janana,*
54. *Sharab wa zalimen kefan warana,*
55. *Laghor livzan sare azhman janana;*
56. *Hazaren takburan Qafir khanana—*
57. *'Giran ail khanan Kahan Hana.'*
58. *Marian bastaghant Hindi manjana*
59. *Qabau umrai pat manjana,*
60. *Sara takbir khutha markh samana;*
61. *Saren Din Mahomed gon banzen bihana,*
62. *Hamara gone Gazane gon Hana.*
63. *Karam Han akhta, Sherani man tarana;*
64. *Mazare hung dathant Haibatana—*
65. *'Janan sathan, iutan na hamana*
66. *Sara buran, khashane zavana,*
67. *Phadh gardi laghor bazhman warana!'*
68. *Shave roshbitho wa bama dhamitha,*
69. *Mari gon Qafjra jang aritha;*
70. *Janokhen tupaq wa topan raritha.*
71. *Subahan rosh dan nermosh charhitha,*
72. *Faringi suraheir liah lahitha.*
73. *Khuthe khalbu man therha chanbaritha;*
74. *Sarena drang man chhaka draritha*
75. *Sara erha pa bana ulhitha.*
76. *Jahan jaskenthage top thawara,*
77. *Zamin zha topakan gardo ghubara,*
78. *Lahitho zartaghe Kohe mazara!*
79. *Sare erkhapto man lahme dighara*
80. *Ganritho watitha muri kirara:*
81. *Razen topan dainia damra*
82. *Chirangen zurthaghaia garipen hawara.*
83. *Marri sar sisto bitha du lara*
84. *Karam Han khapta gon chyargist wa*

chyara.
85. *Mura Han gwastaghe napt guzara,*
86. *Qatal zha topane mar mara*
87. *Karmie rakhitha pa sagh para,*
88. *Hazure pialawan noshe gon Yara;*
89. *Hamodha wajitha Shahe nighara*
90. *Hazur bhaje khapte Qafirara.*
91. *Shahidi khaptaghan warna gharane*
92. *Pira chyargist marenthe sir jane.*
93. *Manan nam nyayan surihane*
94. *Maluken Haibat wa tazi sazane,*
95. *Mura Han sunh sar taj amirane;*
96. *Mazaren Shahali istezaghane*
97. *Barakhen tegh raste an marane*
98. *Saghar goahan thi topan nishane!*
99. *Kuja Lunar hothen Muhammedane*
100. *Halalen dor warthan koh sarane?*
101. *Gihen Jarwar gon Miran Shahalia*
102. *Shuthaghant zaham tara ya diliya.*
103. *Bihishta nishtagant peghambariya;*
104. *Faringi rikhtaghant chhak wa sariya*
105. *Sagharan gahitho ishta Maria.*
106. *Karbi khaptagnant dhundh Qafirane.*
107. *Du sal ser athant abtar garane,*
108. *Warokhen dal arshe khargazahe;*
109. *Dare bokhte shut ha wa guzh naghane*
110. *Hamon jiwar buz arithi muzahane.*
111. *Sakhi Doda, Sardar manghihane*
112. *Ali gon tho madaten quzratane;*
113. *Jahuden Qafirane jang jhora,*
114. *Marian khatiha pa zaham zora.*
115. *Ma kan gon ma tho jangi tak tora;*
116. *Quran nyamaghen Suhri gon bora;*
117. *Du brathon pishtaghun gar pa gwaria*
118. *Ma dar khota ado siman dariya!*
119. *Jathen zaham pa dil zora wathia;*
120. *Shukar jaga khutha dir awariya.*
121. *Thara sobh dathage Shahen Alia*
122. *Kar kalmo farze pa duren Nabia.*

Notes [on this poem]

The language of the poem may be considered fairly representative of poetical Balochi of the period. A few Sindhi words occur, *e.g.* *zamin* (line 33: this may be a corrupt reading, as it does not rhyme) and one, I belicve to be Brahuiki—*liahi* meaning 'hope.' (lines 27 and 62).

There are a number of presumably Baloch words which are entirely unfamiliar to me. I took 'sazane' (line 94) as meaning 'worth hundreds' (of rupees); but am somewhat doubtful of it.

An example of typical poetical diction is line 11—the idea of numbers being so close that they have no room to stand. Compare:

Ma dighara jagah nyath phadha
Hand nyath mardar o nariyanan.

The metre of the poem corresponds with that given as II, by Longworth Dames. Line 91 **is** a good example:

U— — — U — — — U — — —
Shahidi khaptagan warna gharane

Sometimes a 'breath' after an accented word takes the place of an actual syllable, the rhythm being maintained:

U— — —, — — —U— —
Line 7:   Shitabi danh dathi Sahebara

U— —, U — — — —U— —
Line 11: Niya jagh janokhen tupakara

U— — — — — — —, U — —
Line 100: Halalen dor warthan koh sarane

These and other variations give the metre much the same flexibility as the Virgilian hexameter.

One section of the introduction, in Longworth Dames' book, is entitled 'Methods of singing' but it contains little more than a detailed description of the two musical instruments which provide the accompaniment to Baloch ballads. Of the music, he merely says: 'Most of the chants are very monotonous, having a range of very few notes' and this is true of the one example which he reproduces in notation. The description of a Baloch ballad-concert, given by that acute observer, Richard Burton, though in a humorous vein, seizes upon the peculiarity of the manner of singing: 'Each fresh verse is ushered in by a loud howl so strikingly discordant that your every nerve starts at it, and so prolonged that anticipation wearies of looking forward to its close ... the conclusion of the phrase—a descent into the regions of the *basso* till the voice dies away, vaguely growling'—of the melody, however, he says nothing definite.[12]

I believe that a year or two ago a gentleman from Europe toured this part of the country with a gramophone recording apparatus and it is hoped that much of this music may be rescued from obscurity by these means.

My equipment consisted of a tolerably good ear, and pencil and paper: and with some knowledge of the theory of music, this is quite sufficient. Baloch music, like that of most hill-peoples, is simple in character. The elaborate runs, *porta menti* and cadenzas, with quarter-tones, which embellish Indian music of the plains, with its vast variety of *raags* or modes, are here absent. The connection between verse and music is direct: the stresses generally fall on important words, and there is no lingering out of unimportant words, or single syllables over many notes, so often at the caprice of the Indian singer.

The Modes of Baloch melodies do not, so far as I have ascertained, depart from the diatonic Modes (Dorian, Lydian, Phrygian, etc.) on which the modern European major and minor scales are based. The intervals arc all easily recognized tones or semi-tones and there is no serious difficulty in scoring a melody: though the tonal compromise to which a pianoforte is tuned has the effect of making them sound somewhat 'out' when played on it.

The Mode to which the ballad of Naffusk is set is one of the least subject to this deterioration: it is what we know as the first of the 'authentic Modes', the Dorian, proceeding D E F G A B C D. This Mode, to the European ear, sounds better going downwards than upwards: for the latter, it seems natural, to adopt a transposition of the AEolian Mode which, from the same 'final', or key note, would proceed D E F G A B♭C D.[13] This flattening of the sub-mediant note (B) in the melody actually occurred in part of the accompaniment played on the sarinda, on one occasion that the ballad was sung to me by 'manghanhars'. Nevertheless, I am persuaded that the correct setting is in the Dorian Mode and musicians may form their own conclusions from the chant as scored below:

This chant, it will be conceded, is dignified music, perfectly appropriate to the heroic but sombre theme of the poem. To those acquainted with the Anglican Cathedral Psalter, it will recall the Quadruple chant to which one or two of the longer psalms are set. In the actual singing too, there is the common feature of repetition of one line of the chant to allow the music to end together with the words. But while in the Psalm this adjustment is only introduced at the conclusion, the third line being repeated, it occurs several times in the singing of the ballad; so that the introduction of a new subject, or sometimes even the beginning of a new sentence, will be accompanied by the opening phrase of the chant. This is facilitated by the fact that the second and fourth lines of the music are identical. This true and vital union of words and music, in place of a haphazard association, adds enormously to the effectiveness of the ballad as sung: reinforcing the changes of rhyme which, in the verse, announce each new development in the narrative.

A ballad even more popular than that of Naffusk, at least in the Upper Sind Frontier District, is that popularly known as 'Kehar Mehar'. I have obtained three versions of this, two of them in entirely different metres. They record an incident which must have taken place shortly after John Jacob assumed charge of the Frontier. It describes how the foreigners, having taken the country over from the Talpurs, started tyrannising over the Balochis, and 'Jekam' issues orders that he will not tolerate any more looting and raiding. Hearing that Kehar, Mehar, Chibbar and Kora, Khosas, were thieves, he called to Khangarh, but they told the messenger they would not go— 'Jekam' would be lucky if he ever saw them at Khangarh! A sawar came to take them, but they attacked and killed him. They then took counsel of a woman [for] what they should do next—give themselves up, fly, or resist. She said they should resist, and she would fight with them if necessary. Soon a naik and party of sawars came, and a hand to hand fight occurred in which, after killing several of the horsemen, the four Khosas were either killed or captured. Chibbar was brought before Jacob, who was so pleased with his bravery that he gave him a dress of honour and a Jagir. The language in the poems on this subject is unfortunately much mixed with Sindhi.

Another good ballad is that on the storming of Kelat and the heroic death of Mihrab Khan—an event referred to in the poem on Naffusk. Another part of which was recited to me by the late

Sardar Islam Khan, does not seem to be on the repertoire of any Baloch amateurs or their bards whom I have since questioned, and it would be a great pity if it actually has been forgotten. It dealt with the fortunes of the Sardar's namesake, Tumandar of the Bugtis, to whom reference has been made in the earlier part of this paper, and contained many allusions to Jacob and Merewether, describing why the Chief in extremity surrendered to Major Goldney rather than to Jacob.

I have recorded many other ballads commemorating intertribal fights which, perhaps, are not worth remembering by any but the descendants of those engaged.

Another class of poetry which is popular among the Hill-Balochis in particular, is that which deals with miracles of the Prophet, and more particularly those performed by Hazrat Ali. There is a very long poem on the legend of Ali's miracle at Naig in Sehwan Taluka. He was working on earth as a labourer, and the infidel king of this place engaged him to draw water out of a well of fabulous depth, as Ali had admitted that he could do the work of one hundred men. Out of curiosity, the king came in the afternoon to see how he was working and finding him asleep by the well, kicked him angrily, asking him why he was not drawing water. Ali thereupon caused a spring to flow—the water rose out of the well and began to flood the whole countryside, until the king expressed himself a sincere convert to Islam, when it was stayed by Ali. Similar legends are current at a number of places west of the Indus River.

The Balochis also delight in satirical poems and I have recorded an amusing modern one describing how the Chiefs of the most prominent tribes in Balochistan demeaned themselves by drawing the carriage of a departing Agent to the Governor General to the railway station. It may be recorded, as a curious repetition of Marri intractability that the Chief of the tribe flatly declined to participate in such unbecoming conduct!

Most Balochis are more or less acquainted with the classics of their language: the poetry of the heroic age of Mir Chakar and

Gwaharam and to a less degree with poems connected with their own tribe.

Their characteristic emulation is evident when repeating the well-known 'Daptar Sha'r' or ballad of genealogies: if their particular tribe is not mentioned, in the authentic version, they will insert its name in place of another.

Original composition still continues among the Balochi, and I have had the pleasure of recording, from the lips of the composer, a ballad commemorating the exploits of one of the 'Robin Hoods' of late years. This poet is an old man, of no position or education, named Rehan son of Suleiman, Gabol, and lives in a remote valley of the Kohistan. His mind is a storehouse of the classical ballads, and the style of his own compositions is in the old tradition.

Most of his poems are of a quasi-religious type, dealing with dreams and visions. Though their intrinsic merit may be slight, this evidence of culture acquired in the primitive simplicity of the mountains is interesting; and it is disturbing to feel that his compositions, as well as many more still existing from the past, are likely to lapse into oblivion for want of a few connoisseurs, who could surely be found among the many educated members of their race, to record them.

NOTES

1. This event appeals, from internal evidence, to have occurred in the fifties, when Nur Mahomed was the Marri Tumandar. This is to be inferred from the sarcastic lines 'let the leadership at the tribe break into pieces and depart—it does not belong to a woolly sheep.' Sardar Nur Mahomed was of a retiring disposition, a 'fakir' unsuited for ruling so turbulent a tribe. After a few years he was held to have lost his reason and was deposed.

2. These are probably the inferior tribe of this name inhabiting the Khirthar hills.

3. Charles Mason, *Narrative of Various Journeys in Sinde, Balochistan, Afghanistan and the Panjab*, (Vol. II).

4. *Kachhi Gazeteer*; Mason, *Narrative* (Vol. II).

5. This is the story as told me by the Bugtis. The 'Annals of the Mazaris' (Longworth Dames) and 'The Mazaris of Sind' (Mahomed Yasin) give a different version.

6. *Sibi Gazeteer.*

7. This signal of submission was also resorted to by races inhabiting the countries to the westward (see: Tod's 'Rajasthan').

8. E. B. Eastwick's *Dry Leaves from Young Egypt.*

9. Mr Ross Bell, Political Agent Upper Sind; see Eastwick's *Dry Leaves from Young Egypt.*

10. Information received from Wadero Jumo Khan Bugti.

11. *Record Book of the Sind Irregular Horse* (Vol. I).

12. Richard Burton, *Scinde or the Unhappy Valley*, 174–9.

13. The 'final' or key note of this mode is properly A, and it has been used from time immemorial for the well-known melody 'Tonus Peregrinus' for the psalm 'In Exitu Israel.'

11

Historical and Racial Background of the Amils of Hyderabad

S. J. Narsain

IN THE STUDY OF A RACE OR A TRIBE OR A GROUP OF PEOPLE, IT is now universally acknowledged that environment and heredity play an important part. Environment exercises a steady and constant influence upon man and by the application of his intelligence man uses his environment more and more to his advantage. This application of his intelligence by man makes a part of the heredity of man. Thus heredity and environment go hand in hand on the path of progress. They enter into various aspects of life. Hereditary influences operate greatly in making up the history of a group of people. The past and the present history of the Amils reveal the powerful influences of heredity as expressed under particular geographic, social and political environments. It manifests certain outstanding characteristics that give the Amils a distinct individuality of their own.

The Amils of Sindh style themselves after the occupation they held during the regime of the Mussalmans. The word 'Amil' is of Persian origin. 'Amil' in Persian means 'to administer'. The Amils served in the capacity of administrators and revenue officers. Probably this term was always applied by the Mussalman rulers to persons holding such posts. Early in the fifteenth century when Ahmedshah I conquered India, he wished to improve his dominions. At that time 'he appointed the Amils that is sub-divisional revenue officers' for the purpose.[1] As in Sindh, so in the Punjab, the Administrative and revenue officers were called after that name. The cultural affinity between these two provinces is too well-known to require any discussion. In both provinces this class of people have retained this name to themselves.

The Amils of Hyderabad are composed of different classes of people. Majority of the Amils are Lohanas by caste. A few belong to the Khatri caste and an insignificant number to other different castes. But just as their places of origin are unknown, their caste is also not definitized.

Let us first consider the Khatris. The history of the Khatris is obscure. Lack of historical records does not enable us to examine their hereditary qualities in detail. But their high capabilities have been standing put markedly from time to time in the annals of history. This may be indicative of the working of powerful hereditary influences.[2]

Among the Khatris, the different sections assign different origin to themselves. Taking all these accounts of heritage into consideration, the Khatri caste appears to be belonging to the Solar, the Lunar or the Agni cula race.[3] The Khatris of Sindh, however, claim Sri Ramchandra, the hero of Ramayana, as their common ancestor.[4] They declare that Ayodhya was their original home. From there they migrated to Delhi, and thence, to the Punjab where their numerical strength is great even to the present day. The Khatris have come to Sindh from Multan to escape the taxes imposed upon them by the Mussalman rulers.[5]

Evidently, the Khatris belong to the Kshatriya class. Their superiority 'in physique, in manliness and in energy' prove that they are the 'direct representatives of the Kshatriyas of Manu'.[6]

There are several legends connected with the origin of the Lohanas. Originally they are said to have been Rathor Rajputs. It is narrated that once the Rathors fell out with Raja Jaichand, the powerful King of Kanauj. The indignant Raja declared war against them. Conscious of their inadequate strength, the Rathors prayed to Lord Varuna to come to their rescue. After some days of constant and fervent prayer, Lord Varuna was pleased. He ordered them to stay in an invincible fort built by his supernatural power. For sixteen days, the people fought, and came out victorious in the war. But the fort vanished on the twenty-first day as willed by Lord Varuna. And the Lord bade them build an iron fort on the site and call themselves Lohanas (Loh means iron) thenceforward. The Rathor warriors followed this decree to the letter. They built a fort Lohghar (from which it became Lahore) and called themselves Lohanas.[7] Raja Jaichand flourished in the twelfth century. While we come across a number of references to a tribe called Lohana during as well as earlier to his reign.

Certain writers presume that the Lohanas derive their name from some country. Many writers allege that Lohakot or Lohanpur in the Punjab is the place from where they derive their name.[8,] Campbell assumes that the Lohanas take their name from the District of Lamgham in Eastern Afghanistan and 'probably belong to the Lohanis who formerly held the country between the Suleman Hills and the Indus'.[9] The Lohanis are the people of Afghanistan. They are 'mercantile travellors' who drive caravans to and from between Khorasan and Hindustan.[10] In the nineteenth century the Lohanis were famous for their packmanship.[11] It is a fact that before the invasion of the Arabs to spread their new religion during the seventh and eighth centuries, Afghanistan and Baluchistan were the dominions of Hindu kings. Professor Wilson has proved the existence of Hindu kingdom in Afghanistan by analysing the coins and antiquities discovered there.[12] The prevalence of Buddhism in Afghanistan is also substantially proved by the discovery of numerous stupas and Buddhistic statues in the land. Cunningham declares that the Kabul valley enjoyed Hindu suzereignty till the tenth century. He states, 'During the whole of the tenth century the Kabul Valley was held by a dynasty of Brahmins whose power was not finally extinguished until towards the close of the reign of Muhommad Ghaznav.[13] 'In those days therefore, it would appear that a great part of the population of eastern Afghanistan, including the whole of the Kabul Valley, must have been of Indian descent, while the religion was pure Budhism'.[14] But the ferocity of Ghaznavi soon drove out the idolators from the land 'and with them the Indian element'.[15] The close connection maintained by Afghanistan and India in ancient times may go to advance the statement of Campbell regarding the relationship between the Lohanas and the Lohanis. The Lohanis might have embraced Islam in the days of its pristine glory, thus severing all connections with their Hindu brethren. But owing to the lack of any historical proof, nothing very definite can be stated on this point.

There are various other tribes with whom the Lohanas are identified by different writers. The Lamanis, Lohas and Lois are haphazardly mentioned and connected with the Lohanas.[16] The possibility of any relation with all these tribes appears to have arisen in the mind of the writers because of the similarity of their names and occupation.

The Lohanas claim for themselves descent from Lava,[17] the eldest son of Rama, just as Rathors do from Kusha, the younger son of Rama. The tendency to link up the origin with some eminent personage or to infinity is a characteristic of [the] human mind. Men delight to think of a grand ancestry or a distinguished pedigree to which they imagine to belong. The census reports and the gazeteers doubt the claim of the Lohanas to Kshatriya class, on the proposition that the Lohanas everywhere shine in the capacity of traders and businessmen, so they place them under the category of the Vaishyas. But a glimpse at the past history of the Lohana shows that they belong to the warrior class and as such are entitled to declare themselves as Kshatriyas.

The solar race is believed to terminate with Raja Sumitra, the thirteenth in descent from Brihadhal. But many Rajput races attempt to form allegiance with it. Lava, the ancestor of the Lohanas, is supposed to have founded Lavakot or Labokot, the present Lahore.[18] His descendants are believed to have extended over the whole of the Punjab. Tod observes that its Bhalla Branch is still addressed at the time of blessing by the bards as Tatta-Multan Ka Rao (i.e., the Lords of Tatta and Multan).[19] Tatta is a town in Sindh. It was a flourishing and prosperous city in mediaeval times, while Multan formed a part of the province of Sindh till after the expiration of Hindu Raj.[20] This indicates that the abode of the Bhalla Branch was at first on the Indus. But there is some confusion in this matter. For, 'the Bhallas on the continent of Saurashtra, on the contrary assert their origin to be Indusvamsik and state that they are Balicaputras who were the ancient lords of Arore on the Indus'.[21] In the face of these conflicting views Tod concludes that 'it would be presumption to decide between their claims.'[22] But Tod 'would venture to surmise that they might be the offspring of Sehl, one of the princes of the Bharat who founded Arore.'[23] Sehl is again identified with Sehr or Sehires, the early Hindu rulers of Sindh, supposed to belong to the Sodha tribe of the powerful Parmara race, belonging to Agnicula.[24]

There is however an important point that requires careful consideration. Cunningham cites from Reinaud's *Fragments Arabes* that Sindh was divided into four principalities under Ayand, the son of Kafand, a non-Hindu king of Sindh who reigned sometime after Alexander the Great.[25] These four principalities were named Zor, Askalandusa, Samid and Lohana, all of which correspond with the division noted by Hwen Thsang.[26] Hwen Thsang visited Sindh in AD 641. At that time Sindh was divided into four divisions which are described by Cunningham by their geographical positions as Upper Sindh, Middle Sindh, Lower Sindh and Kachh. It appears then that Lohana was once a territorial place in Sindh.

The Lohanas, as they appear before us in the seventh century, are the inhabitants of Brahmanabad situated in the Middle Sindh. Formerly Brahmanabad was the city of the Brahmins who revolted against Alexander the Great when he conquered Sindh.

Consequently they were put to the sword by him.²⁷ Brahmanabad was then known by the name of Hermatelia to the Greeks. History does not disclose the fact when the Lohana tribe came to occupy Brahmanabad.

The Lohanas step upon the stage of history as an influential and powerful class of people in Sindh, ruled by a chief of their own class, Agham Lohana. Naturally, the delight of splendour and grandeur, and the love of self-assertion were ingrained in them. Agham Lohana was perhaps not the first ruler of his tribe; his fore-fathers may have had ruled before him, as is evident from a letter of Rai Chach, the Brahmin usurper to the throne of Sindh to him. It says: 'you consider yourselves kings of the time from your power and grandeur, origin and lineage. Though I have not inherited this Kingdom and sovereignty, this wealth and affluence, this power and dignity from my father and grand-father and though this country has not been ours before, still my elevation and improved fortunes are due to the Grace of God.'²⁸ It was customary with the Governors of the principalities to submit to the supremacy of the King of Alor. Agham Lohana was unwilling to acknowledge the Brahmin usurper as a sovereign. A fierce battle ensued between them. 'There are said to have been some forty thousand fighting men in Brahmanabad who daily issued forth and gave battle to Rai Chach.'²⁹ Finally, the army of Agham Lohana was put to flight and their chief was killed. His son submitted to the King. So Rai Chach placed him on the throne. But the tribe as a whole met with a severe treatment. Rai Chach passed strict laws against them. The martial tribe was deprived of the right of carrying sword; riding on horse with saddles was forbidden; the gorgeous dresses of their palmy days were denied them; and they were forced to put on coarse garments and to go barefooted and bare-headed. Besides, they were to supply firewood to the ruler of Brahmanabad, they had social, economic and political status lowered. A high, ruling aristocratic people were levelled down with the lowliest, though some Lohanas were appointed to respectable posts to effect solid security.

It may be noted here that though Rai Chuch was a Brahmin, Buddhism was the dominant religion in Sindh, as it was then in the rest of India. Numerous Buddhists inhabited in the country. Mr Smith speaks of great many Buddhist monks living in Sindh but they did not lead a pure and a strictly religious life.[30] Brahmanism was also practised in Sindh. There existed no restriction as to the choice of religion. Both were followed with social impunity by the people. Chandar, the brother of Rai Chach, was a Buddhist by religion. He ardently patronized his faith when he ascended the throne. Aghan Lohana professed the dominant faith of the land. It may be that the Lohanas belonged to the same faith with their leader.

The unfortunate defeat was almost like a catastrophe to the high career of the Lohanas. The unfavourable circumstances checked the spontaneous flow of the high capabilities of the Lohanas in Sindh. Their physical and mental energy was suppressed. Some of the Lohanas learnt to adjust themselves to the circumstances. Their mental habits changed with the changed condition of their life. They lived like common folk. Economic degradation compelled them to take to simple means of subsistence. They became agriculturists, menial servants, vegetable-sellers etc. Even at the present day certain sections of Lohanas are found engaged in such occupations.[31]

Sindh was in a state of political unrest shortly after the downfall of the Lohanas. In AD 711 Muhammad Bin Kasim, conquered Sindh. Thereafter Sindh was always subject to political fights and disturbances in which the Lohanas took but little part. A state of disquietude of a different type fell upon the Lohanas in the tenth century. A tremendous geographic upheaval destroyed their place of habitation. The complete destruction of Brahamanbad by an earthquake must have caused a great loss of life and property. It is probable that this compelled its inhabitants to scatter themselves and move to different countries, for the Lohanas had little opportunity to revive their social, political and economic life in the land. They occupied the most degraded position being considered as 'a villanous set of people' quite like the wild men living in some villages of Fars and Payeh.[32] The Lohanas pass out of the pages of history of Sindh at that time, though their prowess and brilliance shine forth in other parts of India.

In the twelfth century, when Prithviraj was the King of Delhi, the Lohanas appear as a flourishing military race. The Delhi Court poet, Chand Badrai, has composed an Epic describing vividly in the old Hindi language the various incidents that mark the grand career of Prithviraj. In this he often mentions the Lohanas taking part in many a battle. 'One of the members of the race is said to have accompanied Prithviraj on his expedition to Kanauj and is enumerated among the wounded.'[33]

The latter history of the Lohanas reveal them as an oppressed class. They were often subjected to the tyranny of the rulers. In the thirteenth century, it is recorded that a number of Lohanas immigrated to Sindh. They are said to have been driven out from Multan by the Mussalman rulers, into Sindh from where they made their way to Cutch.[34]

The Lohanas never left Sindh totally. We catch a glimpse of them in the fifteenth century. A certain celebrated Saint Yussaf-Uddin, a pious man, descendant of Abdul Qadir Jilani, is said to have carried intense religious propaganda in Sindh, and succeeded in converting many Lohanas to his religion. The Saint was an inhabitant of Baghdad. One night he dreamt that his presence was required in India. So he started for his journey, and came to Sindh in AD 1422. Here he preached his religion so fervently and enthusiastically that it appealed to many a heart. It is said that he converted seven hundred Lohana families after ten years of sincere and assiduous effort. These seven hundred families are believed to have followed the suit of two important persons of their caste.[35] It is difficult to state the psychological principle behind such a change of mentality. May be that pure religious sentiment unalloyed by any condition induced them to embrace this religion. Or may be that it was the desire for economic prosperity which allurement is winning over so many people to Christianity and Islam at the present day in India. Or may be that their social position came to play some part in it. The social status of the Lohanas at this period, as is already observed, was degrading and their economic condition was poor. As a class they were despised by their rulers. Probably they considered it preferable to join the ranks of their rulers, thereby rising in social status. Afterwards these Lohanas migrated to Cutch where their number was increased by converts from the Cutch Lohanas.[36]

The history of Sindh shows constant inflow and outflow of people. The struggle for existence has always been the primary cause for emigration. Pitt-Rivers declares that all causes of struggle, strife and supremacy have but one fundamental problem at the bottom, that of struggle for existence.[37] The tyranny of the Government also has often led to emigration. In the latter half of the seventeenth century, small streams of people, emigrated into Sindh from the Punjab, Rajputana, Cutch and other places. These people were Lohanas, Khatris, Bhatias and others, the first being by far in large majority. The struggle for existence found a solvent in this that Sindh provided them with different occupations. Those who emigrated avoiding the tyranny of the Government escaped the iron rule of Aurangzeb and his immediate successors, almost in the manner of Catholics who escaped the tyranny of the Protestant Government in England in the sixteenth century. At this period Aurangzeb took certain drastic measures against the Hindus and their religion. 'In April 1669, he ordered the provincial governors to destroy the temples and schools of the Brahmins ... and to utterly put down the teachings and religious practices of the infidels.' On the second April 1679, the Jazia or Poll tax on non-Moslems was revived and again 'with one stroke of his pen he dismissed all the Hindu clerks from office'.[38] These measures created discontentment and provocation among the Hindus. So, many Hindus migrated to different places to live a peaceful and secure existence.

The new settlers into the land of Sindh must have brought their families with them. If they really fled from the tyranny of a bigoted king, it is highly improbable that they should leave their families behind. Others who came to earn a livelihood may also have been accompanied by their wives and children, looking to the unsafe conditions of the times. It may also have happened that they left their families at their native places like many merchants, to return home once in a period of a year or two. But those who contemplated to establish a permanent abode must have taken away their families to their places of settlement or formed new relations with the natives of the place. A number of Brahmins sufficient to carry on religious ceremonies must have also escorted them. Mr Advani assigns the date of the first immigrants, some of whom are the ancestors of the present Amils, to be about AD 1670.[39]

It would be of some advantage to consider the routes pursued by the immigrants to come to Sindh. In absence of railroads, the main lines of communication, linking cities with cities and forming the highways of commerce must have been the routes for the coming and going of people. Taking Hyderabad as the centre, we shall pursue the different routes that connect Sindh with the countries through which the immigrants came to Sindh. There exists a road from Hyderabad to Multan which is established for the facilitation of carrying merchandise and general traffic. It is a road of high antiquity when the western Punjab constituted a part of the province of Sindh. The road passes through Bahawalpur State, Sukkur, Khairpur and Nawabshah districts, following the bank of the Indus but not very close to it. The road is so clear and prominent that there is a proverb in Sindhi stating that 'the blind men can find Multan'. This road must have permitted frequent migration. A number of our immigrants came by this road.

While this road connects Sindh with the Punjab, there is another road that enables Sindh to maintain communication with Rajputana. This road goes through Tando Allahyar, Mirpurkhas, Shadipali, Umarkot and then passes the great Indian desert to reach Jodhpur. This is a difficult road to travel. The desert forms the worst part of the journey. During the day the heat of the sun is intense and the desert burns like a furnace. At the present day the Jodhpur Railway Company discretely avoids the heat of the desert; trains cross it at night time when the desert is cool. This path must have been rather uninviting when the journey was done at slow speed in bullock-cart or on camel-back. Some of the immigrants came to Sindh by traversing this path.

The route taken from Cutch to come to Sindh is a river and land-route. By crossing the Kori Creek by a boat, the emigrants come to a salt-waste. Passing through it, they enter Sujawal and Saidpur. They cross the Indus and go to Tatta Taluka. Then they catch a road that takes a northerly direction, and reach Hyderabad after crossing the river at Kotri to Gidu Bunder.

Migration leads to excessive selective process.[40] Men who are lazy and unadventurous stay behind. Others, who are less adaptable to new environment and the hardships of the journey, are eliminated. So the weak and the unfit go to the wall. Only the bold and the strong, endowed with energetic spirit and mind, survive. *Desire for migration, for undertaking the troubles and risks of a journey during days when no provision for easy conveyance existed, manifests a mentality above the average type. To migrate means to go to a new—unknown and unfamiliar—place.*

The immigrants possessed the pushing quality to seize any opportunity that came to them and to make the best use of it. They moved in different directions in search of employment. Some of them entered the capital and found employments in the courts of the Mussalman rulers. Others sought the best business quarters. It is probable that two members of the same family took to two different occupations. One joined in business enterprise which was more or less confined to trade only, and the other served in the court. The descendants of the court officials designate themselves Amils, and those of trading class, Bhaibunds (Banias). Therefore, originally there existed no class distinction between the Amils and the Bhaibunds. The distinction was attached to the difference in occupation only.

The Amils who are the object of our study, on their coming to Sindh, served at the then capital of Sindh, Khudabad. It appears that some Lohanas and a few Khatris were employed in the service of the rulers of Khudabad. They displayed considerable proficiency in the management of state affairs. State craft was soon acquired by them.

In the eighteenth century the capital of Sindh was transferred from Khudabad to Hyderabad. So the officials and traders began to shift to the new capital. But some of the officials and traders were unwilling to move out of Khudabad. They stayed behind. As a result the Amils, like the Bhaibunds, came to be divided into two classes. One class remained at Khudabad, the other came to Hyderabad. Gradually time and geographical division brought about definite distinction between the two. The gulf of separation of the two classes became wider till at last they became two separate social groups maintaining no connection with each other. The Khudabadi Amils became a consolidated party, but the Hyderabadi Amils suffered the new officials at the rulers' court to join their community. So while the Khudabadi Amils increased by the slow process of multiplication only, the Hyderabadi Amils increased not only by multiplication but by addition also. The present Amil community is not of the pure Khudabadi genus, but is made up of several classes of people.[41]

The Amils were increasingly employed in greater numbers to posts of every description in the revenue and administrative departments. They carried on State-correspondence, and travelled as State envoys and as ambassadors. Frequently they were sent to pay tribute to the King of Khorasan whose suzereignty was acknowledged by the rulers of Sindh. Besides serving as the Secretaries of Foreign Department the Amils served in the Home Department as well. At times the Amils were found even in the Military Department, though the rulers had scarcely any standing army worthy of mention. In this manner, by their ability and intelligence, the Amils became indispensable to the Mussalman kings of Sindh. The following statement of Burton stated with regard to the Amils bears great truth in it: 'Even the Ameers with all their hatred and contempt for

Kafirs could not collect or dispose of their revenues without the aid of Hindu Amils.'[42]

The Bhaibunds, in their return, carried on trade and commerce of the country. As a matter of fact, almost all Hindus who were not of the official class, and were not Brahmins, took to trade. It was extensively carried on by them. All necessary as well as luxurious articles were provided to the people by them. Therefore the Hindus, as a class, constituted a very important section of people in Sindh during the Muhammadan rule.

Though the reins of Government passed from one dynasty to another, the Amils and the Bhaibunds continued their services and business in Sindh. The Talpurs succeeded the Kalhoras. The Amils who were serving under the Kalhoros now took their posts in the Court of the Talpurs. The reports and accounts of the travellers in Sindh at that time throw a flood of light upon the life and character of the people, both Hindus and Muhammadans. The Hindus had Panchayats for the internal administration of their community. The Panchayat effected social solidarity, exercised judicial authority and settled all disputes and disagreements between the individuals of the community. It was a stronghold for the Hindus.

The character of the people, so far as the reports go, was, to say the least, not praiseworthy. The Sindians were regarded as treacherous and liars; the Baluchis were indolent and debauched but they were sometimes praised for bravery; the Hindus were considered avaricious and over-reaching. The Shikarpuris were characterized by great laxity in respect of their peculiar tenets, flagrant licentiousness and general disregard of principles of morality and decency, though they were considered honest in their mercantile transactions.[43] The Amils played tricks and deception in Court. They learnt to read and write letters in any manner they pleased. They copied documents, forged seeds and took [a] good amount of bribe. They robbed the Government for the slightest gain. 'The Amils,' as said by Burton, 'looked rigidly to their own advantage; and in pursuit of it they were held by no oath, feared no risk, and showed no pity.'[44]

With the annexation of Sindh to the British territory, the Amils took up service in the Government department; already in the Court service, they constituted an important section of people who were indispensable for the administration of the country. The Amils had a fair knowledge of the province and its people. They could therefore render effective assistance to the new rulers. The capacity of the Amils to work efficiently won the admiration of the English. They were described as 'able and energetic, honest and upright, and they displayed an earnest application and devotion to duty.'[45]

Ethnological consideration of the Amil community leads us to a great disadvantage. Sindh [was] sadly neglected by the ethnologists who attempt to investigate the racial types in India. Now Sindh gives a new turn to the established theories of racial types in India. The excavations at Mohanjo Daro shows that the inhabitants of the land at that time were, as judged by their physical features, of Sumerian type. They are Pre-Aryan and non-Dravidian. Considering the later history, it is found that Sindh has suffered from a great admixture of blood. In early times, the mingling of races was the order of the day in Northern India, though India maintained caste rules. North Indians people came in contact with various foreign races and tribes who constantly penetrated through the mountain barriers of India and occupied the land. Bactrians, Scythians, Parthians, Huns and others pushed towards India and adopted Hindu religion and name. The regular affluence of foreign races caused immense admixture of blood. In the Baudhayana Dharamasutra, it was expressed that: 'The inhabitants of Anarta, of Anga, of Magadha, of Saurashtra, of Upavritta of Sindh and Sauvira are of mixed origin'.[46] The races of the north were therefore regarded as impure and it was established that a person going for travel and sometime even for pilgrimage in the north had to change his sacred thread after performing prayasehitta.[47] This kind of order was passed against these countries because the rest of India observed comparative racial purity by observing rigid caste system. Such relative ethnic purity can be preserved in countries which are geographically isolated or economically uninviting. But India, land of gold, developed this unique method for preserving pure blood as much as possible.

Risley in his *The People of India* divides India into its several provinces and attributes particular racial composition to each. He speaks of seven racial types prevailing in India and assigns Scytho-Dravidian element, as preponderating among the people of the Bombay Presidency.[48] Aitken states that 'to this day a large proportion of population is certainly Scythian, not Aryan' in Sindh.[49] It is true that Scythians had come and settled in Sindh in large numbers and that at that time Sindh was known as an Indo-Scythian land.[50] But at present the term 'Scythian', making up a distinct facial type, is being called into question.

Again, if rightly observed, Sindh will be found racially and culturally quite distinct from the rest of the Presidency. To a certain extent, this may be applicable to Gujrat as well and especially to Kathiawar, which has always maintained a close connection with Sindh. On the other hand, great cultural and facial unity exists between Sindh and the Punjab. Extensive amalgamation of blood has taken place between these provinces. And we know that the people of the Punjab, Kashmir and Rajputana are Indo-Aryans.[51] To what extent the Indo-Aryan traits are to be found among the Hindus of Sindh is a question that we are not in a position to settle. The Khatris are, however, unanimously ascribed an Indo-Aryan origin. Havell furnishes with a brief account of the characteristics of an Indo-Aryan as afforded by ethnographic investigations and states that these are markedly to be observed among the Khatris.[52]

The Amils are a strong and healthy class. They are robust and well-built. The physique of the Amils has always been highly attractive. Foreigners describe them as a 'light complexioned, regular featured and fine looking race'. They may be considered to be of an Indo-Aryan descent.

Having considered the racial composition of the Amils, we shall in the end refer to a defective [*sic*] section of people existing in the community. Persons belonging to this class are known as Boodhas.

They possess certain physical deformities. They are an edentate breed having eight teeth, 'round faces, flat noses, thick lips and soft silky hair which does not grow more than six inches. Their skins have no pores and so they do not perspire.' In consequent they feel unbearable heat in the body during the hot season. These physical features are inherited not from father to child but from grandfather to grandchild on the mother's side. All children do not suffer from the same defect. Some are born quite normal. This appears to have existed in the community even during the Talpur regime.[53] There is a supposition that this 'strange product of humanity' will soon get extinct.[54]

NOTES

1. Campbell, *Bombay Gazetteer* (Vol. I), 238.
2. The powerful racial heritage of the Khatris is evident when we find that Guru Nanak, Guru Govindsing, the Great Sikh leaders were Khatris by caste. So were Todar Mull and many of Ranjit Singh's chief functionaries. See: George Campbell, 'Ethnology of India', *J.R.A.S. of Bengal* 3.21 (1866), 109.
3. Horace Arthur Rose, *A Glossary of Tribes and Castes of the Punjab North-West Frontier*, 501–2.
4. *The Ethnographical Survey of Bombay (Monograph No. 3)*, 3.
5. Ibid.
6. Rose, 506.
7. R. E. Ethnoven, *Tribes and Castes of Bombay* (Vol. II), 381.
8. Ibid. 382; Henry Elliot, *The History of India* (Vol. I), 362.
9. James Campbell, *Bombay City Gazeteer*, 226; James Campbell, *Bombay City Gazeteer* 9.1, 122.
10. Henry Bellew, *Afghanistan and Afghan*, 219–20.
11. Charles Masson's *Narrative of the Various Journeys in Baluchistan, Afghanistan and Punjab*.
12. H. H. Wilson, *Ariana Antiqua: A Descriptive Account of Antiquities and Coins of Afghanistan*, 43.
13. Majumdar-Sastri ed., *Cunningham's Ancient Geography of India*, 19.
14. Ibid.
15. Ibid.
16. Ethnoven, 382.
17. Campbell, *Bombay City Gazeteer* 9.1, 121; Tanna, *Lohana Gnatino Itihas* (in Gujarati), chapter 5; Dosani, *Lohana Ratnamala* (in Gujarati), 4.
18. Majumdar-Sastri, *Cunningham's Ancient Geography*, 226–7.
19. James Tod, *The Annals and Antiquities of Rajasthan*, 116.
20. During Hindu regime the boundary of Sindh extended on the cast till the limits of Kashmir and Kanuj, on the west to Makran and the sea, on the south to the sea-port of Surat, and on the north to Kandahar, Seistan, the Suleman mountains and the Kikanan hills (Thomas Postans, 'Of the Early History of Sindh', *J.R.A.S. of Bengal* (1841), 183–97).
21. Tod, 117.
22. Ibid. 46.
23. Ibid.
24. Ibid.
25. Elliot, in his *History of India* Vol. I, speaks of a king Kafand, a non-Hindu King, contemporary with Alexander ruling wisely and efficiently in Sindh (208).
26. Majumdar-Sastri, 285.
27. D. D. Vincent, *The Voyage of Nearchus*, 136.
28. Mirza Kalichbeg, *Chachnamah* (Part I), 32.
29. Henry Cousins' *The Antiquities of Sind*.
30. V. A. Smith, *Early History of India*, 300.
31. Campbell, *Bombay City Gazeteer* 9.1, 122.
32. As Muhammad Kasim, the

first conqueror of Sindh called them (Kalichbeg's *Chachnamah* [Part 1]).

33. *The Revatata Episode (Canto XXVII By).*
34. James Burgess states that the Lohanas emigrated from Kanauj. James Burgess, *Report of the Antiquities of Kathiawar and Kachh*, 193. Ethnoven and others maintain that the Lohanas came from Multan (Ethnoven, *Tribes and Castes of Bombay*, 382).
35. Thomas Arnold, *The Preaching of Islam*, 274.
36. Ibid.
37. Julian Pitt-Rivers, *The Clash of Culture and the Contact of Races*, 1.
38. J. N. Sarkar, *Anecdotes of Aurangzeb and Historical Essays*, 11–12.
39. Bherumal Mahirchand Advani, *Amilan-ji-Ahwal* (in Sindhi), 13.
40. Ellsworth Huntington's *The Character of Races.*
41. Advani, 46–7.
42. *See*: *Bombay Selections* 17.2, 662–3.
43. Edward Thornton, *Gazeteer of the Province Adjacent to India* (Vol. II), 193–4; Thomas Postans, *Personal Observations on Sindh*, 67.
44. Richard Burton, *The Races that Inhabit the Valley of Indus*, 340.
45. Edward Balfour, *Cyclopaedia of India* (Vol. II), 230.
46. Ram Prasad Chanda, *Archaeological Survey No. 31*, 7.
47. *Sindhu Sanvira Sunrashtra tatha pratyaniarasinah Anga Vanga Kahngas LoBa gatva samskaramarhati* (Sanskrit). In some cases, the performance of Sanskara in case of pilgrimage is not asked for. *Tirtha yatra Vina gachhet Samskaramarhati* (Sanskrit).
48. Herbert Risley, *The People of India*, 37.
49. Edward Aitken, *The Gazeteer of the Province of Sindh*, 87.
50. Ibid.
51. Risley, 35–7.
52. Ernest Havell, *The History of Aryan Rule in India*, 32.
53. Lokmandas Manghirmalani, 'Hindus Under the Talpurs of Sindh', *Modern Review* 51 (1932), 267.
54. Ibid.

12

Legends of Old Sind
N. M. Billimoria

THE MOST CELEBRATED SINDHI LEGENDS ARE THE FOLLOWING:

1. Sassui and Punhu (Sansar-ma-sui, heard in the world famous).
2. The tale of Rano and Mumal; two Rajput lovers.
3. The loves of Hir and Ranjho.
4. The story of Marui and the Surara Prince.
5. The battles and death of Mall Mahmud.
6. The conquests of Dulha Darya Khan.
7. The loves of Sohni and Mehar (buffalo keeper).
8. The wars of Dodo and Chanesar.
9. The prophecies of the Samoi or Haft tan.
10. The story of Lilan Chanesar.
11. The legend of the Nang or dragon.
12. The tale of Ghatu or fishermen.
13. The battle of Abdullah the Brahui.
14. The feuds of Subah Chanaiya.
15. The quarrels of Jam Hala and Jam Kehar.

TALE OF SASSUI AND PUNHU

This is a tale of two lovers, who lived at the time when Islam was first introduced into Sindh, about AD 712. The story is known throughout the tract of land lying between Makran and Afghanistan, Jesulmere and Eastern Persia. It exists in the Persian, Jataki and Beluch languages and it is probably the one alluded to by Crow, who observes:

> Meer Fatehaly Khan directed the loves of the Beloch pair as related in some of the country tales to be translated into Persian verse, upon the model of Jami's Eusuph and Zulaykha, that the diffusion of these poems may establish the fame of Scinde, as well in letters as in arms.

The pair is now considered as saints and their tombs are visited by many pilgrims. Their tomb is among the Pub Hills. The popular belief is that no camel can approach the tomb, as the lady will not forgive those animals for carrying away her husband. A pilgrimage to the holy spot secures much happiness to the visitor, and many a devout believer has been fed with bread and milk by a hand stretched out of the tomb. These tales are considered sufficiently established to be chronicled in the historical work of Sind; we find in them moreover that the beautiful lady usually appears to the male, and her handsome husband to the female, pilgrims. Among the Hindoos, Sassui is known by the name of Rul Mui or 'she that died wandering' to distinguish her from another celebrated beauty Sohni, who happened to perish in the Indus, and is therefore called Bud Mui, 'she that died by drowning'. The beautiful verses of Shah Abdel Latif have been translated into English verse by Sir F. G. Goldsmid in 1863 and T. Hart-Davies of the Bombay Civil Service, who was Judicial Commissioner in Sind in 1881, translated fifty Sindhi ballads on Umar and Marui, Saswee and Punhoo and Rana and Mumal &c.

The wife of a Brahmin of Tatta bore him a daughter; she was a lovely child but the astrologers consulted their books and revealed that she would become a Moslem, would marry a foreigner, and would disgrace her family. By the entreaties of the wife the Brahmin did not kill the child but the parents procured a coffer, placed the babe in it with a rich bracelet and committed her to the safeguard of the Indus. The ark floated down to Bhambora, at that time a flourishing city. A washerman who was washing clothes on the bank of the Indus, drew out the coffer, and was astonished to see the beautiful contents. He called to the other washermen and cried, 'See, o ye men, the tricks of the world; to the childless a child is borne by the river.' The washerman had no child, so he adopted the child; after some years Sassooee turned out a beautiful lady, and made a considerable sensation in the female society. As the girl was sitting with her friends, one day, Babiho, a Hindu trader, happened to pass by her watan and the girls asked the merchant to show his wares. While the Hindu is producing his wares, the lady remarks: 'See his beauty, o my friend how handsome he is.' The Hindu modestly declines the compliments in favour of Punhu, the son of his employer, and says: 'What am I? You must see my own lord, of his beauty I have but a fortieth part.' Sassui and the ladies, roused by this assertion, eagerly enquire:

> Banyan by what name did thy parents call thee?
> And who is the youth whose beauty thou describest?

The Hindu replies:

> My parents called me Babihal by name.
> And the youth whose beauty I describe is Punhal Khan the Beloch.

The Lady makes the fallowing request:

> My little Babiho, only bring the Beloch for me to see,
> And I will pay the taxes and duties for all thy caravan.

Babiho at first objects to act as a messenger and begins to raise all kinds of objections:

> He cannot leave from his mother even to the chase,
> How then can I bring to thee that well guarded Beloch?

The lady treats this very lightly and says:

> Hundreds of Cafilas, lacs of people come and go,
> What then is the difficulty for the Beloch to come?

The Hindu merchant says that:

> The beautiful Punhu, with the long flowing locks,
> Has taken to wife two maids, whose voices are sweet as those of the Kokila.

Sassui is not daunted and continues:

> I, too, a maiden, the pride of Bhambora,
> And my accents are not less dulcet than the Kokila's song.

Babiho surrenders and says:

> I now start for Kech. Lady, Allah be thy preserver;
> I have promised to bring the Baloch to thee for the love of the Lord.

Sassui highly pleased, replies:

> My little Babiho, give my best salam to the Beloch,
> And say, Jam, I have sent thee an offering of rich clothes.

This is a delicate hint to come dressed like a gentleman. The first part of the story is ended. The Hindu merchant returns to his master; he takes Punhu aside and gives him the lady's message with rich garments. Punhu prepares to visit Bambhora, fired with love. This is an instance of love, not at first sight, but caused by simply hearing the name of another. The Arabs say: 'And the ears become enamoured before the eye at times' and the Persians often quote these lines:

> Not merely by the eye is fancy bred
> It frequently arise from the ear as well.

It should be borne in mind that these verses are all susceptible of a Sufi or mystic interpretation and must be understood metaphorically as well as literally. A Sindhi would consider Punhu as a type of the immortal spark in the breast of man, which, by the influence of some exciting cause, is suddenly inflamed and burns to unite itself with the source of light. Thus the Beloch becomes a kind of pilgrim who in his progress towards eternity leaves behind him the world and its connections, its pleasures and its pains. Babiho proposes another mercantile trip but refuses to proceed unless Punhu accompanies him. After great trouble the old Jam, Ari, grants permission and when the cafla is ready to start the old mother exclaims: 'O youths, guard my little Punhu with anxious care.' Whereupon the younger wife Ayisa comes forward, seizes the camel's nose-ring and exclaims:

> Husband leave me not thus, for the sake of the Lord. Either pass
> the night with me, or send me home to my father's house. The elder
> wife requests the junior to desist as someone had charmed away their
> husband's affections.

Punhu visited the fair Sassooee, loved her, and lived in her adopted parents' house under the humble disguise of a washerman, till he earned his prize and married his mistress. A world of happiness now lay before the pair. When Ari, the proud old Beloch heard about the abominable conduct of his son, [he] tore off his turban, dashed it to the ground, scattered ashes upon his clothes, rent his skirts, spoiled his shirt-front, and refused to wash. Perhaps privately the old man prepared a rod for the benefit of the young man's pants.

During their married life Punhu once saw Bhagula, the fair and frail wife of a goldsmith (sonar). Punhu became faithless and charged Sassui with faithlessness; she proposed to decide their quarrel by the trial of fire. A pile of burning fire was prepared, Bhagula tried to run away but Sassui seized her by her ears and compelled her to enter the burning fire: virtue triumphed and [the] Sonar's wife was burnt to ashes, her ears which were in the pure hands of her rival only remained. Now we come to the catastrophe of the tale.

The old Beloch, Ari, sent his six stalwart sons to bring the fugitive home. They hastened to Bambhora, and, in no way appeased by the beauty of the sister-in-law, kindness, hospitality and skill in cooking, succeeded, partly by force, partly by stratagem, in carrying off Punhu, drunk with opium, upon the back of a high trotting dromedary. Who can describe Sassui's grief?

> At dawn Sassui looks round, but her lover is not on the couch beside her.
> She searches, yet finds not the camels of her brother-in-law at the place where they alighted;
> Stooping to the ground she gazes, and recognises the fresh footsteps of her Punhu.
> Then she weeps tears of blood, as if sprinkling the hills (over which her husband was travelling);
> Crying, 'alas, alas', she scatters the red gulal over her head.
> How shall her wounded heart survive the loss of him, whom Belochis have torn away from her?

Then comes the consolation of her friends. Sassui declares to her friends to follow her husband's footsteps.

All dissuade her in these words, which graphically depict the dangers of the way:

> Go not forth to the wild, O Sassui, where snakes lurk in the beds of the mountain streams,
> Where jackals, wolves, baboons and bears sit in parties (watching for the traveller);
> Where black vipers in the fiumaras oppose your way with their hissings;[1]
> Fierce hornets haunt the hills, Korars utter their cry
> And Luhars, winding round the trees, swing and sway, (in the wind).[2]
> After which dangers, appear the sheds—Jam Punhu's village home.

Still Sassui adheres to her resolve and starts upon her journey. At last she meets a goatherd, and asks him:

> O my brother, the goatherd, God give thee many goats,
> And may thy name be celebrated (for the beauty of thy flock) at every ford (where the animals are driven to water).
> For the Lord's sake, goatherd, point out to me the path taken by my brothers-in-law.

Now this demon who was very ugly had been told by his mother that one day he would meet in the jungle a beautiful bride, decked in jewels and rich dress. Seeing Sassui, he concluded that she was the person intended for him. He began to make love to the poor girl, who to gain time complained of thirst and begged her ugly admirer to milk one of his goats. He replied that he had no pot. She gave him a lota with a hole in it. The villain did not find that his lota was not full at all. Now Sassui, driven to despair, offered up earnest prayers

---

1. Nai, bed of a mountain stream generally dry but converted by a few hour's rain in a raging torrent.
2. Korar and Luhar are well known kinds of snakes.

to Heaven to preserve her honour; begging to be admitted into the bowels of the earth, if no other means of escape existed. Heaven heard her prayers and suddenly she sank into the yawning ground. The wretched goatherd saw his mistake, and to atone for his sin raised a tomb in honour of the departed fair one.

As usually happens, or is made to happen, in such cases, Punhu, who had escaped from his brothers, was travelling in hot haste towards Bhambhora, arrived at the very spot of his wife's live-tomb exactly five minutes after the monument had been erected. He had his slave Lallu with him. Attracted by the appearance of the tomb, he went up to it, and would have sat down here to rest, when he heard the voice of his bride calling him from the tomb:

> Enter boldly my Punhu, nor think to find a narrow bed
> Here gardens bloom, and flowers shed sweetest savour;
> Here are fruits, and shades and cooling streams,
> And the Prophet's light pours through our abode,
> Banishing from its limits death and decay.

Punhu called up his slave Lallu, gave him the reins of his camel and asked him to carry the tidings of his fate to his father and friends. He then prayed to heaven to allow him to join his Sassui; heaven granted his prayers by opening and swallowing up the lover. Lallu informs the old Jam of his son's last act:

> Separation is now removed, and the friends have met to part no more.
> The souls of those true lovers are steeped (in bliss) and the rose is at last restored to the rose bud.
>
> *Gul wiyo gulzar mein.*

TALE OF UMAR AND MARUI

The next tale is that of Umar, the Sumra prince and Marui, the Sangiani. The Sangi is a Sindhi clan living near Umerkot. The word Marui means the girl belonging to the Maru tribe, a semi-nomadic race living in Malir in the regions about the Thar. One Palino ran away with Mihrada, the mother of Marui from the house of Phula Lako, her husband. Mihrada's condition prevented the celebration of her marriage with Palino till the birth of Marui. The astrologers predicted about Marui: 'Your daughter's fate shall be such that to you, O parents, Umar shall apply with joy.' The young woman grew up and became very beautiful; her first victim was Phog, a shepherd in the service of Palino; the servant was desperate with love and went to his master and told him that he could not serve any longer. Palino did not like to lose a good servant, and understanding the cause of his dissatisfaction, promised him the hand of his step-daughter, Marui.

At first Phog was highly delighted; after some time seeing no prospects of success he went to his master and threatens to complain of his perfidy to the ruler of the land. Palino replied that:

> Umar the just King lives far off,
> And he will not interfere with trade or marriages,
> You will injure yourself by this conduct, O Phog.

Phog undertakes the long journey from the Thar to Omerkot and narrates the deceipt [*sic*] practised upon him and offers Marui as a present to Umar. The ruler, in order to test the veracity of Phog about the beauty of Marui, shows him the female members of his family. Phog exclaims:

> O Umar Sumra, even the charms of thy sister,
> Though faintly resembling are not to be compared to those of
> Marui;
> Her nilufar-like nose, her cheek, rich as the light falling on amber gris

The dark locks on her forehead, the braids which fall below her
waist
Must be seen to be appreciated, believe me, O Umar Sumra.

Umar then went with Phog and at last beheld the outskirts of the
beautiful Malir, a district near Omerkot. There on a tank they saw
Mihrada and Marui drawing water. Umar asked for some water.

Then Marui immediately drew water as clear as milk,
And shrinking backwards poured out the stream;
The Hemir in delight offers up prayers for her happiness.

When a woman or child brings water to a person, the drinker utters
a benediction. After a time, Umar leaped from his camel, seized the
young lady and carried her off to Omerkot, in spite of tears and
struggles. Marui refused to touch food or speak a word but prayed,
as Hart-Davies translates:

Set me, set me free
O Umar, that I may seek my home,
   Let go, Marui,
May none to prison ever come.
   With my darling I
Will pick the fruit of Kubber trees
   Six days have passed by
And yet thou wilt not me release,
   No, this is not well,
How I hate this princely court,
   This to me is hell,
This proudly-rising lofty fort.

Every day she was chained and fettered and when night came,
she was carried to a couch on which Umar slept, a gold dagger,
separating the pair. This lasted for some time, till Marui exclaims:

This is not the way, O Sumra, in which men contract nuptial
alliances.
Thou chainest those whom thou lovest—this is a strange manner
of showing affection.
Alas, Alas, I am dying for one sight of the Tharr;
Ye holy Pirs of Panwar, O grant me to see my friends once more.

Umar then released the prisoner and allowed her to live among the
ladies of the palace. She took an opportunity to request her cousin
Maru to assist her in escaping. Maru came to Omerkot, and entered
the chamber where Umar and Marui were sleeping. Maru wanted
to kill Umar, but Marui dissuaded him from this sin and substituted
a silver for the gold dagger on the couch. A few days after this,
Marui in company of some ladies of the palace went to perform a
pilgrimage nearby. After visiting the tomb and performing the usual
religious rites, Marui pointed to her cousin, and asked the women
'which of you will wander about with my brother the Fakir?' Umar's
sister who had accompanied Marui replied:

Having left (thy cousin) Maru at Malir, thou sayest
I have acquired a new brother here;
Free, indeed, art thou, go thou with this, thy other brother.

Marui, finding some excuse for escaping from her companions,
mounted Mara's camel and hastened to revisit her beloved Malir.
    Umar then gave up the idea of making Marui his wife. He rode
over to the Malir, and adopted Marui as his sister. The platonic
love did not die; for Marui came to visit her adopted brother Umar
during illness. Marui heard accidently the false report of Umar's
death, as she was preparing to visit him. Umar as soon as he heard
of death of her fair lady, expired also.
    Verily we are God's, and unto Him we are returning.

THE TALE OF RANO AND MUMAL

Hamir Sumra, a ruling prince of Sind, called together his friends Don Bhutani, Sinharo Rajani, and his bother-in-law, Rano Mendhro, and proposed a trip on the banks of the River Kak, near Omerkot, and to call upon Mumal a woman of renowned beauty. The party started and met a Fakir on their way;

A Babu (mendicant) met them in the wilderness, one watch after sunrise
When speaking of the Kak, he wept tears of blood (and cried)
'Let no one go to Kak, lest he become what I am.'

Mumal belonged to the Rajput Rathors. Rano was also of the same race belonging to the Sodha clan; there are many Sodhas about Omerkot and the Thar, where they are lords of the country. During the rule of the Amirs, their headman levied grazing fees from the graziers and was never interfered with in his prerogative. Although Hindus, they intermarry with Mahomedans.

Kak, a river which once flowed near Omerkot, but is now dried up. There are ruins of an old town on its banks, and some traces of Mumal's Meri (house with an upper story). The friends asked the Fakir the reason of his complaint of Kak. The Fakir rejoins:

Men (if you go there), the very trees will lament your fate.
The stones will cry aloud, and the waters shed tears for you;
Magis veils, like a lightning's blaze, will obscure your sight
Mir affirms that no one can gaze at Mummal,
Without bearing in his face wounds that never heal.

The Fakir further narrates his woes and adds 'O wise one, I came with my suite from Lodrano, I, the naked pauper, was then a noble but Kak has ruined and beggered me. She ruined all, my friend, I now go forth alone. Shun thou the road to Kak, and avoid the pit into which I fell.'

The advice was disregarded by the friends, who reached the waters of the Kak. When they saw a crowd of female slaves, they went and enquired the name of the stream, the town, &c. Mumal's handmaid, Natir, was indignant at their ignorance, and among other things informs the travellers that here dwell Mumal and Sumal, Sehjan and Muradi, and described their dresses &c.

The friends repaired to a place where they received a message from Mumal; the servant approached with a low salam and placed some toasted *chana* (gram) and raw silk at each traveller's feet. All of them ate the gram and sent back the silk cleaned and spun, except Rano, who told the handmaid to inform her mistress that Rano had twisted the silk into a rope for his horse and threw the gram to the animal. When Mumal heard what had happened she sent some halwa and bread to Rano; the hero punished the maid and asked how her mistress dared to send him a woman's dinner.

Now the friends received an invitation to dine with Mumal, but each of them should come singly. The Hamir started first but returned supper-less being frightened on the road by horrible forms of dragons, lions. The other friends followed, but failed. Rano took a guide with him, the fair Natir, who tried to run away when they were half way on the road but Rano threatened the maid with a dagger. Rano knew that the figures on the road were put to frighten him; he reached Mumal's house where he was offered to sit on a couch. Rano suspected some trick, removed the covering on the cot, and saw a well underneath. He was then ushered into a room where a number of damsels all beautiful and similarly dressed were arranged; Rano nearly failed to discover Mumal but fortunately he saw a Bhumra, a large black bee, buzzing round her head attracted by the fragrance. Rano and Mumal lived happily for a time, but their happiness did not last long. The jealous Sumra waited for a few days and when his brother-in-law left Mumal to return home, requested to see the lady's face even for an hour. Rano consented on condition that the prince should behave and dress as a common servant. The Hamir consented but when Mumal asked him to milk a buffalo, he could not do it. Mumal guessed what had occurred and said to her lover 'Rano, thou hast erred and sadly erred in bringing the handsome Sumra here in such unseemly plight.' The prince felt the indignity and sent a message to Rano:

Art thou coming, O Mendhra, thy friends all sigh for thee;
Or hast thou any message for the lords of Dhat?

To which he replied:

A hundred salams to fair Dhat, twenty salams to my neighbours
In Mumal's love, my lord, we care for nothing else.

Dhat is a province near Omerkot; the people are called Dhati.

In an evil hour, Mumal wishing her lover to be on friendly terms with his lord induced Rano to bid goodbye to his companions. When he went to them, he was seized, bound on a camel and carried off to Omerkot where Hamir confined him in a prison; he was not released till he promised never to return to Kak. Rano, as soon as he got liberty, visited the lady of his heart. One morning his wife found the water in which he had bathed to be of reddish colour, called her mother-in-law and said to her:

Thy greedy profligate son is ever wandering about in pursuit of strange women;
Some foe has been wounding, some enemy beating him;
See how the blood has poured in streams from his forehead.

The old lady was alarmed and carried the vessel to the Prince, who immediately guessed that the colour was of the water of the Kak river; the prince mutilated the fine camel of Rano. At length Hamir's wife interceded and procured the freedom of her brother. Rano took bold of his young colt, for the old mother of the camel had died, and rode fast to Mumal's abode, promising the young colt the best of feed.

Fate willed it otherwise. The fair Mumal, in order to lessen her grief, dressed her sister Sumal in Kano's old clothes and made her sleep on the same couch. At night Rano arrived and saw two persons lying together; he wished to kill them but put a stick by the side of the couch and left the house quietly. When Mumal arose, she saw the sign, and cried in grief:

> Thou hast ridden to Kak, and yet thou believest thy love faithless
> O Jat, hath thy intellect fled forever?
> With grief as thine only Companion hast thou departed, O
> Mendhra.

Mumal is very unhappy and every pleasure now ceases to please. At last Mumual disguises herself as a merchant, goes to Dhat and puts herself in Rano's way. Rano formed friendship with this new comer and invites him to his house. One day when they had been playing at chess, Rano remarked that the merchant was very like the 'Light of love', Mumal. She threw off her disguise, and showed him the ring which Rano had given her in the happier days. Still Rano is hard, when Mumal exclaims:

> Human beings, O, Mendhra, are liable to error,
> But the good do good, and injure others as little as possible.
> They carry on friendship to the last, and never (lightly) break its
> chain.

Rano still remains obdurate: Mumal seizes the hem of his dress and says 'My love, I come to thy abode as a suppliant, and cast thy skirt round my neck.' Feeling sick of life she collects a pyre of wood, and exclaiming 'if we meet not now, I go where our souls will reunite, O Mendhra', sets fire to the mass and burns herself to ashes.

The youth now comes to his senses, repairs to the spot and addresses to the manes of his Mumal:

Our separation now ends, my beloved, our sorrows are over,
Fired with desire of thee, I quit the world which contains thee not
Tell my friends (ye bystanders) that Rano is gone to seek Mumal,
falls headlong into the burning heap of wood.

THE LOVES OF SONI AND MEHAR (BUFFALO KEEPER)

The love story of this unfortunate couple is narrated in Punjabi ballads also; there Soni is called the 'Dub-mui' or 'Drowned Beauty'. Soni, according to tradition, was said to be a Hindu; others say she was the daughter of a Jat of Sangar, a village on the banks of the Sangra river, in the province of Jhang Siyal. She was given in marriage to one Dam, a man of her own tribe. As the nuptial procession was on its way to the river, her husband sent her into the jungle to fetch some milk: there she saw a buffalo-keeper, and fell in love with him at first sight. In order to visit him she was in the habit of crossing the river at night on a *chatti* (earthern pot) such as fishermen use on the Indus, and returning before daybreak, reversing the well-known practice of Hero and Leander. The mother-in-law, the cause of all domestic woes in Sindh as well as in the whole world, discovered the intrigue, and persuaded her own lover, Kodu, a potter by trade, to make a *chatti* of unbaked material exactly similar to the one, used by Soni. The unsuspecting Sohni took the jar substituted by her treacherous relation and attempted to swim the stream; the jar burst and the fair lady there and then met with a watery grave. When she did not turn up as usual and knowing that the night was a stormy one, Mehar sprang into the river and was never seen again.

This tale seems to have come from the Punjab. Mr Kincaid in his 'Tales of Old Sind', names Mehar as Izat Beg, son of a rich merchant of Bokhara: Izat Beg on his way home fell in love with Suhni in Guzrat town on the banks of the river Chinab; as Izat Beg had lost all his wealth, he worked as a buffalo grazier. He used to swim the River Chenab every night to meet her love but once he got himself wounded; from that date the lady used to swim to him, and on a stormy night by the treachery of her sister-in-law, was drowned.

Her praises are generally sung in 'Bait' like these:

Sohni was fair, both in body and mind,
Nor has she one defect you could remark:
She left husband and home in search of happiness
and in quest of love, but found a grave.

HIR AND RANJHO

This well-known Punjabi legend is narrated differently. Ranjho was one of the eight sons of Jam Mahomed, a chief of Jhang Siyal, on the banks of the River Chenab. The father, determined to provide a wife for his son, collected all the beauties, out of whom Ranjho selected Hir, who was already a married woman. Both of them fell in love with each other, and both of them set out on their wanderings. Both lived and died fakirs.

Another version of this love story is as follows: King Chuchak ruled at Jhang Sayal on the banks of the River Chenab. He had a very beautiful daughter, Hir. She lived in a palace on the river, and had a boat in which she would take long trips up and down the river.

At the same time in the Hazar country, there ruled four princes of whom Ranjho was the bravest and most beloved. He heard about the beauty of Hir and went in search of her. He entered her cabin, and being tired went to sleep on her bed. Hir, when she heard about it, wanted to kill the foreigner but at his sight fell in love with him. They lived privately together, but her love for Ranjho got noised abroad. When the king heard about it, he confined Hir and drove away Ranjho from the city, but he lay concealed in a wood in hopes of seeing the princess; as soon as she was free she met him. When this was known they formed a plan to get Hir married to Khiro, son of king Norang of Norangpur. She would not make preparations for her wedding. The father in despair took her to the Kazi, [and Hir said to him] '... love is as old as Adam; why should a lover need books when the mirror in his heart shows him the form of his beloved?' The Kazi screamed: 'take her away and kill her, she is not fit to live'.

The king did not kill her but sent her to Norangpur, where she was married to prince Khiro, sore against her will. In the meantime Ranjho went to Norangpur. When Hir knew about her lover's presence she gave out that she was bitten by a cobra; the court doctors could not cure her, till Ranjho, in the garb of a Fakir, was sent for. He cleared the room of all relations, and met Hir alone. That night both of them fled to Hazara. As Ranjho was the favourite of the people, he became master of his father's kingdom, married princess Hir and together ruled over the people of Hazara for many years.

THE PROPHECIES OF THE SAMOI

The Sammas ruled over Sind for more than two centuries; Jam Tamachi son of Junur was the third prince of the family. He and his family were taken prisoners and confined at Delhi by the Mogul. In the fifth year of Tamachi's rule, Makhdum Baha-el-din, great saint of Multan, was visiting his murids or disciples at Tattah. This sufi of great eminence was born in AD 1182, and died in AD 1267. The murids plotted his destruction in order to secure the blessings of his perpetual presence because, if he died at Multan, the journey to that place was so long and troublesome. The event alluded to is by no means without examples. The people of Multan murdered Shams of Tabriz, the celebrated Murshid (or spiritual teacher) the more celebrated Hafiz, in order to bury him in their town. The Afghan Hazarehs make a point of killing and burying in their own country any stranger who is indiscreet enough to commit a miracle or show any particular sign of sanctity. A follower of the saint discovered the plot and took the saint's place in his bed with his permission.

The murids killed the person, cooked his flesh and wanted to eat it. Tasting the blood and flesh of a holy man is considered by ignorant mystics an act of peculiar religious efficacy. They repented of their resolve, put the remains in a pot, sealed it and cast it into the Indus. This pot was found by seven Mohanas (fishermen) who ate up the flesh in ignorance of its nature. They at once became Siddhas (saints), or Walis and are celebrated to the present day as the Samoi, Mamoi or the Haft-tan. Samoi from the Samma jo Goth, or the remains of ancient Tatta near lake Kinjur, generally called the 'Samoi jo diro' or 'pad', the ruined heaps of the Samma clan. The word Mamoi is translated either as cannibals or revealers of hidden things, and Haft-tan alludes to the seven trunks without the heads.

The seven fishermen came to the court of Jam Tamachi at Tatta, and informed him that under his capital was the head of a snake, whose tail reached to Delhi; and as long as the animal retained its position Sind had nothing to fear from the Lords of India. And at the request of the Jam they secured the serpent's head by thrusting a spit into the ground. But the people of Tatta did not believe this. They pulled out the iron rod, and were struck with horror when they saw the point dropping blood; the people fell on their knees and asked the seven fishermen to intercede with heaven for them, their children and their country. The saints informed them that it was impossible, for the snake had turned his head where stood his tail and that Sind had for ever lost her protecting spell. Jam Tamachi became very angry and ordered the seven Mohanas to be decapitated; the order was obeyed. Each headless trunk arose and holding its head began walking towards the east. They arrived at Amri on the banks of the Puran river. They were buried in the sepulchres which are still to be seen at Makan Amri.

Before they left Tatta, each headless person addressed a short speech to the Jam regarding the future destinies of Sind. The first corpse raising his head uttered these lines:

The Hakro shall become a perennial stream and the dyke of Aror
shall burst
And thus shall productions of lakes and streams be carried to the
Samma clan as presents.

In Burton's time (1851) the prediction was not then fulfilled. The
dyke of Aror had not burst; and the Hakro, a large bed of a river
near Umerkot, had no water in it. Aror is located about four miles
eastward of the Indus at Sukkur and Rohnj. The second line means
that Palla fish and other aquatic chestnut-like roots which grow in
Manchar and other lakes shall thus be conveyed to the inland regions
about Jesulmere and Cutch, occupied by the people of Samma
tribes. This prophecy is fulfilled by the Sukkur Barrage.

The second corpse said:

Long and long shall the Ar remain full of water; but when at last it
shall dry up;
In those days the children of the Beloch shall be cheap and
valueless in the land.

The prophecy is now gradually being fulfilled. The Ar and Awar
are other names for the Baghar Creek, which is becoming more
shallow every year; and the Belochis, who formerly were the lords
of the soil, are regarded with no more favour or respect than the
Sindhis, Jats and other inferior people. This is plainly indicated that
the children of the Baloch shall be sold for five dirhems, or about
half a crown; a low price.

The third head declared:

Karo Kabaro's walls shall view
Fierce combat raging half a day.
The Mirmichi shall routed be
Then, Sindhe, once more be blithe and gay.

The Samas and Arguns met for a final trial of strength in Chachkan
a district in the Eastern Delta country, where a hard fought battle
ended in complete victory of Shah Husayn. Following Mir Masum's
chronology, this battle must have been fought in 1523 so that the entire
period of the Sama dominion was just 190 years. The Fakir predicted
that at Karo Kabaro a battle shall be fought lasting six watches
(18 hours). The Mirmichi shall be beaten. Sindh shall enjoy peace.

I have slightly altered his translation to make it more exact. He
[Burton] says that Sindhis explain this prediction as referring to Sir
Charles Napier's victory at Daba, and the extinction of the rule of
the Talpur Mirs, but that Karo Kabaro cannot be accounted for, no
action having been fought at such a place. He accepts the popular
interpretation of the prophecy, and agrees with the popular opinion
that the inexplicable term Mirmirchi designates the Talpur chiefs.
It is certainly true that the popular views on these points are as
he describes them, but I believe them to be totally mistaken. Karo
Kabaro is not an imaginary name; the place intended is evidently
Khari Khabarlo, a township in the present Tando Bhago Pargana,
part of ancient Chachkhan, and I think it extremely probable that
this was the battlefield in which the pride of the Samas was quenched
and that this prediction (perhaps safely uttered by somebody after
the event) refers to that fatal day. The Mamu-i-Fakirs, as the legend
says, were put to death by the Sama, Jam Tamachi. It was indeed
after the execution that each severed head uttered in succession one
of the well-known prophesies. What more likely than that, some later
admirer of men fully credited with divine inspiration should gratify
his vengeful feelings and his fancy by inventing a mamu-i prediction
in relation to a catastrophe which he regarded as divine retribution
for Jam Tamachi's crime? And if we compare historical facts we
shall find that they support my view much more than the popular
one. The battle of Chachkan is described by Mir Masum as lasting
from early morning till well on in the afternoon. Twenty thousand
fell in the fight—a great exaggeration. The battle of Daba on the
other hand lasted but one hour, and the field is 60 good miles from

Khari Khabarlo. It is therefore difficult to see how the prediction can refer to the case of the Talpur Mirs. The word Mirmichi was a nickname applied to the Sama princes. Mirmichi was never applied to the Talpurs; they never fought a battle at Khari Khabarlo. The meaning of Khari Khabarlo (properly, loi) is place of salt land and Khaber bushes.

The fourth carcase immediately enquired and replied:

The Mirmichi shall be beaten; what are the signs of the Mirmichi?
Below (the waist) they have dark clothes, and dark hair on their heads.

There is a variation which can be translated thus:

The Mirmichi, who may teach ye,
The surest token him to know?
His lady fair wears double tails,
And down his neck the long curls flow.

This is equally ambiguous. The Belochis wear dark blue cloths round the loins, and have dark hair, but so are many other clans.

The fifth body describes the signs of the times to come.

The war shall begin from Lar (the battle shall be fought in Lar)
but from upper Sind
(Siro) the rumour of an army's approach shall come down.
When this occurs, then indeed trouble cometh to our little Sindh
from the south-eastern direction.

This is the celebrated prediction which, after agitating the whole of Sindh from 1839 to 1843, was at last accomplished. Lar or Lower Sind was the scene of the battles of Mianee and Daba; the British force was not sent from the south but marched down from Sukkur. The South-east direction points to the Bombay Presidency.

The sixth corpse predicts:

The thin grey steeds shall come down from the north.
The petticoated females shall go about the streets divided (among the people)
After which the rule of the Tajyani begins.

The natives always remark the fondness of the British for grey horses and the British cavalry had not grown fat at Sukkur in 1843. The second verse alludes to the Beloch women who when of rank wear a petticoat covering their persons from the waist to the ankles.

The seventh body ended the scene with these words:

Come and sit, o ye people, under the protection of the Nagar and beyond the Puran river build no new abodes.

The Nagar is Tatta, the city of Sindh during its prosperity. The prophecy is said to be fulfilled by abandoning Hyderabad, the capital of the Talpurs, and selecting Karachi for the headquarters of Government. Some of these rhymes are of modern growth; others are ancient, handed down from father to son for generations past.

13

Census Reports of Sind for the Years 1931 and 1941:
A Comparison
N. M. Billimoria

IN 1931 THE CENSUS OPERATIONS FOR THE BOMBAY PRESIDENCY (including Sind) were carried on by Mr A. H. Dracup, who owing to ill-health was compelled towards the end of May 1932 to proceed on leave to England and it devolved upon Mr H. T. Sorley, ICS. to complete the work of the census. Mr H. T. Lambrick, I.C.S. was the Superintendent of Census Operations in Sind for 1941.

The smooth progress of census operations must depend on the co-operation of the public. But in 1931 leaders of the Indian National Congress refused to co-operate with the census authorities and disorganized proceedings by interfering with house numbering operations and prevented the collection of information by subjecting census officials to annoyance and in some cases to physical assault and boycotted citizens who were not disposed to accept the Congress dictum. Overt hostility was displayed in four municipal towns only, *viz*. Ahmedabad, Vile Parle, Ghatkopar-kirol and Broach. The census work in 1941 in Sind was carried on smoothly.

AREA, HOUSES, AND POPULATION

The exact area of Sind with which these reports is concerned is in 1921, 1931 and 1941 is 46,506, 46,378 and 48,136 square miles respectively. It will be seen that the total area for 1941 of the province differs from that given for the last two decades. No change in the external boundaries of the province has taken place and the difference is simply the effect of recent revision operations by the Survey of India.

As a new district of Dadu was created, many changes in the internal divisions of Sind since 1931 have taken place. It was formed of parts of the old districts of Larkana and Karachi; the new Larkana district absorbed part of the old Upper Sind Frontier district, while the latter gained some small areas from Sukkur and the old Larkana district. These changes create great difficulty in comparing with the statistics of former years as the boundaries of a number of talukas have undergone alteration.

Mr Sedgwick was the Bombay-Sind Provincial Superintendent of Census in 1921. He observed, 'The Census House is a hopeless hybrid between the family and the building.' Mr Lambrick considers this statement to be in great measure inevitable owing to the diversity in the manner of life among the population. The definitions adopted for the Sind Census of 1941 were as follows:

BUILDING: A roofed structure made of any materials, which is likely to remain in existence on the same site during the census period, whether used for purposes residential or non-residential; being under one undivided roof, or under two or more roofs connected *inter se* by a subsidiary roof.

HOUSE: A building or part of a building which is and likely to remain during the census period, a dwelling regularly inhabited by a human being or a family living together in one common mess, with their dependents and resident servants.

The total number of persons recorded as houseless was, in 1941, 80,689 or 1.8 per cent of the entire population. These elements include seasonal and other temporary immigrants from the countries to the north-west and south-east; fakirs of many descriptions; and wandering tribes such as Ods, Bhats, *Karias* (wandering blacksmiths) and Wagris. Three per cent, of the population in the districts subject to seasonal immigration were recorded 'houseless', the average in other districts being one and a half per cent.

The average number of persons per house in British Sind was a little under five in the urban areas and 5.8 in the rural areas. The latter show a higher rate than the former in every district; and it is also worth noting that it is higher in the Upper Sind districts than in those of Lower Sind, attaining the high average of 7.7 in the rural area of Upper Sind Frontier district. The cause of this may be assigned to the tendency among rural Mahomedans, particularly Balochies, for a family to live together after the sons have grown up and married.

DISTRIBUTION OF THE POPULATION BETWEEN URBAN AND RURAL AREAS

Municipal and cantonment areas, which alone were reckoned as urban areas, numbered 30 in 1931 while they were 29 in 1941. During these ten years, two municipalities, Bubakand [and] Keti Bunder, were abolished, and two, Dadu and Nawabshah, were constituted. But in 1931 these two latter were treated as towns.

A new cantonment of Drigh Road was formed. But for the purpose of the following tables, the cantonments of Karachi, Manora and Drigh Road have been included with Karachi municipal area as Karachi City and Hyderabad Cantonment with Hyderabad Municipal area as Hyderabad City. The number of towns thus appears as 26.

Of the house-dwelling population of Sind, nearly 20 per cent live in urban areas, and a little over 80 per cent in rural areas. Compared with the figures for 1931, they come respectively to 18 and 82 per cent. The urban-rural ratio calculated on the population living in towns of 5,000 and over is 1:4. The percentage rate of increase of the urban and rural population were 27.6 and 14.3 for the ten years 1931–41. In the previous ten years they were 27.9 and 16.6.

Density: Sind has an average density of population 1941 of 94 souls to the square miles; while in 1931 it was 81 to the square mile. More than two-thirds of the area comprised in Dadu district is barren hill country, and two-thirds of Thar Parkar district is sandy desert. About one-third of Sukkur and Karachi districts is barren waste; sand, bare hills, or salt flats. The average density of 'Sind' proper, i.e. the country irrigable from the River Indus may be estimated as 165 souls to the square mile. The area of Sind in square miles is 48,136; towns 26; villages 6,583; Dehs, 5,495, occupied houses, 8,14,315.

Population: 4,535,008 (males, 2,494,190; females 2,040,818).

Percentage increase in population in the five towns in Sind:

Hyderabad	1911 to 1921,	7%	1921 to 1931,	29.8%
Shikarpur	1911 to 1921,	2.9%	1921 to 1931,	12.6%
Sukkur	1911 to 1921,	21.2%	1921 to 1931,	62%
Tando Adam	1911 to 1921,	29.5%	1921 to 1931,	3.9%
Shahdapur	1911 to 1921,	42.6%	1921 to 1931,	47.7.8%

Five of these towns are in Sind and increased irrigation facilities combined with the construction of the Lloyd Barrage at Sukkur and its auxiliary canals must be regarded as partly responsible. In Hyderabad additional reasons are its growing importance as an educational and residential centre. The Census Superintendent of 1931 adds that it is however possible that some of the increase may be due to the depression in the business of the 'Sind Worki' merchants who finding their branches in numerous places outside India unremunerative in years of slump [and] have returned at least temporarily to their native town till business abroad improves.

Variation in Population during Fifty Years:
Net variation 1891 to 1941 for the whole of Sind is +1,659,908.
Percentage variation: 1931 to 1941, +16.7; 1921 to 1931, +18.5;
1911 to 1931, -6.7; 1909 to 1911, +9.4; 1901 to 1941; 41.2.
Density: 1941, 94; 1931, 81; 1921, 68; 1911, 73; 1901, 67.

The above figures show a fairly steady rate of increase all over the province with a single period of ten years, 1911–1921, in which the population suffered a heavy mortality in the influenza epidemic of 1918–19.

The gain in population in Sind during the last fifty years is nearly sixty per cent over the 1891 census figures. Karachi and Upper Sind Frontier have increased nearly one hundred per cent during the fifty years. The increase in Karachi is due almost entirely to the growth of Karachi City itself. Steady development of irrigation facilities is the result of increase in the Upper Sind Frontier which was dependent almost exclusively on precarious rainfall. In the last three decades the changeover in this district from one-third rice and two-thirds dry crop cultivation to the reverse proportions has attracted cultivators.

Nawabshah and Thar Parkar show a gain of about sixty per cent on account of vast improvements in rail communication and irrigation in the half century. Hyderabad district has increased by over 50 per cent; Sukkur by 46; Dadu by 40 and Larkana by 35 per cent. Larkana comprising roughly the tract known as Chandukah in former days has been perhaps the most highly developed part of the province for over a century, and has always been comparatively thickly populated.

The total area cultivated in the province of Sind in 1931–32, the last season before the Barrage canals came into operation, was about three million acres, of which about two million were in what subsequently became the Barrage zone, and one million in the non-Barrage area. By 1937–38 over three million acres were cultivated in the Barrage zone area, while the non-Barrage Area showed a million acres. In 1938–39, the last season for which figures are available, the total area Barrage and non-Barrage under cultivation was four million two hundred thousand acres. An increase of 37 per cent of 1931–32 figures. This vast extension of cultivation has occasioned a demand for *haris* which has attracted numbers of people from adjacent countries in the north-west and south-east. It is possible that people in the province have moved towards this cultivation. On the whole the people of Sind prospered during the ten years, 1931 to 1941.

TOWNS AND VILLAGES CLASSIFIED BY POPULATION

In the census of Sind for 1941, one important introduction was the classification of 'villages'. The basis of the compilation of 1931 was the 'revenue village' known in Sind as the 'deh'. In 1931, Sind returned 5,352 revenue villages, and 5,180 inhabited towns and villages; 2,841 of these having population under 500 souls.

TOWNS: The terms 'town' was applied to all municipal and cantonment areas. Villages in the 5,000 to 10,000 class which are not municipalities and thus not classified as towns are as follows:

Hyderabad—Tando Jam; Matli
Larkana—Shahdadkot
Nawabshah—Kandiaro
Sukkur—Khanpur; Pir-jo-Goth
Thar Parkar—Mithi

CITIES: The three cantonment areas in and in the vicinity of Karachi Municipal district have been treated as component parts of Karachi City; and Hyderabad cantonment as part of Hyderabad City.

Total number of cities, towns and villages	6,609
Total number of Dehs	5,495
Population of Sind	4,535,008

CITIES CLASSIFIED BY POPULATION WITH VARIATION SINCE 1891

The most noteworthy phenomenon recorded in the census of 1941 is the increase of the population of Karachi (Municipal area) during, the past ten years. It amounted to 45 per cent, the highest decennial rate ever recorded since the ten years 1881–91, though it attained 43.5 per cent in 1911–21. Mr Sorely in his report for 1931 writes that the rise in population in the fifty years 1881–1931 by 261 per cent was one of the most striking features in the census history of the Bombay Presidency. The figure for the fifty years 1891–1941, 266.2 per cent, is even higher.

We will consider the main causes of this high rate of increase in Karachi:

1. Equable climate of Karachi and its freedom from congestion.
2. Karachi has gained greatly from immigration; people came over not only from other parts of Sind, but also from Baluchistan, Cutch, Rajputana, Gujarat, United Provinces and the Punjab.
3. The Hindus of Sind, [who] generally preferred to live in towns and villages, migrated to Karachi and settled there permanently because Karachi is the only modern and progressive place in Sind. The advantages of mild climate are now appreciated.
4. Karachi became the headquarters of a provincial government in 1936. Many new government offices opened; and this development has directly or indirectly caused many persons to settle in the city.
5. The demand for housing caused many buildings to be erected. The development of the Artillery Maidan Quarter has attracted many masons and labourers from Cutch; and these people live in municipal limits. The present war did not slacken the activity of buildings; a large number of military buildings are being erected.
6. The growth of [the] Karachi fishing industry has brought many Makrani fishermen to settle in the Lyari Quarter in the past

few years. The demand for Karachi fish has increased all over north-west India.

7. The development of the barrage area has benefitted considerably the entrepot trade on which the prosperity of Karachi depended. The number of bales of cotton annually exported through Karachi has risen by nearly one hundred per cent on the average since 1932. Also exports of wool, hides and skins, and iron ore show heavy increase.

8. Carrying and forwarding business of Karachi is thriving and agency business of every kind has increased during the ten years.

9. The only obstruction to the further development is the inadequate supply of water. But if the Indus water supply scheme is completed in the next few years, the growth of Karachi may become even more rapid. Mr Lambrick writes: 'Given virtually unlimited water, no place could be found better suited for development of the textile industry, and it is not unreasonable to contemplate a time when Karachi, with a huge cotton growing tract almost at its backdoor, may compete successfully with Ahmedabad and Bombay.'

Mr Sorely refers to the same subject in his Census Report for 1931: 'The high percentage[s] in Sind are noticeable. In addition to the natural increase induced by the benevolence of the seasons during the decade under review ... the insistent demand for labor for the Sukkur Barrage has resulted in an appreciable influx of persons, particularly from Baluchistan and the Punjab; and the general stimulus to trade, caused by the disbursement of considerable sums of money in the shape of wages, may reasonably be expected to have swelled the population in urban areas. Further, there have been indications that on this occasion the Moslem element in the population has taken the census more seriously than usual and Muhammadans throughout Sind have been at pains to render individual household returns accurately. In an area where the home is especially sacrosanct and in which the female members of a family are not generally accorded the freedom granted to the womenkind of other castes, the influence of this spirit of co-operation is not unlikely to have been effective.'

TOWNS ARRANGED TERRITORIALLY WITH POPULATION BY COMMUNITIES

The number of places classified as cities increased in 1941 by one; it was anticipated that Hyderabad's population would exceed one lakh; it has in fact surpassed this figure by a large margin.

The number of places classified as towns was reduced by one, the municipalities of Bubak and Keti Bunder were abolished after the census of 1931, while the cantonment of Drigh Road came into existence. During the decade, the municipalities of Nawabshah and Dadu were constituted.

The total urban population of the province increased by 27.5 per cent; the increase during the ten years 1921–31 was 29 per cent. The magnetic influence of Karachi City was never greater. The considerable proportion of increase of Hyderabad is drawn upon the mofussil (rural or provincial area) but their development is shadowed by the rising towns in Barrage Area, namely Nawabshah and Mirpurkhas. The former has gained by 149 and the latter by 92 per cent.

The following five towns in the Barrage Area have developed during the last ten years, viz. Dadu, Tando Allahyar, Ratodero, Shahdadpur and Tando Adam. Tando Mahomed Khan and Jacobabad outside the Barrage Area are thriving. The following four towns are decaying, viz. Sehwan, Matiari, Nassarpur and Tatta. The attractive influence of Karachi and Hyderabad have ruined them. Matiari, Nassarpur and Tatta are centres of [the] handloom weaving industry, which is passing through hard times and the trade which prospered Sehwan and Tatta has shifted to other centres.

The indigenous Hindu population, i.e. the Lohanas, Bhatias,

etc. have a tendency to live in large villages and towns while the Muslims live in villages and hamlets. Mr Lambrick states that this distinction is becoming more sharply defined for while there is a strong centripetal movement among Hindus, a centrifugal tendency has begun among the Muslims.

Total and Percentage Increases, 1931–1941:
1. Hindu urban population, over lakhs, or by 40%.
2. Hindu rural population, a little over one lakh, or 15%.
3. Muslim urban population, a little over one quarter of a lakh, or 9%.
4. Muslim rural population, over 3½ lakhs, or 14%.

Proportion of Hindu Urban Population to Their Total Population:
1. 1931 urban, 36.9%.Rural 63.1%.
2. 1941 urban, 41.6%.Rural 58.4%.

Proportion of Muslim Urban and Rural Population to Their Total Population:
1. 1931 urban, 10.2%.Rural 89.8%.
2. 1941 urban, 9.8%. Rural 90.2%.

The Hindu figures include for 1931 the 'depressed classes' and for 1941 the 'scheduled castes'. In Sind, 'scheduled castes' include the various Bhangi castes and Menghwars and very few others. Of these 11 per cent live in towns and 88 per cent in the mofussil; and if we separate them from the 'other Hindus', it will be found that almost half of the 'caste Hindus' live in towns; the figures for the urban and rural areas amounting to 48 and 51 per cent, of their total population (I have left out the decimal figures).

We may add that Bhils and Kolis, who are considered as 'caste Hindus' in Sind, form a very great proportion of the Hindu community dwelling in the rural areas of Thar Parkar, Hyderabad and Nawabshah. Among them there are many immigrants from

Cutch, Marwar etc. but a greater number come from Thar in Sind. 7,205 Bhils and Kolis were recorded in cities and towns, and 176,369 in the rural areas.

The large increase in the Hindu community in towns is made up chiefly by migration from smaller towns and villages in Sind. The percentage of increase was as follows: Nawabshah 150; Mirpurkhas 90; Dadu 70; Tando Allahyar 50.

I have shown above that the average increase in the urban population of the Muslims is 9 per cent; this is due to very great gains in a few flourishing places, while in the majority of towns Muslims have decreased. The cause of this may be attributed to the development of the Barrage Zone. In 1931–32 the area irrigated was twenty million acres. It has risen under the Barrage to thirty-two million acres. The vast extension of cultivation demanded more *haris*.

The effect of the introduction of the Barrage irrigation has attracted the Muslims out of the towns on to the land. And the Hindus previously living in small villages are induced to concentrate in the towns and larger villages which are handling the growing transit trade in agricultural produce.

Of the other communities, the Sikhs show much increase in Dadu, Hyderabad, Karachi, Larkhana, Nawabshah, Shahdadpur, Tando Adam, Mirpurkhas, Jacobabad and Khairpur Mirs. It is well-known that the Sikhs are very skillful in matters connected with engineering.

COMMUNITY

Community has been adopted as a more suitable term than 'religion'. Hindus are now divided into 'scheduled castes' and 'others' instead of the old division of Hindus into Brahmanic, Aryan, and Brahmo. In 1931, the 'depressed classes' which correspond fairly closely with the 'scheduled castes' were not shown separately in the table for religion, but appeared in table Caste, Tribe, Race, or Nationality.

Tribes: The tribal of 1931 Table (XVI) religion, were primitive people who were understood to worship animistic Deities distinct from the Hindu Pantheon. The tribes in the 1941 community table are in Sind, exclusively Thakurs, who are classified as a primitive aboriginal caste in Sind, though there would be equal justification in including the Bhils, Kolis and similar people of Eastern Sind.

Hindu Scheduled Castes: The 'depressed classes' in 1931 amounting to 99,551 included Menghwars, Bhangi, Mochis, Mahons and Dheds. In 1941, the same castes were counted as 'scheduled castes'. Their numbers are nearly doubled.

Muslims: Sunnis and Shias are no longer tabulated separately.

Jains: In 1931 they amounted to 1,144 while in 1941 the figure comes to 3,687; this may be due to the immigration of persons from Gujarat to Karachi; perhaps this may be [the] result of more accurate enumeration.

Parsees, Jews and Others: No increase or change worthy of remarks.

RELATIVE STRENGTH OF THE MUSLIM AND HINDU COMMUNITIES IN SIND

The information on this subject is very important and interesting. The proportion of Muslims to the total population has declined from 76 per cent in 1931 to 71 per cent in 1941. The proportion of Hindus (including Scheduled Castes) has increased in the same period from 23 to 27 per cent. All other communities have improved from .4 to 2 per cent.

Hindus from Shikarpur, Sukkur and Rohri have gone to settle in Karachi. We find that Hindus (including scheduled castes) have increased by ten and Muslims by 11 per cent, roughly. The above figures may be further tested by assessing the increase of Hindus in the most predominantly Muslim tracts, i.e. on the right bank of the Indus; and the increase of Muslims in a tract on the left bank where Hindus are comparatively numerous. For this purpose we will examine the figures; we find an increase by 14 per cent of Hindus in Upper Sind Frontier, Larkana and Dadu Districts, and of Muslims by 10 per cent, in Hyderabad District. We can conclude that the natural rate of increase in the indigenous Hindu population is higher than among the indigenous Muslim population. The conversion from Hinduism to Islam in former years has ceased to be of importance.

The population of Muslims is greater in Upper Sind Frontier where there are nine of them for every one Hindu; and the two communities in Thar Parkar are almost equal in numbers. In Hyderabad there are rather more than two Muslims to one Hindu; in Sukkur five Muslims to two Hindus; in Nawabshah three to one; in Larkana and Dadu five to one. These figures, in form of percentage compared with those of 1931 in Upper Sind Frontier the Muslims, are more than the Hindus but in the south-eastern districts the reverse is the case:

		Muslims	Hindus
		(Percentage)	
Upper Sindh Frontier	1931	89	10
	1941	90	94
Dadu, Larkhana & Sukkur	1931, 1941	Steady	Steady
Hyderabad	1931	69	30
	1941	67	32
Nawabshah	1931	76	23
	1941	75	24

It may be mentioned that in the census of 1891 Muslims and Hindus were in the proportion of nearly four to one; in that of 1881, they had appeared as six to one. This sudden decline in Muslim predominance is really due to the fact that in 1881, 127,000 persons were recorded as Sikhs of whom more than one lakh should almost certainly have been shown as Hindus.

When Sir Bartle Frere was Commissioner in Sind, Census of the Province of Sind was held in February 1851. The percentages of the Muslim, Hindus and 'other' population to the total population were then 74, 21 and 5 per cent. The following note to that Census was as follows:

> The great disproportion between the males and females in this schedule may be in part accounted for by the dislike of orientals, and especially Mussalmans, to speak of anything connected with the Haram. It is probable that not a few wives and female attendants are thus passed over.

Growth of education may have decreased this tendency of concealment but the number of Muslim females to 1,000 Muslim males in Sind actually appears less in 1931 than in 1851; namely 781 against 787. Among Hindus, 1,851 census showed 810 females to 1,000 males, the figure for 1931 being 792. The causes of the deficiency of females in Sind are discussed by Mr Sorley in his Census Report for 1931. I will quote some of the interesting points mentioned by him:

> It is interesting to note in the Punjab Census Report for 1921, which was the work of two officers, one, Mr Middleton, believed that the census figures for total population are subject to very little error, while the other, Mr Jacob, thought that 'there is good ground for doubting that the census figures possess the extreme accuracy which is claimed for them.' He added that as a district officer in Jullunder he noted 'the concealment of the existence of female children as a matter of continual report and observation.' Personally I am inclined on general grounds to agree with Mr Jacob's view. In a Mussulman land like Sind, which returns the greatest deficiency of females in the Presidency, it is well known that female children are thought very little of and in some cases the parents would be unwilling to admit that they possessed an abnormal number of daughters. But it is not so much the prejudice against female children that may vitiate the accuracy of the statistics in Sind and elsewhere as the utter

indifference which characterises anything relating to female children. There would indeed be little cause of surprise if it were found by objective test (could that be devised for some local areas in a later census) that large numbers of female children are not mentioned in birth returns, in census returns, or in death returns. That is to say, it would not be extraordinary if in many areas girls were born, lived and died between the ages of 0 and 15 without the fact ever appearing on any kind of public record. If, however, a girl in such circumstances survives the age of 15 she becomes valuable as a bride and hence she is likely to figure in public returns for the first time. The age-groups are notoriously unreliable for the lower ages. Even a cursory glance at the comparative numbers of children in the age-groups from 0 to 15 is enough to show that there is something wrong with the figures and it is likely that the numbers of girls between the ages of 5 and 10 and between the ages of 10 and 15 are greatly understated. After 15 another set of influences begins to operate because the girl is then being married or being prepared for marriage and bargainings go on about her, which means that individually the girl now receives attention she did not have before. Very likely too the age of the girl will then tend to be overstated so as to make her out to be a more mature wife than if she were shown to be just reaching puberty. It must be clear on quite general grounds, and it is indeed a matter of ordinary observation that these influences are powerful and they must have some effect on the census figures and, later on, upon the vital statistics. Quite another cause of wrong enumeration of girls of early age occurs when the children of both sexes are dressed alike, as happens sometimes.

Furthermore, there may be quite a strong tendency in certain places and with certain races and tribes to enumerate girls as boys. Enumerators in all areas, whatever instructions were, are not likely to have subjected to a minute corroborative examination the sex and age of every child. If all these influences operate together, as they may very well do, the disturbance to the normal distribution of sexes in the age groups from 0 to 15 may be considerable and the result would be to understate that number of female children, especially in Mussalman lands. A priori, therefore, there exist strong reasons for thinking that the female population is somewhat underestimated especially in the lower age groups, and this would unduly depress the sex ratio and lead to a belief that there are more females in deficit in India than is really the case. It is probable therefore (1) that there is a considerable concealment, mostly through sheer indifference of female births and female deaths and female existence, (2) that the concealment works unequally in different age groups which makes the exact location of the sources of error hard to find, (3) that after a certain age, though indifference is still at work, indifference works less powerfully, so that the figures for females are nearer the truth in middle and late life than they are in early life. As, however, the important thing in a growing population is the number of births as compared with the number of deaths, any great error in the enumeration of females in the earlier age groups is like to lead to fellacious [sic] conclusions as to the general deficiency of women in the population ... the age statistics and the sex statistics depend much, upon each other. If the age statistics are inaccurate many of the most valuable conclusions that might be drawn from the sex statistics are rendered hopelessly speculative. It is alleged that conditions in the educated classes differ conditions amongst the poorer classes and the primitive and hill peoples in respect of the treatment of girls from the age of five on till the age of puberty. But there is no evidence to show what some anthropological examination of typical castes and a few test examinations of census statistics in a representative number of villages in various parts of the Presidency, it is hard to see how any advance toward certainty can be achieved.

Mr Sorley adds:

The lowness of sex ratio amongst females in the Muslim Community is worthy of note.

As regards local distribution of the sex ratio it will be noted that the female ratio is higher than the male in the 0 to 5 age group in all divisions except Sind, where it is as high as 995 which shows that the deficiency of girls in the early stages is not very great. It is probably therefore what happens after that accounts for the very great deficiency of women in Sind. The figures for all natural divisions present the same general features. The female ratio is usually most unfavourable in the 40 to 60 age-group. This is probably due partly to a heavy mortality of women soon after the age of child-bearing has passed, and is doubtless partly the result of the married woman in India, in almost every community, having too hard a life, bearing too many children and not having enough care taken of her when she is required to labour with her hands as well as nurse and maintain children and to do the household cooking. Even the Zoroastrians who are more careful in all their domestic and social arrangements than any other community, show the same very heavy mortality of married women once the period of maternity has been passed. There is therefore a means by which the deficiency of females in India can be remedied. More care needs to be taken of married women, especially at the end of their child-bearing period. An inspection of Imperial Table VIII will show for selected cases how heavy the mortality is amongst married women over 43. In this respect widows offer a complete contrast and the most plausible explanation of this is that a widow has had less arduous marital demands made on her and has had much less hard work to do. As the greater part of the female population between the ages of 18 and 43 is married, the effect of only a slight improvement in female mortality during married years would be a considerable lessening of the deficiency of females generally. The evidence of the census and the vital statistics on this point is not however entirely satisfactory because no detailed figures are available for the death rates amongst unmarried, married and widowed women between the various ages vital for a study of the present question.

   In the case of unmarried women of the Marathas, Sind Lohana and Baluch the gross figures are probably too small to give reliable results, and they have probably resulted in distortion very favourable

to unmarried women in the case of the Marathas and unfavourable
to unmarried women in the case of Sind Lohanas and Baluchi.

In the 1921 Census Report for Bombay, Mr Sedgwick has
discussed very fully the comparative influence on the proportion of
the sexes, of racial character, climate and social customs (which are
considered as influences of permanent character) and of migration,
famine and diseases with sex selection. He showed fairly satisfactorily
that the main permanent factor in producing and maintaining
inequality of the sexes is the racial factor, though this is liable to
permanent modification by (1) geographical or climatic conditions
and (2) social customs and temporary modification by some minor
causes (Bombay Census Report, 1921, pp. 103–108). There can be
little doubt that the main cause of the difference between the Sind
figures for Muslims and general Presidency figures is a difference of
racial characteristics. Whether this can be modified much is open to
question. But there is no doubt that social customs in Sind are not
conducive to female predominance and that a great improvement in
the female ratio would occur if much preventable waste of female
life were stopped.

The explanation of the increase in female mortality, relative to
male, between the ages of 3 and 15, when girls might be expected to
be as healthy and as robust as boys, has been given in the Census of
India Report for 1911, page 218, and the reasons may be accepted
as sound. They may be briefly quoted here as follows: 'The neglect
of female infants is of two kinds. There is the deliberate neglect with
the object of causing death which is practically infanticide in a mote
cruel form; and there is the half unconscious neglect, partly due to
habit and partly to the parents' greater solicitude for their sons. The
boys are better clad and when ill are more carefully tended. They are
allowed to eat their fill before anything is given to the girls. In poor
families when there is not enough for all, it is invariably the girls
who suffer. In this way, even when there is no deliberate intention of
hastening a girl's death, she is at a great disadvantage as compared
with her brothers in the struggle for life.

The life of the female population is, in fact, rather like a fire that starts off with a blaze, is quenched to a dull glow and finishes in a smouldering old age. The life of the male population is like a fire that starts modestly, burns with a bright flame for most of the time and dies quickly without smouldering.

VARIATION IN POPULATION OF SELECTED TRIBES

BHILS

The total population, of the Bhils has increased by 21 per cent. Ever since the Barrage canals opened these people settled on the lands as *haris*, instead of wandering about looking for casual labour, doing cotton picking etc. and then returning in their old homes in the Thar. The increase in their numbers in Nawabshah is over 33 per cent.

The majority of Bhils speak Thareli or Dhatki, the dialect of Sindhi characteristic of the Thar. They do not mix with other tribes but live in their own hamlets and encampments in huts of wattle and grass matting. Like other Hindus, they marry with the caste but not within their own 'Nukh'.

KOLI

The number of the Kolis has increased from 60,562 in 1931 to 101,456 in 1941. Like the Bhils they are most numerous in Thar Parkar district. Since the Barrage canals opened, like the Bhils, the Kolis try to settle on the land instead of wandering about. Hindu Zamindars in Hyderabad District have encouraged them to become their *haris*. In 1941 there was continued scarcity in Cutch, Marwar, Palanpur, and even Gujarat, and that induced the Kolis to immigrate to Hyderabad.

The Kolis, like the Bhils, are accepted as true Hindus in Sind. They speak Gujarati, Tharali or Kachhi, and live in their own villages. Like the Bhils they marry within the caste but outside the 'Nukh'.

BALOCH

The increase of the Baloch in 1941 is about 75 per cent, more than in 1931. The Barrage irrigation has occasioned a huge migration from the barren hills of the Mari-Bugti country or from the dry plains of Kachhi.

While the Kolis and Bhils in Sind are for the most part confined to the districts on the left bank of the Indus and a bulk of the Brahuis are to be found in districts on the right bank, Balochis are scattered over the entire province from Kashmor to the Indus delta and from the hills near Karachi to those of Nagar Parkar. Proportion of Baloch to total population in Sind and Khairpur State is 23 in 1941 and 25 in 1931, per cent.

The tribes which belong exclusively to Sind are the Talpors (including Nixamanis), Chandias, Buledhis and Karamatis. The Tumandar of the Rinds (of Shoran in Kachhi) has practically made over the chiefship of his tribesmen to his brother who lives in Nawabshah district. The Bugtis, Dumbkis, and Mazaris everywhere in Sind recognize the authority of their tumandar.

The Khosas, Jatois, Lagharis, Lunds and Bozdars are numerous in Sind. Mr Lambrick adds that there is a tendency for Baloch tribes in Sind to lose their cohesion and for *muqadims* of sections to set up as independent *sardars*. This has been noticed in respect of the Buledhis. Another instance is the Jamali tribe which is very numerous and widely scattered in Sind; this has one *sardar* in Dadu district and another in Nasirabad tehsil in Baluchistan, while the Gabols have two *sardars* both living in the same place.

SOCIAL CUSTOMS OF THE BALOCH IN SIND

The system of 'Phori', by which every tribesman contributes something for the benefit of the chief on occasions of marriage or death ceremonies in the chief's family, is still followed.

Among several tribes the old custom that females cannot inherit land is still prevalent. An elder son gets a share in addition to his due as 'mehman navaz'—his obligation to entertain guests.

Marriage: A youth marries his father's brother's daughter. If first cousin is not available, he will seek in remoter relations; at last he goes to a family of the *paro* or clan but never beyond the 'paro'. The traditional obligation of a Baluch husband to put his wife to death for infidelity is still prevalent especially in Upper Sind.

The Baloch mother is very anxious to change the shape of her child's head and to make it beautiful, just as the Brahuis. The Baloch mother allows her child to spend about the first six months of its life, flat on its back with the head resting on hard ground when the bones of the skull are soft, from which position the child is prevented from rolling over. The back of the head is flattened producing a broad forehead and wide-spaced eyes—a sign of beauty amongst the Balochis and Brahuis.

Occupation: Most of the Balochis in Sind are *zamindars* and *haris*. Some of the tribes depend more on their animals than land; the Lunds of Dadu take out their camels for hire; and the Kapirs (Marris) of Thar Parkar graze sheep and goats. Many of the hill-Balochis gain their livelihood by selling mats, and women of many tribes weave 'falasis' and camel-trappings for sale.

MAKRANIS

No separate figures for this Western Baloch tribe were made this year. There are many in the Karachi City and depend on manual labour; several of them move into Eastern Sind to work in cotton ginning factories, and when the factories are not working maintain themselves by field and casual labour.

Language: Out of about eight lakhs of people of the Baloch race in Sind, perhaps one-quarter speak Siraiki—often differing little from Sindhi; and this is particularly marked among the tribes living in Sukkur, Nawabshah, and Thar Parkar districts. Others speak only Sindhi; it is often found that in a single tribe, for instance the

Chandias, particular sections speak respectively Balochi, Siraiki, and Sindhi as their mother tongue. The Makranis are, on the whole, more tenacious of their mother tongue. Western Baluchi, which differs a good deal from the Eastern and Northern dialect, and are not inclined to speak Sindhi.

BRAHUIS

The census returns for 1941 show 82,326 Brahuis in Sind. The tendency of the Brahuis is growing more to settle in Sind.

Occupation: The Brahuis who are permanently settled in Sind are *zamindars*, cultivators, engaged in camel-transport, blacksmiths and *kalaigars*, and labourers.

Tribes: Most of the Brahuis found in Sind hail from Jhalawan province of Kalat State; and the Mengal and Zahri tribes supply the great majority. The following among others are also regular visitors: Muhammad Hassanis, Bizanjavs, Sasolis, Bajis, Jattaka (permanent near Tatta) and Pandranis, who are settled permanently in Upper Sind. A fair number of Sarawan tribesmen are found, for instance Lahris and Langava.

Until recent years the Brahuis were accustomed to sell their girls to Baluchis and Sindhis in marriage; as the girls were good-looking in youth, the market was brisk, and the temptation to make easy money was great. HH the Khan of Kalat has ordered all Brahui sardars to put a stop to this practice. (About the language, etc. of the Brahuis, please see my paper on the subject, *Sind Historical Society Journal Vol. IV*, No. 2, September 1939, pages 61–65.)

THE JATS OF JATI AND SHAHBUNDER TALUKAS

The Jat tribe in the Delta of the Indus have given the name of Jati Taluka and probably they are the oldest inhabitants of Sind. The Malikani section have their headquarters at Raj Malik, where their chief lives. They wander about the taluka with herds of female camels. They live almost on the milk of the she-camels; they eat no bread and drink no water. They sell their young camels at fairs. The Jats living in Shahbunder taluka, particularly the Fakiranis, follow a similar manner of life. The language of these Jats is considered to be Seraiki.

Other Jat Tribes: Tribes such as the Lishari and Jiskani are found all over Sind. They spend most of their time transporting grain from one place to another. Mr Lambrick reminds that students of Baloch legendary history will recall that the war of the Rinds and Lasharis was mainly due to the rivalry of the two chiefs of this tribe—Chakar and Gwahtam—for the favours of Mai Gohar, a rich camel-owning Jatni.

Variation in Population of Selected Tribes:

Sind	1931	1941	Variation
Bhil	67,963	82,118	+14,155
Koli	60,562	101,456	+40,864
Baluch	427,869	748,797	+320,928
Brahui	71,610	82,326	+10,716
Jat		84,372	

VARIATION IN POPULATION OF SELECTED TRIBES

DADU DISTRICT

Dadu and Johi talukas were irrigated before the opening of the Barrage by the tail reaches of the Western Nata Canal; increase in population is merely 9 per cent. Kakar shows an increase in population by 29 per cent, though his taluka like Mehar was, in the pre-barrage period, well irrigated by inundation canals. Kohistan Mahal received rain fall in the year 1940 increased by 37 per cent.

HYDERABAD DISTRICT

Tando Allahyar taluka gained much in population since the Cartage, for Nasir Branch flows right through the middle of the taluka on the high level; an increase of population by 50 per cent has been noted. Dero Mohbat, known as Matli has the highest rate of increase in the whole of Sind, viz. 62 per cent. On account of the growth of the Hyderabad City, the taluka has gained by twenty per cent. Hula in pre-barrage days was well irrigated; between 1921 and 1931 there was an increase of population by 19 per cent. At present the population has remained stationary. Tando Bago of which about a third now falls within the Barrage zone, gives a modest increase of eight per cent. The population of Guni is almost stationary, and Badin at the tail of the Fuleli system has actually lost by 12 per cent.

KARACHI DISTRICT

On account of the rise in the Karachi City, there is an increase in the Karachi Taluka by 45 per cent. Ghorabari lost during the ten years 1921–31, and during 1931–41 a further fall has taken place. Jati and Tatta had an increase in population during 1921–31 [but] have now decreased to the same extent as Ghorabari. Shahbunder and Sujawal which had registered an increase during 1921–31 are now stationary. Keti Bunder has lost heavily. Mirpur Bathoro and Mirpur Sakro are the only talukas which show a gain in the past ten years. The irrigation facilities in Mirpur Bathoro area are better than in any taluka of the district; and in Mirpur Sakro the development of the Nari Chach during the last ten years has attracted settlers. There is no doubt that the general decrease in population in the district of Karachi is due to the effect of the Barrage.

LARKANA DISTRICT

The taluka constituting the present district of Larkana were among the most prosperous in the whole of Sind in pre-barrage days, under the Ghar and Western Nara systems. The exceptions were Shahdadkot (then part of the Upper Sind Frontier) and Warrah served by the tail branches of the Begari and Ghar respectively. Shahdadkot has attracted a large number of Brahuis from Kalat State and Balochis from Nasirabad tehsil and Kachhi, especially the Magsi country, who have bought land and settled.

NAWABSHAH DISTRICT

Nawabshah district had gained 19 per cent increase during the ten years 1921–1931. This rate is not quite maintained during the ten years 1931–41 but the percentage of increase continues to be high in all talukas except Kandiaro and Sakrand where it is eight per cent. Nawabshah shows the highest rate of increase, 35 per cent, but in the last decade it had gained 48 per cent. Moro had an increase of 10 per cent during 1921–31; during 1931–41 it has gained 22 per cent. Sinjhoro had increased from 12 to 17 per cent. Nawabshah has benefitted greatly from the introduction of Barrage irrigation, especially the three towns, Nawabshah, Tando Adam and Shahdadpur.

SUKKUR DISTRICT

Sukkur District is outside the Barrage zone except a small portion of Rohri Taluka and the greater part of Garhi Yasin taluka. During the ten years 1921–31 the population had increased at 22 per cent; the actual overall increase for the district in 1931–41 is eleven per cent. In the previous ten years the talukas of Rohri and Sukkur were great gainers, because in 1931 several thousand of workmen were engaged in the construction of the Barrage. Now they appear almost stationary. Garhi Yasin has advanced from 10 per cent in 1921–31 to 16 per cent in 1931–41, and Gotki and Pano Akil, dependent exclusively on inundation canals have both improved; and the increase in Mir pur Mathelo and Ubauro are high. Shikarpur Taluka records a 12 per cent increase after gaining by 20 per cent in 1921–31.

THAR PARKAR DISTRICT

In 1921–31 this district showed a rate of increase of 18 per cent but under the ten years under review it has advanced to 24 per cent or by far the highest in British Sind. It was in this district that the success of barrage irrigation was instantaneous and its progress most rapid. In the Umarkot taluka the highest rate of increase in population was recorded; in the last ten years it has gained by 55 per cent. Jamesabad shows an increase by 34 per cent; Mirpurkhas has recorded a gain by 45 per cent.

Digri, Khvpro, and partially irrigated taluka of Biplo all show high rates of increase. Also there has been a gain in Samaro and Sanghar.

Of the purely desert talukas, Chachro continues to increase 21 per cent as against 22 in 1921–31. Mithi has remained stationary; and Nagar Parkar records a loss of 22 per cent. The increase in Diplo by 35 per cent is almost entirely due to the opening of a canal in the strip between the Thar Parkar and Dhoro Naro. The increase in the population of Thar Parkar district can be safely ascribed to the effect of the inauguration of the Barrage.

UPPER SIND FRONTIER DISTRICT

About one half of Garhi Khairo taluka receives irrigation from the Barrage; in this taluka the population has increased by 25 per cent. Jacobabad and Kashmor have gained; also Kandhkot which gains 17 per cent; the figure for Thul is small only 11 per cent.

Mr Lambrick concludes that 'the prosperity in this non-Barrage district is due to constant local improvements in irrigation and more particularly to the progressive removal of restriction on the growing of rice. From its position close to less favoured lands, it continues to draw a fair number of settlers from outside the province.'

In the 1931 census report Mr Sorley mentions four infirmities—insanity, deaf-mutes, blind and lepers. The largest number of deaf-mutes is in Sind. Of the districts in the Presidency returning more than 600 deaf-mutes each, there are 13 in all, of which 6 are in

Sind. In 1911 it was noted that the largest proportionate number of deaf-mutes was found in the Sindhi Bohra community, which showed 177 deaf-mutes per one lac of the caste. The 1921 census showed deaf-mutes, Lohanas in Sind 224 out of 426,697; Baluchis in Sind 403 out of 562,394; Samons in Sind 254 out of 421,583. In 1931 the highest local incidence of deaf-mutism for males was in Thar and Parkar District (209 per 100,000); for females in Thar Parkar District 119 per 100,000. The Sind figures as compared with the Bombay Presidency figures are interesting. In Sind there are 164 male deaf-mutes and 88 female deaf-mutes per 100,000 of the population as compared with only 95 and 61 for the Presidency as a whole.

Blindness: The figures for blindness are almost certainly more accurate than those for the other three infirmities. The figure for the blind in Sind in 1931 was 8,123. In Sind the incidence is .21 per cent, of the total population of Sind. If the incidence of blindness be considered with reference to 100,000 of the population it will be seen that Thar Parkar returns the highest figures.

Infirmities: The number of persons afflicted per 100,000 of total population in Sind.

1931				1921				1911			
Insane	Deaf Mute	Blind	Leper	Insane	Deaf Mute	Blind	Leper	Insane	Deaf Mute	Blind	Leper
66	131	209	6	66	57	223	5	61	106	218	6

Leprosy: Number of lepers per 100,000 persons in Sind, 1881 to 1931, omitting 1901:

1881	11
1891	7
1911	6
1921	6
1931	7

There are 14 leper asylums in the Presidency, which provide for the admission of 1565 lepers. Hiranand Leper Asylum, Mango Pir, Karachi is the only one in Sind. It treated 66 patients in 1921 and 112 in 1931.

Insanity: Insanes per 100,000 (both sexes) 1931

Hyderabad	93
Thar Parkar	79
Karachi	69
Nawabshah	58
Sukkur	55
Larkana	53
Upper Sindh Frontier	45

Accommodation for lunatics: Hyderabad in 1921, 300; in 1931, 159.

Original Citations from the *Journal of the Sind Historical Society*

1. A. B. Advani, 'The Kalhora Dynasty and Its Overthrow by the Talpur Chiefs of Sind', *Journal of the Sind Historical Society* Volume 1.2 (October 1934), 7–23.
2. A. B. Advani, 'Crime and Punishment in the Days of Talpur Rulers of Sind, 1783–1843', *Journal of the Sind Historical Society* Volume 3.4 (December 1938), 59–62.
3. A. B. Advani, 'Diwan Gidumal and Seth Naoomal Hotchand', *Journal of the Sind Historical Society* Volume 4.2 (September 1939), 82–9.
4. A. B. Advani, 'Mirza Khusro Beg', *Journal of the Sind Historical Society* Volume 1.3 (March 1935), 51–61.
5. H. T. Lambrick, 'Lieutenant Amiel and the Baluch Levy', *Journal of the Sind Historical Society* Volume 2.1 (January 1936), 18–61.
6. H. T. Lambrick, 'The Sind Battles, 1843 (Part 2)', *Journal of the Sind Historical Society* Volume 6.4 (September 1943), 393–438.
7. Ramjee Gunnoojee, 'Memorandum of Occurrences Which Took Place at Hyderabad in Sind Between the 14 and 18 February 1843', *Journal of the Sind Historical Society* Volume 6.1 (June 1942), 54–8.
8. John Jacob, 'General John Jacob's Notes on Sir William Napier's *Sir Charles Napier's Administration of Scinde and Campaign in the Cutchee Hills (with Foreword by Patrick Cadell)*', *Journal of the Sind Historical Society* Volume 3.3 (June 1938), 73–83.
9. Patrick Cadell, 'Letters Received by John Jacob, 1840–1858 and Sir Bartle Frere's Letters to John Jacob (with Foreword by H. T. Lambrick)', *Journal of the Sind Historical Society* Volume 8.1 (June 1947), 13–29.
10. H. T. Lambrick, 'Observations on Baloch Poetry of the Sind Border',

Journal of the Sind Historical Society Volume 5.4 (February 1942), 173–93.

11. *S. J. Narsain*, 'Historical and Racial Background of the Amils of Hyderabad, Sind', *Journal of the Sind Historical Society* Volume 1.3 (March 1935), 35–49.

12. N. M. Billimoria, 'Legends of Old Sind', *Journal of the Sind Historical Society* Volume 3.4 (December 1938), 29–45.

13. N. M. Billimoria, 'Census Reports of Sind for the Years 1931 and 1941: A Comparison', *Journal of the Sind Historical Society* Volume 6.4 (September 1943), 361–87.

Index

N

Naffoosk (*also* Naffusk Nafoosk) 196, 224–7, 230, 232, 235–6
Nang 258
Napier, Sir Charles 49, 59–62, 64, 80, 119–28, 132–5, 139, 141–2, 144, 147–52, 154–9, 161–4, 168–9, 171–6, 178, 180, 184–9, 191–2, 196, 198–9, 202–4, 207, 209, 215, 220, 278
Napier, Sir William 71, 138, 140, 143, 146, 153, 160, 165, 167, 170, 179, 182–3, 200–1
Narayanan, Vashuda 10
Nareja 128, 130, 132–3, 135, 138–9, 144, 146–9, 170
Natir 270
Nawabshah 249, 283, 285–6, 289–91, 293, 299–301, 305, 308
Nerun Kot 23, 41
Newport, Major 75–6, 82, 89–90, 100, 109
Newspaper 8, 200
Nimach 199
Nizamani 138, 300
Norangpur 274–5
Nukh 299

O

Outram, James 48–9, 64, 119–20, 122, 151, 170–1, 173–6, 178–9, 188, 194–208, 212, 216

P

Palino 266
Pamnani, Hassaram Sunderdas 7
Panchayat 252
Panchayatana 13
Panwar 268
Paro 301

Parsee 112, 292
Parthiraj, Rana 46
Partition 3, 5, 7–9, 12–13
Persia 21, 33, 42, 53–5, 63–4, 151, 206, 212–13, 259
Persian Gulf 213–14
Phog 266–7
Phori 300
Phulaji 69, 74, 79, 95–100, 102, 104–5, 107, 110–11, 220
Phuleli Canal 41, 62
Pir Ari 9, 155, 157–8, 160, 164
Pir-jo-Goth 286
Poetry 10, 218–19, 237
Political Agent 70, 74, 76–7, 79–80, 83, 92, 94, 99, 106, 110, 116, 225, 229, 239
Population 3–4, 7, 13, 68, 88, 99, 211, 214, 243, 254, 282–94, 296–7, 299–300, 303–7
Porebundar 45–6
Postans, Thomas 32, 74, 78, 90–2, 95, 110–12, 114, 230, 256–7
Pottinger, Henry 47–8, 59, 65, 67–8, 72, 172
Pringle, R. K. 203, 208–9, 215–16
Prisoner 15, 27, 30, 38, 54, 59, 60–1, 74, 89–90, 92, 111, 117, 123, 142, 155, 157, 159, 164, 166, 223, 268, 275
Pub Hills 259
Punhoo 259
Punhu 258, 260–5
Punishment 25, 35–8, 121, 132, 173
Punjab 40, 69, 195–6, 198, 203–4, 210–11, 213–14, 216, 241–2, 244, 248–9, 254, 256, 273, 287–8, 294

Q

Quetta 211, 214, 216